POPULAR IMAGES
OF
POLITICS

A Taxonomy

DAN D. NIMMO
University of Tennessee

PRENTICE-HALL, INC., ENGLEWOOD CLIFFS, NEW JERSEY

Library of Congress Cataloging in Publication Data

NIMMO, DAN D.
    Popular images of politics: a taxonomy.

    Bibliography: p.
    1. Politics, Practical.   2. Political sociology.
3. Public opinion — United States.   4. Voting — United
States.   I. Title.
JK1976.N52   301.5'92   73-20457
ISBN   0-13-687095-3
ISBN   0-13-687087-2 (pbk.)

JK
1976
.N52

© 1974 by Prentice-Hall, Inc., Englewood Cliffs, New Jersey.

PRINTED IN THE UNITED STATES OF AMERICA

10 9 8 7 6 5 4 3 2 1

PRENTICE-HALL INTERNATIONAL, INC., LONDON
PRENTICE-HALL OF AUSTRALIA, PTY. LTD., SYDNEY
PRENTICE-HALL OF CANADA, LTD., TORONTO
PRENTICE-HALL OF INDIA PRIVATE LIMITED, NEW DELHI
PRENTICE-HALL OF JAPAN, INC., TOKYO

contents

70145

Politics as Social Order, 143
The Illusions in Mass Images, 148
Self-Competence and Adaptive Imagery, 149

A BIBLIOGRAPHIC NOTE   156

APPENDIX   156

INDEX   178

preface
and
acknowledgments

In contemporary politics people frequently speak of the images of governing officials, political candidates, and other public figures. How many times have we heard that a particular politician "projected" a "good" or "bad" image, how a public official encountered "image trouble," or how another "merchandised" a new image? From such comments have come alternative points of view. One is that an image is something a politician, or his aides, creates, projects, and sells; if the image has no mass consumer appeal, the politician simply creates a new one. The other view posits that the mass mind is not so easily manipulated, that images of politics reside instead in the minds of people, and political leaders adapt to them—since "beauty is in the eye of the beholder."

This book is an introduction for undergraduates to the various types of images people have of selected political objects, what they are and how they are formed, communicated, and distributed. It offers another outlook to the two views noted above, i.e., any image is complex and multifaceted, but that image is a concept useful to students in organizing and synthesizing a great number of ideas about how people perceive not only public figures, but all types of political objects. The focus on political imagery emphasizes that popular responses to political symbols permeate all politics regardless of whether the motives of political actors are benevolent or malevolent.

A reviewer of an early draft of this work described it as *taxonomic.* Since a taxonomy classifies according to some concept or system, such a characterization is correct. The attempt here is to examine the oft-used concept of image and to classify how people imagine and respond to leaders, governments, social movements, ideologies, parties, policies, etc. Given that this taxonomic effort is conducted at an introductory level, more knowledgeable readers may object that the text offers them nothing new, that it merely recasts selected materials in a slightly different framework. To be sure, the kinship of the concept of image to such other notions as symbols or attitudes is undeniable. However, there is something to gain by taking an albeit vague concept that undergraduates have at least heard of (such as that of image) and refining it to introduce them to selected research and speculation in several areas of political behavior: attitudes, socialization, communication, voting, and leadership. Critics may label such an exercise as forced or contrived, but perhaps other readers will pause long enough to entertain the possibility that in the future an explicit and more comprehensive concern with popular images of politics is warranted.

Several people have provided assistance in the preparation of this volume. From Professor James Combs of Valparaiso University came numerous insights in discussions of political dramaturgy. Roger Emblen of Prentice-Hall first asked me to explore the possibility of such a work as an introduction for students interested in how people respond to political symbols, and Milton McGowen has provided continued encouragement. And, Barbara Christenberry, who understands well the problems of communicating to contemporary undergraduates by way of the written word, provided indispensable editorial assistance.

introduction

At sporting events in this country it is a tradition for spectators and athletes alike to stand, face the Stars and Stripes, and in response to the public address announcer's invitation, "join in the singing of our national anthem." But we live in controversial times, and once unchallenged long-standing customs are no longer readily accepted. Witness the remark of one professional athlete: "The whole anthem-flag ritual makes me un-comfortable. . . . A flag, after all, is still only a cloth symbol. You don't show patriotism by showing blank eyed love for a bit of cloth. And you can be deeply patriotic without covering your car with flag decals."[1]

Contemporary assessments of Old Glory are not always so measured. More direct defiance takes the form of people setting the flag ablaze, blowing their noses on it, wearing red-white-and-blue bikinis, or using the flag as a patch on trouser seats. Defenders of the flag also have distasteful tactics, exemplified by bumper-sticker slogans adorning flag backgrounds: "Love It Or Leave It, America" and "If Your Heart Isn't In It, Get Your Ass Out Of It." It is not always easy to distinguish protesters from patriots on the basis of their treatment of the national banner; after all, the ever protesting Abbie Hoffman and the aging patriot Roy Rogers both wear flag shirts as part of their show business attire. There are city ordinances which

[1]Jim Bouton, *Ball Four* (New York and Cleveland: World Publishing, 1970), p. 59.

label the wearing of flag patches upside down on trouser seats as "desecration" punishable by fine and imprisonment, but which see no crime in displaying the Stars and Stripes on battered, dirty garbage cans. One clear result of this confusion is that the controversy has made the flag a highly successful commercial commodity. Countless novelties (ash trays, pencils, cigarette lighters, etc.) bear flag decors; flag decals come with gasoline and potato chips; flags themselves set sales records; and, as the quintessence of the interest in the flag in the market place, there is even a toilet paper decorated in the Old Glory motif.

For some people the American flag is thus an instrument of commercial exploitation, for others a standard for evaluating the sincerity of loyalties to the community, and for still others a means of personal and social expression. It is "a cloth symbol" but certainly with diverse meanings, or what we shall call *images,* for various people.

In 1955 Kenneth E. Boulding wrote a short treatise entitled *The Image.*[2] In it he argued that each person possesses a store of subjective knowledge about the world, that is, a store of things he believes to be true. This subjective knowledge constitutes his image of the world, and his behavior depends upon his image. Actually a person has many images, because he possesses subjective knowledge about various facets of the world in which he lives. One facet of a person's world is politics.

This book is about people's images of politics and how they are communicated, learned, and distributed in a mass society. Following Boulding and others who have written on the subject, we examine the notion of images in detail. We shall use that notion as a device for introducing selected research and speculation in several areas of political behavior, notably in the areas of political attitudes and opinions, communication, socialization, leadership, and voting. Moreover, we incorporate views from several sister disciplines of political science — social psychology, sociology, anthropology, the communication sciences, and dramatic criticism. Although our emphasis is clearly upon images in American politics, we will cite examples from other political systems as appropriate.

The complexities of modern life intensify today what journalist Walter Lippmann noted a half-century ago: "the attempt to see all things freshly and in detail, rather than as types and generalities, is exhausting, and among busy affairs practically out of the question."[3] Instead of a comprehensive view of what is going on, we select from our news media, organizations, markets, and homes only partial pictures; we often recognize only vaguely familiar characteristics in those pictures to which we add interpretations of our own: "we notice a trait which marks a well-known type, and fill in the rest of the picture by means of the stereotypes we carry

[2]Kenneth E. Boulding, *The Image* (Ann Arbor: University of Michigan Press, 1961) p. 6.
[3]Walter Lippmann, *Public Opinion* (New York: Macmillan, 1960, © 1922), p. 88.

about in our heads."[4] This tendency to selectively perceive, interpret, and give meaning to what we observe, especially when what we see has no precise, fixed meaning clear to everyone, is the process of imagery explored in this book. We will ask several questions about it.

First, *what are political images?* What are their characteristics? Of what assistance to us are our images of politics? In Chapter One we present a fuller definition and description of political images and the functions they perform in political thinking, feeling, and acting.

Second, *how are images of politics normally communicated* among people in a mass society? What are the principal means of interpersonal and mass communication we use to become aware of the images of others? In Chapter Two we consider these means and describe the content, media, and styles of image communication.

Third, *how do people learn their images of politics?* What types of images do they acquire, and when in life do they acquire them? What is the significance of images acquired in early life in a person's capacity to change his political views in later years? We explore these questions in Chapter Three as we consider the development of political images in children and young adults.

Fourth, *what are the principal patterns of political images distributed among the members of a mass society?* What images do people have that *support* their political community, its regime, and its leaders? How do people indicate their *concerns* about politics? In Chapters Four and Five we look at the distribution of images in contemporary society.

Finally, *what problems and possibilities occur in political imagery?* From what perspective is it helpful to draw conclusions about the functions of political images? Are political images merely political illusions or can images be more than illusions? In Chapter Six we introduce the notions of dramatic perspective, symbolic play, and self-competence to assist in dealing with these questions.

The overall content of the following chapters, then, provides readers with an introduction to five key areas dealing with the general question of how people look at politics: what political images are, how they are communicated, how they are learned, how they are distributed, and what problems they inject into our efforts to cope with our political environment. In each area we shall develop a principal theme: (1) in discussing the overlapping nature of political symbols and political images, we suggest that our *images of politics provide significant aids for obtaining material gain, evaluating politics,* and *expressing ourselves;* (2) in outlining the processes of image communication, we note that the *means and styles of communicating often take precedence over content;* (3) we shall see that in developing our political images we *learn how to relate to politics emotionally,* but we

[4]*Ibid.,* p. 89.

often fail to acquire evidence to support our emotion-ladened views; (4) our description of the distribution of political images will indicate that our *support* for political systems and our voicing of political *concerns* also *involves images with great emotional content;* and (5) we will see that *politics is as much public drama and play as minded, adaptive behavior.*

One other introductory remark is necessary. Political images are not the whole of politics. In getting a start on understanding political imagery the reader will have no revealed secret explaining all of politics. But there is a dimension to all political behavior which includes how people perceive the world, that is, the "pictures in our heads." Those pictures sometimes differ sharply from the immediate world in which we do things that have observable consequences. Those pictures and how they can relate to our actions are the subject-matter of this book, not the whole of observable actions and consequences which also comprise politics.

Moreover, it should be evident that "image" is a nonpejorative term in this text. It is not the premise of this discussion that images are somehow evil concoctions used by political sorcerers to fool the masses. And, when contemporary politics is described as public drama and play there is no intention to declare all politics, or even some, fakery or foolishness. Rather, the focus on political imagery simply accepts "the recognition of the symbol as a fact of political life" and that recognition as "perhaps the major contribution of twentieth-century political science."[5] We shall recognize that fact by describing political images as personal responses to political symbols regardless of the benevolent or malevolent motives of the actors involved.

[5]Abraham Kaplan, *American Ethics and Public Policy* (New York: Oxford University Press, 1963), p. 55.

1

political imagery

To begin to understand political imagery we need a more detailed definition of political images along with some idea of their general characteristics. We can then turn to a discussion of how images help us in relating to politics.

IMAGES AND IMAGERY

In the Introduction we said that Kenneth Boulding characterized a person's image as his store of subjective knowledge of the world, things he believes are true. Images thus are primarily mental. People relate to their surroundings in large measure through their senses — taste, touch, hearing, smell, and sight. But they do more than directly experience the world. They *represent it* to themselves, both by interpreting it and giving it personal meaning. These representations are images, i.e., "an image is a natural representation, in that it embodies or recaptures some of the perceptual experiences actually associated with what it represents."[1] Following this line of reasoning, *an image is a subjective representation of something previously perceived.* It is an interpreted sensation or, in other words, a

[1]Bernard Berelson and Gary A. Steiner, *Human Behavior: An Inventory of Scientific Findings* (New York: Harcourt, Brace & World, 1964), pp. 188-89.

5

meaningful impression, appearance, semblance, or similar mental representation of our perceptions.

Once formed, our images influence what we see and how we see it. They influence the formation of new images. As our images encounter new sensations, they may change. In rare instances our images undergo radical change. Boulding writes, "A man, for instance, may think himself a pretty good fellow and then may hear a preacher who convinces him that, in fact, his life is worthless and shallow as he is at present living it. The words of the preacher cause a radical reformulation of the man's image of himself in the world, and his behavior changes accordingly."[2] But by and large our images are resistant to change; modifications in images are more frequently minor reformulations, clarifications, and additions of new, usually supportive, information.

A *sign* is a sensation that we interpret on the basis of our images (and which may in turn affect those images). When our images give meaning to a sign (as in giving meaning to a colorful cloth such as a flag), the sign comes to stand for something other than itself. It becomes a *symbol.* Hence, we "call a combination of sign and meaning a symbol, thus distinguishing the principal component parts of a symbol while recognizing their unitary character."[3]

The relationship between symbols and images obviously is close. "Images have all the characteristics of symbols. . . . We do not take . . . [symbols] for bona fide sensations, but attend to them only in their capacity of *meaning* things, being *images* of things — symbols whereby those things are conceived, remembered, considered, but not encountered."[4] Indeed, the meaning of a specific symbol (a flag, a holiday, a folk tale, or even a revered public figure) flows from the images of those perceiving the visible sign; simultaneously those images are stimulated by the sign itself.

Thus, we say that the *symbolic aspect* of any act consists of the significance placed on it by the person performing it, or by persons regularly performing it. For instance, the act of voting has subjective — that is, *symbolic* — significance to voters apart from the mere physical operation of marking an "X" on a ballot; yet, the ballot is a *visible sign* that helps call forth the symbolic significance.[5] *The transaction between signs and images that results in symbols is called imagery.*

Imagery is inherent in all behavior. When a person acts he has an image of the present in which the act occurs, an image of the past preceding

[2]Kenneth E. Boulding, *The Image* (Ann Arbor: University of Michigan Press, 1961), p. 8.

[3]W. Lloyd Warner, *The Living and The Dead: A Study of the Symbolic Life of Americans* (New Haven: Yale University Press, 1959) p. 455; see also William C. Mitchell, *The American Polity* (New York: The Free Press, 1962), p. 123.

[4]Suzanne Langer, *Philosophy in a New Key* (Cambridge, Mass.: Harvard University Press, 1942), p. 144.

[5]Harold D. Lasswell and Abraham Kaplan, *Power and Society* (New Haven: Yale University Press, 1950), p. 10.

the act, and an image of the future subsequent to the act. In effect, he presents to himself, tentatively and before acting, alternative possibilities of the future that he anticipates resulting from his choices. He imagines the future in combination with his impressions of the past and present. He does not simply respond directly to stimuli, but constructs his purposeful behavior in his mind through interpretation of signs and imagination of conditions.[6]

Therefore, imagery is not a voluntary matter. We engage in imagery simply by behaving. What is implied is that when one person relates to another, he imagines what the impact of his behavior will be on the other person. He anticipates the impressions the other person will have of him. Such anticipation demands some understanding of the intentions of the person with whom he is dealing. However, since he has no way of gaining certain knowledge of such intentions, he constructs an image of those intentions from available clues. And images, as mutually interdependent exchanges of meanings, are inherent in communication, for the images of one person affect and are affected by the other. The expressions a person makes govern the impressions others have of him; in turn, the impressions of others influence the expressions a person makes. Hence, in relating to others several of our images are engaged (as well as the images of the others) — our images of our past and present conduct, our image of intentions of others, our image of our own intentions, our image of the impression we will leave on others (i.e., how they perceive us), and our image of the future consequences of our acts. Imagery is a process of complex, active imagination; in short, it is a minded, not a mindless, behavior.[7]

By the same token, political imagery is interpretative behavior. We do not simply respond in predetermined or conditioned ways to flags, anthems, political advertising, patriotic and/or revolutionary appeals. Instead we interpret political signs, at some times arriving at meanings shared by most members of the community and at other times reaching different, even conflicting, images. In any event, each sign does not simply "stand for" something else; it becomes a symbol with an image of its own to each citizen, a meaning apart from the visible referent. The symbol is a goad to action that generates expectations of how things are and will be, thus influencing political behavior.[8]

[6]George Herbert Mead, "The Function of Imagery in Conduct," in *Mind, Self & Society,* Charles W. Morris, ed. (Chicago: University of Chicago Press, Phoenix Books, 1962), pp. 337-46; Hugh Dalziel Duncan, *Symbols and Social Theory* (New York: Oxford University Press, 1969), pp. 210-13; Robert W. Friedrichs, "Phenomenology as a 'General Theory' of Social Action," *Journal of Value Inquiry,* Vol. 2 (Spring 1968), 1-8; Walker Percy, "Symbol, Consciousness, and Intersubjectivity," *The Journal of Philosophy,* Vol. 55 (1958), 631-41.

[7]Bernard N. Meltzer, "Mead's Social Psychology" in Jerome G. Manis and Bernard N. Meltzer, eds., *Symbolic Interaction* (Boston: Allyn & Bacon, 1967), pp. 5-24.

[8]Herbert Blumer, "Sociological Analysis and the 'Variable'", *American Sociological Review,* Vol. 21 (December, 1956), 683-90; Alfred North Whitehead, *Symbolism: Its Meaning and Effect* (New York: Macmillan, 1927), p. 63.

An image is an "interiorised imitation" of the external world,[9] what we believe about our surroundings. To the extent that our images correspond poorly to the details of the environment, argue some students of images, we live in a "pseudo-environment" filled with "pseudo-events."[10] There is a germ of truth in this argument. Certainly it is rarely possible to be fully informed about political situations, to have access to all relevant evidence, and to anticipate accurately the consequences of our own actions, to say nothing of those of others. Generally we rely on hints and clues that reinforce our image of what to expect: "since the reality that the individual is concerned with is unperceivable at the moment, appearances must be relied upon in its stead. And, paradoxically, the more the individual is concerned with the reality that is not available to perception, the more must he concentrate his attention on appearances."[11] As long as "the way in which the world is imagined determines at any particular moment what men will do,"[12] inaccurate images can create problems. This is a line of thought we develop in detail in Chapter Six.

COMPONENTS OF IMAGES

Images bear a close relationship not only to symbols but to attitudes. Social psychologists refer to attitudes as predispositions, or tendencies, of people to act in response to specific stimuli in specific ways under specific conditions. Images are also predispositions, but predispositions to a particular type of activity — i.e., perceiving and interpreting stimuli. If attitudes are tendencies to behave in overt ways, images are tendencies to *perceive* and *interpret*, mental processes not so readily visible.[13] Since images are like attitudes, we can describe their components much as social psychologists describe the components of attitudes — the perceptual, cognitive, affective, and conative.[14] These components are interdependent and separation of them is artificial, but it is necessary for an understanding of the characteristics of images.

[9]Jean Piaget, *Play, Dreams* and *Imitation in Childhood* (New York: The W. W. Norton & Co., 1962), p. 5.

[10]Walter Lippmann, *Public Opinion* (New York: Macmillan, 1960, © 1922), p. 13; Daniel J. Boorstin, *The Image* (New York: Atheneum, 1962), pp. 11-12.

[11]Erving Goffman, *The Presentation of Self in Everyday Life* (New York: Doubleday, 1959), p. 249.

[12]Lippmann, *Public Opinion*, p. 25.

[13]See Thomas N. Ostrom, "The Emergence of Attitude Theory: 1930-1950" in Anthony G. Greenwald et al. (eds.), *Psychological Foundations of Attitudes* (New York: Academic, 1968), pp. 1-31; Marvin E. Shaw and Jack M. Wright, *Scales for the Measurement of Attitudes* (New York: McGraw-Hill, 1967), pp. 1-14. The view that images are predispositions to perceive is developed in Robert O. Anderson, *A Rhetoric of Political Image Communication* (Unpublished Ph.D. dissertation, University of Missouri, 1971), pp. 11-12.

[14]These four major aspects of images as conceived in this work are spelled out by both social psychologists and other social scientists. For example, see Theodore M. Newcomb,

By the *perceptual* component we refer to our direct observation and/or manipulation of a cue or combination of cues. Such cues may be persons, places, events, ideas, or any other object. Through perception we take account of our environment, but perception is not independent of our thinking nor a process occurring prior to thinking; rather, it is a component of thinking. Some have argued that we first see and then define, others that we define first and then see, but it is best to keep in mind the simultaneity of perception and other mental processes rather than to seek temporal priorities. Perception of objects seldom catches *all* details; rather we perceive in the objects "the particulars, *kinds* of thing, general qualities, rather than uniqueness."[15]

The *cognitive* component refers to our *thinking about* and *interpreting* the referent of an image. We may think of the cognitive component as involving a belief-disbelief aspect; that is, cognition involves our information and knowledge of the environment. There is also a time perspective in cognition that governs our expectations of what things will be like in the future, as well as how they appear at present.

The *affective* component refers to our feeling about an object, person, or other referent. It thus involves the emotions of liking and disliking, love and hate, warmth and fear. Our feelings about others may vary in direction (as like or dislike) or in their intensity (as when we feel strongly about some issues but are passive about others).

Finally, by the *conative* component of an image we refer to our proposed action when given a specific cue. Faced, for example, with the opportunity to vote in a local election to institute a sales tax in his community to raise revenue, a man can propose to vote against the tax, to vote for the tax, or not to vote at all. Through such proposals a person expresses the interplay of his perceptions, cognitions, and affections.

Our opening discussion of current controversies over the American flag provides an illustration of how the various components of images are integrated. Taking but one possibility, a man sees (perception) in the flag an emblem of the way of life he fought for, and almost lost his life for, in World War II. He believes (cognitive) that way of life is threatened by persons who burn, tear, or otherwise desecrate the flag. He thus opposes (affective) desecration and favors laws prohibiting such acts. He ends up

Ralph H. Turner, and Philip E. Converse, *Social Psychology: The Study of Human Interaction* (New York: Holt, Rinehart, & Winston, 1965), pp. 230-38; Robert B. Denhardt and Philip W. Jeffress, "Social Learning and Economic Behavior: The Process of Economic Socialization," *The American Journal of Economics and Sociology,* Vol. 30 (April 1971), 113-25; Ulf Himmelstrand, *Social Pressures, Attitudes and Democratic Processes* (Stockholm: Almquist and Wicksell, 1960), p. 76; M. Brewster Smith, "The Personal Setting of Public Opinions: A Study of Attitudes Toward Russia," *Public Opinion Quarterly,* Vol. 11 (Winter 1947), 507-23; Richard R. Fagen, *Politics and Communication* (Boston: Little, Brown, 1966), pp. 70-71.

[15]Rudolf Arnheim, *Visual Thinking* (London: Faber and Faber Limited, 1969), pp. 9-10.

supporting (conative) a city council candidate who favors passage of an ordinance to imprison and fine "the Commie flag desecrators."

THE USES OF POLITICAL IMAGES

These perceptual, cognitive, affective, and conative components of images blend together in highly intricate ways for any individual. They provide him with a picture of the world covering a full range of environmental influences he experiences. They orient him, as Boulding says, to the world in several ways:

> We have first the spatial image, the picture of the individual's location in the space around him. We have next the temporal image, his picture of the stream of time and his place in it. Third, we have the relational image, the picture of the universe around him as a system of regularities. Perhaps as a part of this we have, fourth, the personal image, the picture of the individual in the midst of the universe of persons, roles, and organizations around him. Fifth, we have the value image which consists of the ordering on the scale of better or worse of the various parts of the whole image. Sixth, we have the affectional image, or emotional image, by which various items in the rest of the image are imbued with feeling or affect. Seventh, we have the division of the image into conscious, unconscious, and subconscious areas. Eighth, we have a dimension of certainty or uncertainty, clarity or vagueness. Ninth, we have a dimension of reality or unreality, that is, an image of the correspondence of the image itself with some "outside" reality. Tenth, closely related to this but not identical with it, we have a public, private scale according to whether the image is shared by others or is peculiar to the individual.[16]

Political images also assist us in orienting ourselves, by helping us take into account and respond to our political surroundings. Depending upon whether we emphasize the cognitive, affective, or conative component of images, we can speak of three major ways our images assist us in politics.[17] First, our cognitive beliefs govern our perceptions of what is real or unreal, possible or impossible, attainable or not attainable; thus *images are tools that assist us in defining goals and reaching them.* Second, our values (the affective component) aid us in judging what is good and bad, desirable and undesirable, liked and disliked; in assisting us in basically moral assessments *images are standards for evaluating our environment.* Third, the conative dimension, relating to what we actually propose to do about objects in our surroundings, gives us a chance to express

---

[16]Boulding, *The Image,* p. 47-48.

[17]This classification is a modification of that employed by Talcott Parsons and Edward A. Shils in "Values, Motives, and Systems of Action" in their jointly edited volume *Toward A General Theory of Action* (New York: Harper & Row, 1951, Torchback Edition, 1962), pp. 160-67.

our individual self, our identity, our needs, wishes and desires; *images thereby serve as means of self-expression.* Keep in mind that these instrumental, evaluative, and expressive images are different perspectives from which to discuss images, not separate, independent kinds of images; any image may predispose us to see our world from a vantage point involving a combination of our beliefs, values, and inner selves.

We encountered these perspectives on imagery in the Introduction when we spoke of the imagery surrounding the American flag. Those using the flag for commercial exploitation, attaching the flag motif to every conceivable product, use the flag image as an *instrument* to reach mometary goals. Others see in the flag a symbol deserving of respect and are quick to *judge* persons who desecrate the flag as unpatriotic and/or immoral. To still others the flag is distinctly "American" and by flying the flag or decorating their automobiles, "hard hats," and bodies with flag decals, they *express* their identities as Americans. Let us examine each of these uses of imagery in greater detail.

Images as Tools

The place of imagery in politics has been a principal concern to several generations of political scientists. By and large political scientists have concentrated primarily upon images as *instruments* in the pursuit of tangible interests. Realizing that one of the reasons governments exist is to allocate material benefits and costs, political scientists tend to treat images as tools used by elites to justify their own interest and class gains while lulling deprived masses into accepting an inferior lot.

Take, for instance, accounts of how images figure in democratic elections. Candidates devote vast quantities of money (estimates run well above $100 million for some election years) to offering an appealing image to prospective voters through radio, television, and other means of mass communication. The instrumental aspect of such a commitment of resources is not hard to discern. In effect, the candidate exudes an image that says, "vote for me and get this," the "this" being such goals as lower taxes, withdrawal from war, an improved environment, better highways, and other material gains; of course, if successful in his appeal, the candidate's benefit is election to office. But there is an imagery in democratic elections beyond the symbols connected with candidates, political parties, or issues. The election process itself is an exercise in imagery, one in which people believe that they participate in self-governance through selecting rulers. The image of popular control over policy by means of elections is not widely questioned even though seldom accurate. The differences voters detect between competing candidates are usually not on policy stands (indeed, few voters are informed of such matters), but differences in the style and partisanship of the contenders. Voting "is participation in a ritual act; however, only in a minor degree is it participation in policy formation"; the imagery of elections draws "attention to common social ties and to the importance and apparent reasonableness of accepting the public policies that are adopted." This imagery makes it possible for the polity to "survive and retain the support or acquiescence of its members."[18]

Images play a key role as instruments in the proposal, advocacy, and defense of policies: "he who captures the symbols by which public feeling is for the moment contained, controls by that much the approaches of public policy."[19] "Bureaucracy" is an example of a label that carries an odious popular image that was a potent negative force used for decades by opponents of increased federal activity in policy making. In the 1920s and 1930s opponents of federal regulation of child labor feared no good could come of creating federal agencies; federal agencies would mean only more red tape and bureaucratic bungling. And, as late as the 1970s, advocates of President Richard Nixon's proposals to return federal revenues to the states for state use in solving urban and welfare problems justified the policy in part on grounds it would "debureaucratize" the federal government.[20]

But bureaucrats also fully recognize the usefulness of appealing images in winning public support. So they make every effort to capitalize on dramatic symbols in creating supportive images. A highly publicized example occurred during the Eisenhower presidency in the 1950s. Efforts were made to identify the federal postal service (then the Post Office Department) with images of national patriotism rather than with images of a predominantly military bureaucracy. To accomplish this postal boxes used for mailing letters and parcels were repainted from their militaristic olive drab color to a striking red-white-and blue. When the postal service was converted from the Post Office Department into a more self-sustaining public corporation in 1970, a new symbolism reflected the shift. The strategem was to repaint all postal boxes and afix a decal of the American eagle, thus suggesting that the postal service, while still a part of the federal establishment, had a new semi-independent identity. We can't say whether or not the new symbol produced a popular image of the improved quality of postal service; perhaps Americans base that judgment on more direct experiences, such as whether or not they get their mail on time.

Policy makers frequently use images as tools in a controversy to mask

[18]Murray Edelman, *The Symbolic Uses of Politics* (Urbana: University of Illinois Press, 1964), p. 3; see also Charles E. Merriam, *Political Power* (New York: Collier Books, 1964, © 1934), p. 125.

[19]Walter Lippmann, *Public Opinion,* pp. 206-7.

[20]Thurman Arnold, *The Symbols of Government* (New York: Harcourt, Brace & World, 1962, © 1935), pp. 207-8.

from popular attention what is really at issue. Political scientist Murray Edelman cites the federal income tax as an excellent example of "the divergence between a widely publicized symbol and actual resource allocation patterns." On the one hand, the image that each man should be taxed in accordance with his "ability to pay" is widely shared; yet, in fact, through a variety of exemption devices, those with higher annual earnings (especially over $25,000) pay much lower percentages of their income in taxes than if the "ability to pay" principle were practiced as widely as it is imagined.[21]

Images thus play an important part in getting people to accept the election of one set of rulers rather than another and to acquiesce to policies from which they benefit relatively little in the way of actual material goods. And as manipulated by rulers as symbols, images are crucial in building popular acceptance of and respect for governing institutions. Often the more authority associated with a level of government, the more formalized are the symbols and images associated with it. Thus, we find considerably more pomp and ceremony surrounding the inauguration of the President of the United States than with the administering of an oath of office to a governor of a state or mayor of a local community. The wider scope of power exercised at the federal level, particularly as frequently perceived by the citizen, seems to call for more elaborate imagery. The impact of federal policy making upon the citizen's material well-being is widely publicized and must also be widely justified. Additionally, a citizen is likely to experience directly his local community environment, perhaps visiting the courthouse, a city office, or even knowing the mayor or other governing official personally. But the greater geographical and social remoteness of key federal officials makes direct experience unlikely. Thus, images of governing authority replace actual encounters.

Specific governing institutions tend to have images in the citizen's mind peculiar to the functions these institutions perform and to the forms of popular support officials require to conduct their affairs. Courts, for example, make nonarbitrary decisions where there are controversies over enforcement and interpretation of law. Judicial robes, the elevated bench, paneled chambers, formalized seating arrangements, the gavel, and other signs represent the impartiality, fairness, objectivity, and justice associated with the judicial function. Bureaucratic offices offer signs of objectivity and fairness, but in a context of symbols conveying routinized labor, efficiency, strict organization, chains-of-command, minimal discretion, and uniform standards for evaluating individual cases. Hence, "file cabinets, desks, and machines dominate the scene,"[22] The image of

[21]Edelman, *The Symbolic Uses of Politics,* pp. 28-29.

[22]William C. Mitchell, *The American Polity* (New York: The Free Press of Glencoe, 1962), p. 174; the discussion of images associated with governing authority draws up Mitchell's analysis.

bureaucratic order contrasts sharply with that associated with the legislative function. As tribunes of the people, legislators carry on in a tradition of free discussion and extended and elaborate deliberation of policies. The legislative scene has an image of semi-disorder, informality, and openness as legislators meander about the floor, caucus informally, peruse their mail, and write letters, seemingly oblivious to the sometimes heated, often dull, debate of their colleagues. Finally, wrapped up in the office of a nation's chief executive, particularly in the United States, is the image of effective, dynamic leadership. With his official residence of the White House, his coteries of personal guards and reporters whenever he appears in public, his virtually unlimited capacity to command the nation's television spotlight at a moment's notice, and such other visible signs as the seal of office, Air Force One, etc., the President builds acceptance of his role as America's chief decision maker.

One function of political images, then, is as tools to explain and rationalize the relationship between rulers and ruled, between the "haves" and the "have nots," and between people and their governing institutions. As instruments they can be used to mobilize support for candidates, policies, and institutions; by the same token they are used to oppose political objects (as, for example, in the 1960s when the image of an "unresponsive Establishment" served as a rallying cry for diverse groups dissatisfied with what they regarded as immoral American involvement in Southeast Asia, unrelenting poverty, impersonal mass education and mis-ordered priorities.) Whether they are used as instruments of support or attack, our images influence our expectations of the political environment.

Images as Standards

The cognitive component of images carries information and beliefs permitting people to know and manipulate their environment; the affective component consists of the values and feelings that enable people to evaluate that environment. Actually people make political judgments without having much information to support these judgments. Americans, for example, make quick judgments about what the federal government is doing or about their rights as individuals; yet studies indicate that only about one-fifth of the American people knows what the three branches of the federal government are called or know anything said in the Bill of Rights. Moreover, a 1956 study found that only two-thirds of a national sample could be called familiar with political issues; that is, only two-thirds possessed an opinion *and* knew what "government is doing about" the problem in question.[23] Images thus are as likely to be based on ignorance

[23]Robert E. Lane and David O. Sears, *Public Opinion* (Englewood Cliffs, N.J.: Prentice-Hall, 1964), p. 61, and Angus Campbell et al., *The American Voter* (New York: John Wiley 1960), pp. 171-76.

as to be informed. Yet, informed or not, images are standards for judging right and wrong, good and bad, desirable and undesirable.

The evaluative use of imagery is especially important in politics. If we concentrate solely on political images used as tools to assist interests in material conflict or to justify elite rule of the masses, we miss a key function of political imagery. Governments dispense intangible as well as tangible goods, legitimacy as well as material allocations; i.e., governments legally define what is moral or immoral, who is loyal and who disloyal, who shall be free and who imprisoned, who shall die and who shall live. Clearly, more than material matters are involved when governments decree the sale of marijuana illegal, insist that no alcoholic beverages be sold inside the confines of a constituency, prohibit people from running around the streets nude, ban smut mail, regulate abortion, or frown on homosexuals, prostitutes, and other sex "offenders." The areas in which governments define legitimate behavior are numerous, broad in scope, and complex in their diversity, as comprehensive as life itself. People are often far more interested in having their own way than in material gain. That is, they want their behavior regarded by authorities as legitimate and even mandatory for everybody. In sum, to view images as mere opiates leading people to acquiesce to their lot misses the point that *images are prized for themselves* when they confer legitimacy and that "people covet both symbolic and material goods."[24]

When used as tools for advancing material interests, political images create and/or reinforce distinctions between social classes — i.e., aggregates of people sharing approximately the same level of material well-being as measured by their incomes, material possessions, educations, occupations, and style of life. As evaluative standards, images create and/or reinforce distinctions in social status — differences between people in prestige, "good name," social acceptance, reputation for being moral, and social position. Status puts people into hierarchies, into higher and lower rankings; governments confer or withdraw legitimacy from the rankings through laws. Thus, "any act of government can be imbued with symbolic import when it becomes associated with noninstrumental identifications, when it serves to glorify or demean the character of one group or another" for "the political agent, as representative of the society, symbolizes the societal attitude, the public norm, toward some person, object, or social group."[25]

There are various examples of how images act as evaluative standards in politics. Joseph Gusfield supplies an excellent illustration in his account of the Prohibition movement. In 1919 the United States added the Eighteenth Amendment to its Constitution. The amendment permitted Congress

[24]Joyce M. Mitchell and William C. Mitchell, *Political Analysis and Public Policy* (Chicago: Rand McNally, 1969), p. 145.

[25]Joseph R. Gusfield, *Symbolic Crusade* (Urbana: University of Illinois Press, 1966) p. 171.

to pass the Volstead Act prohibiting the transportation, sale, and consumption of intoxicating liquids in interstate commerce (Prohibition). The change marked a victory for temperance forces, which represented beer, wine, and liquor consumption as immoral, as a filthy habit of the poor, the alien, and the downtrodden, and as a threat to the family structure and respectability of the middle classes. The advent of Prohibition legitimized the image of things held by temperance forces: "It established the victory of Protestant over Catholic, rural over urban, tradition over modernity, the middle class over both the lower and the upper strata."[26] To be sure, drinking and intemperance continued, bootlegging became big business, and the law was not enforced (or unforceable). Yet, Prohibition conferred status; it demonstrated who controlled policy making, whose values were America's legitimate values, and, in short, who deserved deference and who degradation in the society. In 1933 the Eighteenth Amendment was repealed. This too was a status conferral giving new legitimacy to lower class values at a time of deep economic depression. Yet, even today, the image propagated by temperance forces in an earlier era holds sway as a legal standard in many local communities, counties, and states.

We witness something very similar to the Prohibition example, insofar as status images are concerned at least, in contemporary America. Much of the concern over use and abuse of drugs stems from a genuine worry about potentially harmful effects on both minds and bodies; yet, there are also those in the antidrug movement more worried about status. To these people drug users represent threats to basic values — threats signified by long hair, beards, rock festivals, mass protests, sexual permissiveness, and "dropping out." Legalization of the sale of drugs, as these antidrug forces perceive it, would constitute a threat to established, middle-class values along with a loss of control over policy making and a diminution of status.

Many of the most celebrated examples of the politics of status images involve judicial trials. In the 1920s, for instance, a school teacher in Tennessee, Scopes, was tried and convicted of violating a state law by teaching the theory of evolution. The Scopes trial represented a major clash of status (as well as a clash of what Boulding refers to as relational images, i.e., the picture of the universe and man's place in it). A rural, biblically oriented, fundamentalist America held off the challenge of a secular, modernizing, scientifically oriented, and skeptical America. A half century later, in 1970, a trial with equally significant, although different, overtones of status imagery occured when a self-styled hippie, Charles Manson, was found guilty of planning and directing the murder of a Hollywood starlet and her companions. Within the courtroom the question of guilt or innocence was at issue, but as reported in America's mass media (and as acted out by

[26] *Ibid.*, p. 7.

Manson himself) the trial unfolded as a dramatic encounter between "straight" and "deviant" cultures. Manson appeared to many as more than an accused killer; he represented a widening renunciation of heretofore unquestioned morals and values; his long hair, admitted use of drugs, alleged hypnotic powers, sex orgies with multiple concubines, and fascination with rock music epitomized what many Americans perceived as the malevolent symptoms, perhaps even the sinister causes, of society's unrest, violence, and turbulence. Given the Manson image, more than a single man was on trial; a whole subculture of truculent, unruly, deviant "freaks" was challenged and some might say, put in its place.

A society's treatment of convicted murderers, condemned to die in the gas chamber or electric chair, also involves an image of right versus wrong. The death penalty is the final retribution against those who refuse to defer to the laws of a civilized society. It is levied not simply to remove a threatening element from the community, but to symbolize ultimate degradation of one who flouts the standards of morality; it dramatizes the distinction between those of status who make and obey the laws and those too degenerate to obey those laws. If the condemned man attempts to take his own life, say, by slashing his wrists or hanging himself, no expense is spared to save him, nurture him, and seek his speedy recovery. For what purpose? So that he may be executed in the appointed manner. Thus is preserved the superiority of a society's images of proper behavior.

In assisting us in reaching judgments, then, our images are standards of legitimacy (i.e., standards of what is morally right and wrong) and of status (i.e., standards clarifying to whom we defer and whom we degrade). In politics, in large measure, "law" is a body of such images: "It is a way of writing about human institutions in terms of ideals, rather than observed facts. It meets a deep-seated popular demand that government institutions symbolize a beautiful dream, within the confines of which principles operate, independently of individuals."[27] Our views of customs, traditions, conventions, ceremonies, rituals, institutions, and habits are likewise images giving meaning to our political lives beyond simply pursuit of material gain. Although a sense of legitimacy and status is less tangible than the material profits associated with using images as tools for profit, that sense is no less subjectively rewarding.

Images as Personal Expressions

As Boulding points out, one of the aspects of an individual's image is his *personal* image, the picture he has of himself. This image of self includes how the individual identifies himself in a world of others, his definition of

[27]Arnold, *Symbols of Government*, p. 33.

personal needs and wants, his inner satisfactions, tensions, and anxieties. Frequently, what an individual proposes to do in a situation (the conative dimension of an image discussed earlier) *expresses his personal image.* When so used, an image is "a highly condensed form of substitutive behavior . . . allowing for the ready release of emotional tension in conscious or unconscious form" as, for instance, "the apparently meaningless washing ritual of an obsessive neurotic."[28]

By way of illustrating the differences between images when used as tools, standards, and personal expressions, let us return to the imagery surrounding the American flag. Merchandisers use the flag image as a device to increase sales of novelties; ruling interests in a community pass antidesecration orders and thus recognize certain images of the flag as morally proper. But when a person salutes the flag it may be an expressive act, a spontaneous outpouring of his patriotic fervor, love, and identification with the nation rather than any desire to achieve material profit or set standards for others. He simply finds the expression itself satisfying and requires no further reward: "The distinctive feature of 'expressive symbolism' is the allocation of energy among various symbol acts which themselves are gratifying (tension-reducing), the referents signified being of secondary importance in this respect."[29] Through such expression a person declares before the world who he perceives himself to be — *his* conception of self, *his* commitments, *his* identity, and *his* notion of *his* role in the social milieu.

As means of self-expression, images help people to identify with a nation, institutions, or groups. Merely by flying a flag, singing their national anthem, visiting monuments, observing holidays, and participating in commemorative ceremonies and rituals, individuals express, "I am an American," "I am a Russian," or "I am Chinese," and get great satisfaction. Political rulers are just as prone to use images for expressing their loyalties to established ways of doing things. In the British House of Commons, for example, there is a period set aside as "Question Time"; i.e., a period when House members put questions to cabinet ministers. Beyond providing a forum for members to debate, explain, and criticize policies, the ceremony "expresses and heightens their emotional commitment to the system, strengthening their trust in one another and also the hold of the system on them."[30] Similarly, the televised press conferences of the President of the

[28]Edward Sapir, "Symbolism," in *Encyclopedia of the Social Sciences* (New York: Macmillan, 1930), pp. 492-95.

[29]Ulf Himmelstrand, "Verbal Attitudes and Behavior: A Paradigm for the Study of Message Transmission and Transformation," *Public Opinion Quarterly,* Vol. 24 (Summer 1960), 233.

[30]Samuel H. Beer et al., *Patterns of Government,* 2nd ed. (New York: Random House, 1962), p. 43.

United States permit reporters and spectators alike to express their interest, concern, and respect for the Presidency.

When images facilitate a people's expression of national loyalties, they serve the broader interests of the entire community. Political leaders understand this and in times of national crises make appeals to such images. Leaders thus employ the same images as tools for demanding sacrifice and courage that the masses use in expressive ways. Even in less critical times leaders make such appeals. The formation of the Peace Corps in 1961 provided a political institution which thousands of young Americans identified with; in voicing their approval of the Peace Corps these Americans expressed their loyalties, hopes, and aspirations for the entire political system. In movements directed against established governmental regimes, leaders also capitalize on the images by which people express themselves, but in this case those expressions are frequently feelings of aggression, fear, hate, or disappointment and deprivation.

Physical signs often stimulate display of personal affection toward a movement, nation, or leaders. The Nazi swastika is a case in point. Nazi leaders originally selected the swastika to symbolize their movement precisely because it was a sign free of inherited images and could therefore be used to carry new meaning. In time people imbued it with emotional connotations that expressed their image of the essentials of the movement. The tilting of a flag-figured swastika in a white circle upon a red background provided a striking, distinctive, and simple picture that permitted a combination of attributed meanings. The tilting conveyed the dynamic quality of Nazism; the black figure in a red and white setting struck responsive chords of nationalism by harking back to the flag of the defunct German empire; red served to represent the blood of revolution; black became associated with the motif of storm-troopers' shirts; the geometric shape reflected both Prussian efficiency and functional design. Educated persons compared the swastika with a similar symbol from India and evoked an image of the Aryan race. Finally, some people imagined the swastika to be a broken cross symbolizing the "true" nature of Christianity in the modern world in the face of Nazi aspirations for racial dominance and world conquest.[31]

In summarizing the uses of political imagery, it is helpful to think of governments as involved in allocating material goods, defining legitimacy, and mobilizing supports. Although there is an obvious combination of instrumental, evaluative, and expressive facets in any political image, it is helpful to think of images being used as tools when associated with the information and beliefs related to material allocations among social classes; to think of images as evaluative standards when involved in defin-

[31]Arnheim, *Visual Thinking,* pp. 143-44; Carl Joachim Friedrich, *Man and His Government* (New York: McGraw-Hill, 1963), p. 101.

ing morals and alloting social prestige; and to think of images as forms of self-expression when they reveal emotional responses to political leaders, institutions, and communities.

POLITICAL IMAGES IN SOCIETY

We have discussed thus far the general characteristics of images and the uses individuals make of them in politics. What of the general function of images, especially political images, in society as a whole? As we have seen, to the people who hold them, the usefulness of an image "lies precisely in the fact that it is not what it is," but that people acting cooperatively "can use it to mean something else."[32] This cooperation comes about through the mutual exchange of the meanings people attribute to signs, or more simply, through the communication of their images.

Imagery is thereby fundamental in human communication. It is fundamental to society as well. Society consists of people relating to one another in various settings. These relationships take various forms, but following the sociologist Hugh Duncan,[33] we say they are basically hierarchical. People divide themselves into ranks, classes, levels, statuses, and so forth, and then perceive themselves and one another as superiors, inferiors, and equals. The images people have of social superiority, inferiority, and equality (and the ways they behave in accordance with those images) define the social order. By communicating their images of the way these relations are and should be, people accept, question, or reject that social order. Thus, to recall once more the imagery surrounding the American flag, some citizens reaffirm their faith in the status quo by patriotic display of the flag while dissenters raise questions about the social order by treating it as a mere piece of cloth or manifest their rejection of "the system" or "the establishment" by flag desecrations. Thus, society originates with the communication of meaningful images, and the social order is accepted, questioned, or rejected through image communication.

Challenges and reaffirmations of the social order imply conflicts. These conflicts become public through image communication, the exchange of views of the world which are not widely shared; indeed they contradict one another. It is here that a particular variety of social activity, politics, enters. Politics is that activity whereby the members of society endeavor to regulate their conflicts and maintain a sufficient level of consensus to make living together possible. Although not the only "regula-

---

[32]Warner, *The Living and the Dead,* pp. 456-57.

[33]Hugh Dalziel Duncan, *Communication and Social Order* (London: Oxford University Press, 1962), and *Symbols in Society* (New York: Oxford University Press, 1968), pp. 44-150.

tor" (religious, economic, and artistic activities being but a few of many others), *politics is a chief method of maintaining and revising the social order* by making decisions regarded as binding upon all community members.

The political images associated with government actions to allocate material goods, distribute legitimacy, and mobilize the masses in support of the community are primary factors in the social regulatory process. Although political images are not consumed in the way tangible goods are — such as income, land, commodities, etc. — they are *imagined* goods, and these intangibles are at least as crucial to most people and far more important to many. In each of their instrumental, evaluative, and expressive uses, political images unite people at certain levels and divide them at others.

Viewed in this light political action (and the imagery associated with it) is significant not only because it is a means to an end, as when a corporation lobbies for a lucrative government contract, but because it awards deference to some groups in social hierarchies and degrades others, and because it recruits the loyalties of some members of the social order and alienates others. The communication of political images, therefore, is directly associated with efforts to achieve social order, for it is through images that people justify the distribution of material goods to satisfy material demands, of legitimacy to secure moral and status deference, and of identities to solidify the community's membership. The communication of images is an intricate but key aspect of politics, and we shall consider it next.

2

communicating
political images

Political images become public, and thus shared by people, through communication. In this chapter we want to examine the communication of political images in detail. We seek answers to several questions. What is communication all about? What are the major aspects of communication? What is the general character of the process by which we communicate political images?

WHAT IS COMMUNICATION?

Communication is "the transmission of information from one person or group to another (or others) primarily through symbols."[1] But, "communication is not just the passing of information from a source to the public; it is better conceived as a re-creation of information ideas by the

---

[1]George A. Theodorson and Achilles G. Theodorson, *A Modern Dictionary of Sociology* (New York: Thomas Y. Crowell, 1969), p. 62; similar definitions occur in J. W. Aranguren, *Human Communication* (New York: McGraw-Hill, 1967), p. 11 and David K. Berlo, *The Process of Communication* (New York: Holt, Rinehart & Winston, 1960), p. 12.

public, given a hint by way of a key symbol, slogan, or theme."[2] This characterization of communication has certain implications that we should make explicit.

That it involves "a re-creation of information ideas" by the public is a first major characteristic of communication. We can think of "information ideas" as images. Basic to the "re-creation" of images is the phenomenon of a person *taking-something-into-account* (in this case a message in symbolic form; i.e., words, gestures, pictures, etc.): "The phenomenon basic to and underlying every situation in which human communication occurs is simply this: that an organism (an individual) took-something-into-account, whether that something was something someone did or said or did not do or say, whether it was some observable event, some internal condition, the meaning of something being read or looked at, some feeling intermingled with some past memory — literally anything that could be taken-into-account by human beings in general and that individual in particular."[3]

In emphasizing the "taking-something-into-account" that occurs in re-creating the images of one person by others, we note that persons are active participants in communication, not simply passive recipients of messages. This introduces a second crucial characteristic of communication; its *relational* or *transactional* properties. Communication is not a process in which one person (the source) acts and another (the audience) reacts; people who communicate are not isolable beings acting independently upon one another. Rather, people take one another into account: "When we talk about communication we are not talking about a situation in which John acts and Mary reacts to John's action and in turn John reacts to Mary's action in some simple, ongoing, one-after-another sequence. . . . John does not communicate to Mary, and Mary does not communicate to John; Mary and John engage in communication."[4] To be sure, we usually talk about this continuous, nonintermittent, process of communication *as if* it consisted of isolable, discontinuous units; but in doing so we should remember that the "units" are really assembled in an interdependent complex, and overlapping process.

A third major characteristic of communication follows from the transactional quality involved in taking-something-into-account. This is the *impossibility of not communicating.* Whenever we are in the presence of

[2]William Stephenson, *The Play Theory of Mass Communication* (Chicago: University of Chicago Press, 1967), p. 8. For the reasoning that leads to the view that images and "information ideas" are closely related see Albert J. Sullivan, "Toward a Philosophy of Public Relations: Images," in Otto Lerbinger and Albert J. Sullivan, eds., *Information, Influence, and Communication* (New York: Basic Books, 1965), pp. 240-49.

[3]Lee Thayer, *Communication and Communication Systems* (Homewood, Illinois: Richard D. Irwin, 1968), pp. 26-27.

[4]Ray L. Birdwhistell, *Kinesics and Context* (Philadelphia: University of Pennsylvania Press, 1970), p. 12.

another person, unless we are totally oblivious to our environment and he to his, we take him into account just as he takes account of our presence. Our behavior in that situation, regardless of its form (words, movement, gestures, or whatever) possesses symbolic, or message, value. Think how silence itself is even a way of communicating. "The man at a crowded lunch counter who looks straight ahead, or the airplane passenger who sits with his eyes closed, are both communicating that they do not want to speak to anybody or be spoken to, and their neighbors usually 'get the message' and respond appropriately by leaving them alone. This, obviously, is just as much an interchange of communication as an animated discussion."

Following this logic, then, any way we behave in the presence of another, whom we consciously or unconsciously take into account, gives him signs, signals, and cues. He reads meanings into those messages, meanings derived from his images. Thus, *we engage in communication by giving off signs which others interpret;* since we cannot behave toward others without giving them signs of some variety, we "cannot not communicate."[5]

But, saying that one cannot help communicating does not mean that there is always a perfect correspondence between what one person transmits and another person receives and re-creates. Obviously, the subjective picture of politics held by the recipient of a communication may differ considerably from that of the source of a message. This possibility leads us to a fourth characteristic of communication; that is, *consensually valid* communication between persons and/or groups requires that the symbols in which messages are encoded reflect and trigger *shared* images. In the absence of shared meanings communication occurs, but misunderstanding is a frequent result.

In sum, *communication is a process of exchanging messages between people who take-something-into-account, engage unavoidably in communication, and read meanings into signs that, once interpreted, become symbols.* We can graphically contrast this perspective with an action-reaction notion of communication by considering two persons, A and B, communication (designated by - - →), and a result, X. Action-reaction views state that A transmits something to B with some result (A - - →B = X). In contrast, we suggest that A and B *engage* in communication about something (the transaction depicted by a reciprocal arrow, thus ← - - →) and the "something" is the "message." Therefore, communication is characterized by A ← - → "message" ← - - → B = X. Thus we keep in mind the mutually reciprocal and overlapping qualities of sources, messages, receivers, and effects.[6]

[5]Paul Watzlawick, Janet Helmick Beavin, and Don D. Jackson, *Pragmatics of Human Communication* (New York: Norton, 1967), pp. 48-51.

[6]Thayer, *Communication and Communication Systems,* pp. 23-28.

KEY ASPECTS OF COMMUNICATION

Communication theorists generally divide the study of human communication into three areas, which they label semantics, syntactics, and pragmatics.[7] The semantics of communication refer to the *meanings* attributed to messages. Syntactics concerns ways of *transmitting* messages regardless of what meaning they have for persons; such transmission includes the media of communication, the languages and coding of messages, and the factors that influence the character of message exchange. The pragmatics of communication cover the *effects* of communication upon behavior, specifically the ways interpersonal and mass communication relate people to one another and structure their behavior. Recalling the distinctions we offered in Chapter One among the cognitive, affective, and conative aspects of imagery, the semantics of political communication generally involve affective aspects, syntactics emphasize cognitive aspects, and pragmatics deal with conative aspects.[8] With these distinctions in mind we turn to a more detailed description of the meanings, transmission, and effects of communicating political images.

Messages and Meanings

People communicate through messages. The content of those messages consists of any variety of symbols that people find meaningful. By now it should be clear that the meaning in a message lies not only in the symbols, but in our human responses to them: " . . . *human* responses because, so far as we know, human beings are the only creatures that have, over and above that biological equipment which we have in common with other creatures, the additional capacity for manufacturing symbols and systems of symbols. When we react to a flag, we are not reacting simply to a piece of cloth, but to the meaning with which it has been symbolically endowed."[9]

The meaning in a message, then, depends upon the interpretations we give it, and those interpretations, in turn, depend upon our images. But, sometimes we forget that meaning depends upon our images and instead think of symbols as having intrinsic meanings, i.e., real properties

---

[7]Charles Morris, *Introduction to Semantics* (Cambridge: Harvard University Press, 1942).

[8]George N. Gordon, *The Languages of Communication* (New York: Hastings House, Publishers, 1969), pp. 19-32; Kenneth Burke, *A Grammar of Motives* (Berkeley: University of California Press, 1969 edition), pp. xvii-xviii; Watzlawick et al., *Pragmatics of Human Communication*, pp. 21-22.

[9]S. I. Hayakawa, *Symbol, Status, and Personality* (New York: Harcourt, Brace & World, 1953), p. 6.

that mean something apart from our interpretations. As an example, think of the highly publicized controversy between the "hairs" and the "hard hats" in the late 1960s.

Many people associated long hair on youth with disruptive, revolutionary, unpatriotic goals and the protective steel hats worn by construction workers with displays of pro-status quo, patriotic stands of organized labor. With little difficulty the words "hairs" and "hard hats" took on a meaning that represented "real" divisions in society: "hairs" and "hard hats" became social types, categories into which people grouped others for ready reference (similar social types in America have included the "Easterner," "WASP," "Acid Head," "Nice guy," "Tennis Bum," or "Jerk"). The words "hairs" and "hard hats" affected what some Americans thought about ("crisis" in the "system"), how they thought ("we" vs. "they"), and what they expected to happen (an "inevitable confrontation between generations"). The words "hairs" and "hard hats" — or more precisely what people took as the intrinsic meanings, or qualities, of persons in those categories — replaced direct contact with reality, at least until some people encountered a "hard hat" who, upon removing his protective chapeau, released long curly locks falling to his shoulders. The example indicates how we symbolize something-taken-into-account, name it and, having named it, assume (rightly or wrongly) that we "know" it; our messages then take on meaning.[10]

Political leaders realize that the symbols employed in communication can be used to trigger images which they believe to have widespread, common, and sympathetic public meaning. By attaching popular symbols to their proposals, politicians seek mass support. The tactic is so characteristic of the imagery in political communication that one illustration will suffice. On August 15, 1971, President Richard M. Nixon, in the face of rising prices, threats to the stability of the U. S. dollar at home and abroad, and increased levels of unemployment, went before the American people on radio and television and announced a 90-day freeze on wages and prices, imposed a 10 percent surcharge on imports, proposed changes in tax laws, and revealed a "New Economic Policy." There was no assurance that images conjured up by "wage-price freeze," "surcharge," or "New Economic Policy" would necessarily be supportive. To be sure, the practice of attaching the symbol "New" to presidential programs had a long and honorable tradition dating back to the "New Freedom" of Woodrow Wilson and through the "New Deal" of Franklin D. Roosevelt. Yet, the phrase "New Economic Policy" also had a long and perhaps less honorable tradition, being introduced as a major program by the 10th Congress of the Communist Party for the Soviet Union in 1921. But Nixon ran little risk in

[10]John Dewey and Arthur F. Bentley, *Knowing and the Known* (Boston: Beacon Press, 1949), p. 298.

using the slogan since the Soviet New Economic Policy is scarcely known by that name to Americans; had he used the more widely recognized symbol of Soviet economic policies, making reference to a Five Year Plan, he undoubtedly would have evoked negative responses.

The Nixon administration quickly moved to cloak its program in phrases with seemingly widespread symbolic appeal. The President's appeal for mass support through such imagery came in his Labor Day radio message of September 6. The President tied his New Economic Policy to the promise of a "goal we have rarely been able to achieve in the past 40 years — a new prosperity without war and without inflation." And, what must a nation do to achieve a new prosperity? It must possess one of the "basic elements that gives character to a people . . . the competitive spirit." The "competitive spirit goes by many names," but "most simply and directly, it is called the 'work ethic'. . . . As the name implies, the work ethic holds that labor is good in itself; that a man or a woman at work not only makes a contribution to his fellow man, but becomes a better person by virtue of the act of working." Are Americans possessed of the work ethic? Yes, said the President, it is "ingrained in the American character" and that is why we consider it "immoral to be lazy or slothful," immoral to "avoid work by going on welfare," and are willing to manifest "reaffirmation of our competitive spirit, the willingness to make a personal sacrifice in pursuit of worthy goals." As evidence of the reaffirmation the President offered a letter from a state employee in Texas (a state in which the Governor had threatened to oppose the President's wage freeze for state employees) which read: "We were both due for salary increases in September . . . but we will survive. If it is necessary to cut our income in half, I still know of no other country I would choose to call my own. I've heard the young people using a phrase that might fit: 'Right on.' " Such responses as these, said the President using a phrase that suggests the rankings of college football teams, would permit America to be "number one" rather than "resign ourselves to being number two or number three or even number four."

Now, what is going on here? Many things, of course. But one thing is that a decision, originally couched in symbols that emphasize, perhaps exacerbate, economic resentments ("wage-price freeze," "surcharge," or "taxes"), is merchandised in the imagery of morality (the "work ethic," it is "immoral to be lazy or slothful"), of status ("personal sacrifice in the pursuit of worthy goals by the man in the street, the worker on the job, the homemaker trying to balance the family budget"), and of national power, status, and pride (America can be "number one in the world economically"). Such imagery fits well the widely shared concerns and aspirations of Americans (see Chapter Four). This is not to say that the President, or any political leader, is aware of empirical evidence on such matters. It is simply to offer the view that in political communications leaders adjust symbols to conform to the images that they think prevail among the populace. Nor could we assert that the President was successful in building support for the New Economic Policy; yet it is of some interest that approval of Nixon's handling of economic affairs, as measured by published polls, rose from 32 to 47 percent during the period of his public appeals.[11]

In addition to the tendency of political leaders to adjust their symbolic messages to the predispositions of their audiences, there is a second major aspect of political communications related to their semantic properties. This is the common tendency for politicians, especially candidates for office, to employ *ambiguous symbols* in the absence of any solid notion of what is on the minds of followers. For example, any political candidate wants to be attractive to voters, but it it difficult to know what voters find attractive. The candidate often deems it better to pose as a relatively undefined something-taken-into-account by appearing cool but courageous, self-confident but not egotistical, articulate but not verbose, or handsome but not too cute. With such an ambiguous or low profile the candidate is a political object that voters find just attractive enough to permit them to discover in him the qualities they find most desirable in themselves.[12] In short, realizing that voters impart meanings to their appearances, candidates endeavor to strike poses sufficiently undefined to permit beauty to come from the eye of the beholder!

How Images Are Exchanged: Means and Languages of Communication

How people transmit images among themselves has been the problem studied by the information theorist. The definition of information scientists employ differs from the popular view that information is simply knowledge. Instead, students of communication *define information as a pattern of events or data which reduces uncertainty or disorganization.*[13] For example, the "picture" we see on a television tube consists of tiny dots, or more accurately, electric impulses. The dots in themselves do not constitute information but the pattern of relationships between those impulses does. When television is referred to as a "cool" medium, the implication is that television is low in information; that is, the capacity of the screen to transmit electric impulses is relatively low. With fewer

[11]News Release, *The Harris Survey,* September 6, 1971.

[12]John W. Fox, "The Concepts of Image and Adoption in Relation to Interpersonal Behavior," *Journal of Communication,* Vol. 17 (1967), 147-51; G. Jahoda, "Political Attitudes and Judgments of Other People," *Journal of Abnormal and Social Psychology,* Vol. 49 (1954), 330-34.

[13]J. R. Pierce, *Symbols, Signals and Noise* (New York: Harper & Row, 1961), p. 24; Wilbur Schramm, "Information Theory and Mass Communication," *Journalism Quarterly,* Vol. 32 (Spring 1955), 131-46; Karl W. Deutsch, *The Nerves of Government* (New York: Free Press, 1963), pp. 75-97.

impulses at hand from which to detect a clearly defined pattern, the viewer must supply his own interpretation to complete the picture, to reduce the uncertainty in the television pattern. Thus the viewer not only watches television, he *engages* in it in virtually the same sense that persons engage in communication. The viewer is involved rather than passive. There is a close parallel to the low information content of television and what we described in the last section as the ambiguity or low profile used by political candidates — one possible reason (in addition to its capacity to reach large numbers of people) for the seeming popularity of campaigning by television.[14]

Generally information theory is too esoteric to assist us here in describing how people exchange images, but certain notions are relevant. An image possesses relative degrees of information. We might, for example, speculate that the image of Adolph Hitler in Nazi Germany (as a strong, decisive, firm and ruthless leader) contained high information to the degree it assisted Germans to reduce the uncertainty produced by war and economic crisis.

To the degree that images incorporate information, the notions of entrophy and redundancy in information theory are useful. *Entrophy refers to uncertainty or disorganization and the lack of predictability in events; redundancy is the opposite, the relatively high predictability in a situation.* Communication reduces entrophy, but this is not always the case, certainly not in politics. The politician who straddles all sides of an issue does little to lessen our uncertainty as to what he will do if elected. Indeed, the amount of redundancy to use, and hence the degree of uncertainty to dispel, is one of the great strategic questions faced by any politician. In his 1968 campaign for the presidency, Richard M. Nixon walked a tightrope between entrophy and redundancy in his statements about the Vietnam war. On the one hand, he endeavored to reduce uncertainty over whether or not he had a position on the war at all by asserting repeatedly (in redundant language) that he had a plan for ending the conflict; on the other, he removed little entrophy by refusing to spell out that plan until "after I am elected."

In addition to entrophy and redundancy in communication there is noise. *Noise is anything in the transmission that interferes with the exchange of information.* "Snow" on the television screen, static on the radio, daydreaming during a class lecture, pathological distrust among people are all examples of noise. We might generally assume that, since noise is disruptive, people try to avoid it. Yet, at least in political communication, noise may be purposely included: "The final paragraph of many political speeches (containing appeals to 'God and country', confidence in the 'wis-

[14]Marshall McLuhan, *Understanding Media: The Extensions of Man* (New York: Signet Books, 1964).

dom of the people' and 'the grand heritage of democracy') is also just so much logical static hardly even functioning as a punctuation mark."[15]

Information theorists not only lead us to ask how much information, entrophy, redundancy, and noise there is in political communication; they also direct our attention to the ways people communicate and code their messages — the means and languages of communication.

The Means of Communication

In thinking about how people communicate about politics what first comes to mind is *talk* — people using words to tell each other things. The political oration, the stump speech, the rally in the shopping center, the administrative decree, or the Supreme Court opinion are all examples of political talk. A distinctive feature of talk is that people usually exchange ideas in a sequential, or story, way. It is primarily through narrative that we exchange cognitive images laden with facts, logic, and reason. This is not to deny the capacities for emotional expression in verbal or written talk, but to say that, as a matter of emphasis, in politics there is a tendency to rely on the narrative in transmitting facts, as in parliamentary debates, position papers, agency reports, question-and-answer sessions, presidential addresses, government documents, and other means of exchange.

Pictures are a particularly effective means for communicating emotions. Whereas words, the elements of political talk, often acquire shared meanings (as indicated by our common responses to them), pictures leave more room for individual interpretation. The meaning in a picture *"depends upon the character and disposition of the recipient of the communication and the values he learns from his culture."*[16] Examples of transmission of images through pictures are not hard to find — photographs of political leaders, posters, political commercials on television, billboards, etc. The American Medical Association was seeking in the late 1940s to defeat a proposed plan for federal subsidization of the doctor-patient relation. A primary method for doing this was the distribution of thousands of prints of a painting of a country doctor at the bedside of a sick child captioned, "Keep Politics Out of This Picture."[17]

In addition to talk and pictures, people exchange messages through their *actions*. We said earlier that anything a person does, even remaining silent, carries meaning for those interpreting his behavior. In politics a variety of actions serve as ways of communicating. Marches, rallies, dramas, dances, and rituals are but a few of these. The elaborate rallies in Nazi

[15]Gordon, *The Languages of Communication,* p. 40.

[16]Gordon, *The Languages of Communication,* p. 142.

[17]Stanley Kelley, Jr., *Professional Public Relations and Political Power* (Baltimore: Johns Hopkins, 1956), p. 77.

Germany's Nuremberg were explicit efforts to dramatize the values of unity, authority, self-sacrifice, and obedience basic to the Nazi regime. Communicating through actions emphasizes the conative dimension of images — acting out, often to the point of making a ritual of them, desired habits of behavior.

Communication theorists postulate that the ways people exchange messages by their talk, pictures, and actions have important social consequences. Word-of-mouth communication, for instance, produces "oral" cultures where persons exchange images in small and intimate groups. Politically this tradition is reflected in parliamentary bodies or the "Town Hall" tradition of New England. President Lyndon Johnson was reputed to be a leader of the oral tradition who liked to speak chin-to-chin, eyeball-to-eyeball, and hand-to-hand with political friend and foe alike in attempting to persuade them to follow him.

Print tends to produce a dependency upon the word as physically displayed on the page, not as discerned by the ear through oral exchange. Print breaks thoughts down into elementary symbols, usually words, presents them in sequence, and thereby may even influence us to see the world in accordance with such a model of independent, linearly arranged units. Print has another effect: " . . . print encourages individualism and specialization. To live in an oral culture, one acquires knowledge only in contact with other people, in terms of communal activities. Printing, however, allows individuals to withdraw, to contemplate and mediate outside of communal activities."[18] Thus, the print culture contributes to developing the type of citizen revered by some theories of democracy, the person who forms his images of politics in solitary contemplation of the information provided by newspaper, magazine, books, and public documents. Print also has the capacity to store in written form the images of one era so that they can be communicated to another; rather than relying upon word-of-mouth to hand down the fable of George Washington and the cherry tree, for example, it is preserved in children's books.

Just as print removes time as an obstacle to preserving political images, moving pictures on screens (as in film or television) removes space as a barrier to transmission. Instantaneous transmission of political words, pictures, and actions to millions of viewers around the world, and even from the moon to earth, enhances the transfer of political symbols across space (recall the first televised pictures of the American flag beamed from the moon!).

[18]James W. Carey, "Harold Adam Innis and Marshall McLuhan," *Antioch Review* (Spring 1967), pp. 5-39.

The Languages of Communication

The languages we use to communicate are tools for reflection that assist us in thought, reasoning, and problem solving. But, they are even more. Languages are modes of action, our means of behaving toward one another. This is particularly true in politics where *the types and styles of languages we use shape our political relationships.* Recall that in Chapter One we said political images are instruments that assist us in obtaining tangible rewards from politics; they also are evaluative categories and standards that help us to judge ideas, people, and programs; and, our images give us a way to express our innermost identities, needs, wants, fears, and aspirations. It is through the types and styles of political language that we use images in these three ways.

TYPES OF POLITICAL LANGUAGE

We usually think of language as a body of words used by a people who agree on what objects those words refer to. So long as there is widespread agreement on the relationships between words and their referents, we have an *object language* that facilitates the transmission of information. But there is another type of language, *protolanguage,* in which the referents for signs are not so clear. Protolanguage includes such nonverbal signs as gestures, body movements, and silence (note the embarrassment when a politician remains silent in responding to a difficult question in a TV interview). Protolanguage conveys information, but due to the absence of agreement on the relations between signs and referents, it involves a high degree of entropy. Protolanguage provides a greater latitude for each person to interpret the meaning of what others transmit than is the case with object language.[19]

Although people transmit images through both object language and protolanguage, much of our political symbolism rests upon protolanguage. Nonverbal communication permits a wider latitude in transmitting vague images than does explicit verbal language. Verbal communication emphasizes the cognitive side of our views, but protolanguages give more leeway in expressing our emotions. Take as an example our oft-cited case of flags:

"Suppose that, instead of displaying the Stars and Stripes, we were to write the words 'American flag' across a piece of cloth and to display that. While the symbols would display the same meaning, the effect would be

[19]Robert C. Carson, *Interaction Concepts of Personality,* (Chicago: Aldine, 1969) p. 19; Alfred L. Baldwin, *Theories of Child Development* (New York: John Wiley, 1968), pp. 232-33; Watzlawick et al., *The Pragmatics of Human Communication,* pp. 60-67; Harley C. Shands, "Outline of a General Theory of Human Communication" in Lee Thayer, ed., *Communication: Concepts and Perspectives* (Washington, D.C.: Spartan Books, 1967), pp. 108-12; Ernst Cassirer, *The Philosophy of Symbolic Forms* (New Haven: Yale University Press, 1953), pp. 177-97.

quite different. To translate the rich visual mosaic of the Stars and Stripes into written form would be to deprive it of most of its qualities of corporate image and of experience, yet the abstract literal bond would remain much the same."[20]

Protolanguage has another advantage over object language for transmitting images. Whereas words are the sign basis of object language, protolanguage incorporates a greater variety of signs. Aside from gestural and postural signs of which there are many (the human face alone can make some 250,000 different expressions),[21] we communicate through odor-producing-olfactory means, through tactile means (vascularity, oiliness and dryness of skin), through muscular means (flaccidity, rigidity, and tone), and through costuming (such as military uniforms) and grooming (as in the case of hair length). We have already noted that there is a language of silence; e.g., the failure of a president to return a call to a cabinet member may make the latter anxious about his political position (as, in 1970, when President Richard Nixon did not respond to the messages of his Secretary of the Interior, Walter Hickel, then requested Hickel's resignation). And, although we seldom think about it, time and space are languages. A political speech that seems too long to an audience (like many delivered by Hubert Humphrey in his 1968 quest for the presidency), arriving early or late for appointments, putting off seeing people until "later" — all these actions use time as a very eloquent language. Space also "speaks." It speaks in the distance people keep between one another when conversing, the position of an official's desk in his office, the location of a politician's office in a building (whether near the top or in the basement), and the size of quarters (as whether a candidate can afford plush headquarters or must run his campaign from an isolated tenement).[22] In governmental bureaucracies the allocation of large offices versus cubby holes, preferred parking spaces, and the fabled "key to the executive washroom" are all ways of transmitting the sense of hierarchy, or the pecking order, from superiors to subordinates.

One of the principal forms of protolanguage is body movement. Research suggests that a particular body language, as with verbal language, is learned. A person's culture has much to do with what gestural and postural movements he uses to communicate. Probably no gesture or body motion has the same meaning in all societies (a smile in one may reflect what is communicated by a grimace in another). Moreover, the meanings in body language are such that "*no position, expression, or movement ever carries meaning in and of itself;*" body language, in short, acquires its

[20]McLuhan, *Understanding Media*, p. 85.

[21]Birdwhistell, *Kinesics and Context.*

[22]Don Fabun, *Communications: The Transfer of Meaning* (Beverly Hills: Glencoe Press, 1968).

meaning from the context it is in and the response people make to it (just as is the case with messages transmitted verbally).[23]

Despite research findings indicating that there are no body movements that serve as universal symbols transcending contexts, there are patterns in interpersonal body language that exist, patterns apparent in politics. Politicians often use body language, for instance, to include or exclude individuals from a group. A politician at a caucus who finds others turning their backs on him, walking off to greet others, or gazing past him to others in the room while conversing with him quickly infers loss of membership, status, and power. How people arrange themselves — face-to-face, side-by-side, leaning toward or away from one another, etc. — also communicates something in politics. Kremlinologists (those students of the politics of the Soviet Union who infer from various indications what is going on in the USSR) study photos of government leaders reviewing parades from the Kremlin in hopes of detecting power changes by such signs as who stands beside whom, who toasts whom, etc. Whether to hold political negotiations at square tables or round tables is another example of this pattern; round tables, requiring at least partial face-to-face seating, symbolize equality of status for all participants while square or rectangular tables raise questions of who sits at the "head," "side," and "bottom."

People also communicate by adopting distinctive body movements. A leader may employ unusual and striking gestures (as did Adolph Hitler) for emphasis and dramatic impact; yet, these distinctive gestures also set him off from the rest of the group as one of higher status and power. To the joy of many mimics Richard Nixon uses an exaggerated series of stilted, almost mechanical, body movements; amusing though they may be, they provide him with a style that some read as a clue to his politics as well as his posture. A politician also uses body language to identify with followers, to convey the image that he is one of them. Fiorello LaGuardia, former mayor of New York City, transmitted a down-to-earth image through body movements that suggested he could adjust to the ethnic composition of his audience.[24]

Nonverbal means of communicating are partly expressive; that is, a person's posture, gestures, perspiration rate, dress, hair, or whatever, are outward manifestations of inner emotional states or psychophysical problems. But, the protolanguages serve instrumental and evaluative functions as well; as with object language they provide politicians with means to transmit symbolic appeals for votes (as Fiorello LaGuardia did), make judgment about politics (as did members of the Yippie movement through their clothing styles), as well as express their identifications with groups (as did the "Afro" hair style for many American blacks).

[23]Birdwhistell, *Kinesics and Context,* p. 45 (italics in original); Julius Fast, *Body Language* (New York: M. Evans and Company, 1970).

[24]A. E. Scheflen, "Human Communication," *Behavioral Science,* Vol. 13 (1968).

There are examples in American politics when protolanguages have been significant: the Kennedy-Nixon debates in 1960 when Richard Nixon's pale and transparent skin highlighted a heavy beard and his constant perspiring communicated apparent tension; the gaunt figure of Governor George Wallace at the Democratic National Convention in 1972 delivering his prepared speech while seated because of his fatigue and weakness following recovery from a nearly fatal attempt on his life; or the ever-present and seemingly spontaneous smile of Dwight Eisenhower that communicated warmth to so many Americans.

The widespread use of protolanguages in politics, however, does not deny the fact that verbal forms of communication are always present as well. Research suggests that in America the emphasis is on words for carrying the central meaning of an interaction while nonverbal forms are only a complement (albeit a significant one).[25]

Certainly in American politics words count for a great deal. First, they have instrumental value. Through words policy-makers sanctify, as well as explain, their decisions allocating the rewards and costs associated with material resources. President Nixon's rhetoric in building support for his New Economic Policy is but one of many instances.

Second, using political words we make judgments on policies, programs, and the "good" and "bad" guys. Think, for example, how different is the reaction of interests to policies depending upon whether the word "compulsory" or "voluntary" is attached to the proposals. The physician has a much different reaction to "voluntary health insurance" than to "compulsory health insurance." To submit voluntarily a labor-management dispute to arbitration implies something quite different than "compulsory arbitration." And, a "volunteer" army seems less repulsive than the "draft" or a "conscript" army. To be sure, the words themselves imply tangible differences in policy; they also evoke immediate conditioned responses: "Language becomes a sequence of Pavlovian cues rather than an instrument for reasoning and analysis if situation and appropriate cue occur together."[26]

Finally, words are definitely expressive. What better way to express pent-up frustrations and fears than to yell "Niggers," "Commies," or some other epithet. Popular television supplies us with an example of this form of expressive behavior. In the 1970s there appeared a television series, *All in the Family,* whose main character, Archie Bunker, was a relatively uneducated, marginally successful,

[25]Birdwhistell, *Kinesics and Context,* p. 55.

[26]Murray Edelman, *The Symbolic Uses of Politics* (Urbana: University of Illinois Press, 1964), p. 116.

bigot who made much of taking his frustrations out on his college-educated son-in-law (Archie dubbed him "meathead"), his wife ("Dingbat"), and the neighbors ("Spiks," "Hippies," "Darkies," "Pollacks," and "Wops"). With each word Archie expressed his reaction to what he perceived as a not-too-friendly world.

RHETORICAL STYLES

In exchanging images people assume a stance both toward each other and toward the content of what they are communicating. *Through their style people reveal such stances.*[27] We are all familiar, for example, with the college professor, well-versed in his subject but with very low regard for the intelligence or enthusiasm of his students, who practices a didactic style ("inclined to teach or to lecture others too much" according to the dictionary). To the notion of style we add that of *rhetoric,* or *the effective use of language.* What we are interested in is the variety of rhetorical styles common to political imagery.[28]

An *exhortive* style urges, or exhorts, a person to some course of conduct. It reflects the belief of those using it that something should be done and that the audience should act. We encounter this style when politicians appeal for mass support. Exhortation often involves a reasoned message — formally stated premise, inferences, and conclusions in the form of threats or promises. To get the attention of the audience and to make an impression, politicians usually resort to an abstract and/or dogmatic statement (e.g., "democracy" or "international conspiracy"). Metaphor is a favorite tactic in exhortation as politicians promise a "war" on poverty (Lyndon Johnson), an economic "game plan" (Richard Nixon), or a "crusade" against crime, corruption, and Communism (Dwight Eisenhower).[29] Political speeches typify exhortive rhetoric. A candidate asserts the premise that his opponent is a "big spender" and accuses him of "fiscal irresponsibility." He then infers that if his opponent is elected it will mean a "sky-rocketing national debt and runaway inflation." He promises, if elected, to "stem the tide," halt spending and lower the cost of living. The implication of the imagery he uses is that the politician makes mass appeals because he (a) needs public support and (b) wants popular participation in decisions. Although neither may be the case, his pleas foster a myth of popular control over policy making.

The *legal* style is the formal language in which lawmakers couch their decisions, as in statutes, constitutions, treaties, etc. The style

[27]Gordon, *The Languages of Communication,* pp. 190-203.

[28]The styles discussed are largely those considered in Hayakawa, *Symbol, Status, and Personality,* pp. 103-19 and Edelman, *The Symbolic Uses of Politics,* pp. 130-51.

[29]Murray Edelman, *Politics as Symbolic Action* (Chicago: Markham, 1971), pp. 65-83.

permits officials to give the impression that decisions once reached are forever binding, for they are stated in apparently complex and precise language. In fact, as the very existence of the judiciary indicates, the language is usually ambiguous with a great deal of room for interpretation. The "law" which is symbolized as sacred and immutable is "what the judge says it is," or, as frequently implied, "what the judge discovers it is." The legal style communicates images that, on the one hand, serve the instrumental purpose of building respect for the law, government, regime, and authority and on the other serve an evaluative purpose, because legal style "provides a vocabulary in which organized groups justify their actions. . . ."[30]

In the *bureaucratic* style a highly technical language communicates rules and regulations, and the limits of their application, to the general public and between administrators. The intricate jargon implies that persons who can understand the language constitute an educated, skilled body of technicians. Penetrating the complexities of bureaucratic rules and procedures seems magical, and bureaucrats are magicians. So long as the magicians perform pleasing tricks (supplying a draft deferment, a social security check, or other benefit) the awe and mystery remains; but, as so often happens when witch doctors fail, respect for administrative personnel vanishes when rules say "no" to clienteles rather than "yes".

Bargaining is the give-and-take in politics and, therefore, the style that promotes the compromises requisite to policy making. We associate bargaining with congressional committees, state legislatures, and lobbyists. It is the least public of the rhetorical styles in politics, taking place in the privacy of the backstage, where political leaders negotiate deals that their constituents might not readily approve. Once the bargain is consummated, exhortations win public support, legal language permits changes, and bureaucratic jargon helps cloak the program in impartiality.

The *emotional* style reflects expressive imagery whereas other styles are more instrumental or evaluative in tone. It shares with exhortation the use of abstract rather than concrete symbols to focus upon what "should" or "ought to" be done instead of accurately describing "what is." But, whereas exhortive abstractions are impersonalized symbols such as "democracy" or "communism," the emotional style relies upon personifications such as "they," "the junkie," or "hairs." The emotional style usually reflects a firm commitment between alternatives ("Rather Dead than Red" or "Love It or Leave It"), cites traditional authority (the Bible, Marx, Freud) rather

---

[30]Edelman, *The Symbolic Uses of Politics,* p. 139.

than evidence to prove points, and reflects a concern with selfish interests rather than a social orientation.[31]

There are, to be sure, other styles of political communication; the humorous style of Will Rogers, Abraham Lincoln or Adlai Stevenson, the strident style of the "radical chic," the shock (or four-letter-word) style of some militants, and the "insider" style of *Time* or *Newsweek* only begin what could be a very lengthy list. The point is that the rhetorical style used helps dictate meaning; put another way, *what* a politician says (content) may seem less important to an audience than the *type of language* (verbal or nonverbal) he uses and *how* (style) he says it. Perhaps the image we have of former President Lyndon Johnson will always be shaped more by our recollection of his Texas drawl and elderly, high school principal appearance than by all the things he ever said or wrote during and about his presidency.

The Homophily Principle

A variety of factors determine the types of ways, languages, and rhetorical styles people use in communicating their images of politics. According to communication scientists, one of the most important factors is the degree of similarity between persons engaged in communication. This is called the homophily principle. *Homophily* "refers to the degree to which pairs of individuals who interact are similar with respect to certain attributes, such as beliefs, values, education, social status, etc." *Heterophily* is "the degree to which pairs of individuals who interact are different with respect to certain attributes.[32] Generally people who share similar objective attributes (age, status, etc.) and subjective images (beliefs, values, and predispositions) communicate with one another more frequently than persons who differ in these respects. For instance, in presidential elections persons similar in age and social status influence each other;[33] in state legislatures members interact most frequently with those of similar age, prestige, and partisanship.[34] In short, people who are alike and who agree with one another talk to one another (the homophily principle). Moreover, there tends to be a more accurate exchange of images among such people.

[31]Robert E. Lane, *Political Thinking and Consciousness* (Chicago: Markham Publishing Company, 1969), pp. 53-55.

[32]Everett M. Rogers and Dilip K. Bhowmick, "Homophily-Heterophily: Relational Concepts for Communication Research," *Public Opinion Quarterly,* Vol. 35 (Winter, 1970-71), 523-38.

[33]Paul F. Lazarsfeld et al., *The People's Choice* (New York: Columbia University Press, 1948), pp. 137-39.

[34]John C. Wahlke et al., *The Legislative System* (New York: John Wiley, 1962).

People who are alike then, have a basis for a reasonable amount of certainty in what to expect from one another, and entrophy is thereby less. Complete homophily, however, implies redundancy, since each person "would already know the message content, and it would contain no information for him."[35] Effective communication probably depends upon a balance between similarities and differences in participants. To permit communication at all, participants must be similar in relevant ways; but to assure that the message contains new information, they also must be different in other ways. Members of tight-knit, closed ideological groups (such as many of the local clubs of the John Birch Society, an ultra-conservative movement of the 1960s) meet often but learn little from one another that they do not already know; arbitration of a labor-management dispute, on the other hand, brings together contestants who have sufficient goals in common to permit arbitration but who differ on means and, as a result, are available for a give-and-take of information. Politics itself is a communication process reflecting homophily on relevant variables, heterophily on others; i.e., persons share a common desire to live together but a diversity of special interests.

One factor which tends to bridge dissimilarities between communicators is their ability to empathize with one another. Empathy is the ability of a person to see things from another's vantage point, to put himself "in the other's shoes," or project himself into the role of the other. The empathetic person need not hold images identical to those around him, but he is able to *entertain* their images and see the world as they see it. Thus, a political leader may not have the beliefs, feelings, and tendencies of his constituents; yet, if he has empathy with them, he can visualize their thoughts and couch his messages accordingly. Generally communication is more effective if the source of a message (say, a political candidate) has greater empathy than the receiver (say, the electorate); voters need to empathize with the candidate less than he needs to with them.

The homophily principle assumes that there are objective and subjective differences and similarities between people. In interpersonal communication the source-receiver relationship is direct and people are generally aware of what unites and divides them. In interpersonal relations the homophily principle generally applies. But, in mass communication the source is far removed from his audience; informal social relationships intervene between source and receiver. Mr. Smith may not, for example, hear or see a presidential address himself but may hear about it through family members, friends, neighbors, or associates. Thus, the similarity-dissimilarity of Mr. Smith to the President is of lesser importance to the

[35]Rogers and Bhowmick, "Homophily-Heterophily," p. 530.

communication than his social relationships with others and, in turn, their relationships to the President. In mass communication, therefore, the homophily-heterophily relationship is complicated by the intervention of social *networks* that transmit political images.

The complications introduced by mass communications influence how political images get diffused throughout populations. Evidence suggests a *two-step flow of communication* whereby, first, images reach relatively well-informed individuals through the mass media and, second, images are transmitted from those persons through interpersonal channels to others who are less directly exposed to mass media.[36] But, the two-step flow is probably more characteristic of routine news events than of striking ones. In fact, studies indicate that almost 90 percent of persons acquire their initial awareness of a major news event (e.g., the launching of Sputnik in 1957, the assassination of President John Kennedy in 1963, and the slayings of Martin Luther King or Senator Robert Kennedy in 1968) through the mass media. This near-saturation is accomplished within 48 hours, with up to 10 percent remaining uninformed thereafter.[37]

The Effects of Communication

The distinction between interpersonal and mass communication is useful in examining the effects of communication upon the relations between people, particularly between political leaders and followers.

Interpersonal Communication

In any interpersonal exchange we can assume that each individual possesses some image of himself — some picture of what he is like, what he aspires to be, as well as what he has become. Consciously or not everyone engaging in communication tries to protect and enhance his *self-image*. When his messages get through to others, it is not only because he has employed appropriate symbols, means, channel, languages, or style. It is also because he strikes a responsive chord in the self-images held by others. Put simply:

"If the content of your message is seen by your listener as enhancing to his self-concept, it will be received and welcomed. If, however, the ideas you are

---

[36]For a discussion of this process see Elihu Katz, "The Two-Step Flow of Communication: An Up-to-Date Report on an Hypothesis," *Public Opinion Quarterly*, Vol. 21 (Spring 1957), 61-78; see also Bruce H. Westley, "Communication and Social Change," *American Behavioral Scientist*, Vol. 14 (May/June 1971), 719-44 and Melvin L. DeFleur, *Theories of Mass Communication* (New York: McKay, 1966), pp. 119-38.

[37]Percy H. Tannebaum and Bradley S. Greenberg, "Mass Communication" in Paul R. Farnsworth, ed., *The Annual Review of Psychology*, Vol. 19 (1968), 351-86.

trying to present are seen by the listener as threatening, all he will do is rigidify his defenses against you. . . . No man or woman can easily be persuaded to do something, to accept something, which violates or threatens his self-concept. . . . This resistance is not so much proof of his cussedness as it is evidence that, like yourself, he sees what he sees, he understands what he understands, and he is not likely to change his perceptions just because someone else tells him to."[38]

If people enhance and/or threaten self-images through communication, then if we want to get our points across to people it helps to have some idea (built up from our experiences with others) of what their self-images are. We must imagine, in short, what the other person perceives, imagine how he will respond to our messages, and mentally rehearse our response to him. The overall process, in which empathy obviously plays a central role, is not simply stimulus followed by response, but involves alternating and circular responses that also determine stimuli. Conversation, for instance, is something like a prize fight. In conversation "each opponent has to put himself in the place of the other so as to decide what to do himself. He must imagine his adversary attacking at one point or pretending to do so and then really attacking in another, and then try to defend himself adequately at the same time anticipating his actions. For only by putting himself in his opponent's place can he anticipate him and in due course make a fitting reply."[39]

In examining political communication at the interpersonal level it is useful to keep in mind a critical distinction — i.e., the distinction between the meaning of the *content* of a message and the *relational* meaning of a message. The information we exchange with another person as *content* may have relatively little to do with what we are saying about how we want to *relate* to him. Let us assume John Doe runs for public office and that he needs substantial financial backing from Mr. Jones. Doe telephones Jones, exchanges pleasantries with him, and reminds Jones of their longstanding, warm friendship. Doe states his desire to seek office and asks Jones's reaction. Jones responds favorably, "If there is *anything* I can do to help, let me know." Thereupon Doe asks for a sizable contribution and for an appointment to arrange it. Jones explains that "My calendar is booked solid until after the election, John; I just don't think we can possibly get together. But, check back with me in a few days and I'll try to squeeze you in." Doe does, but learns from Jones's secretary that Jones is "in conference," "out of town," "ill today," or otherwise unavailable. The content meaning of Jones's supportive message ("If there is *anything* I can do . . .") has been replaced with the relational meaning ("Don't call me, I'll call you" or "Don't come to me for a handout").

---

[38]Hayakawa, *Symbol, Status, and Personality*, pp. 45-46, 48.
[39]Aranguren, *Human Communication*, p. 18.

Relational messages communicate two principal types of images, both important in politics.[40] First, they communicate differences in status between people in particular contexts. That is, we infer from the way people treat us whether they regard themselves (their self-images) as superior, inferior, or equal to us. We learn from relational messages whether they think it appropriate to dominate us or defer to us. Although Mr. Jones in our example accepts equality with his old acquaintance Doe at the content level, the relational message is that Jones is the superior and only he can initiate support for potential candidates. Second, relational messages communicate affection between people. We can, to use the polar opposites, say "I love you" or say "I hate you" by relating to others in ways over and above what we say to them. Candidate John Doe is not only "put down" in status by Jones's refusal to return his calls, Doe soon gets the message that Jones's "friendship" may be only lukewarm.

When the relations between people lead them to accept one another as equals in status and affection, their messages usually reinforce that equality. Very often, however, when Person A communicates with Person B he invites B to accept him as superior or inferior in status and as worthy of like or dislike. In short, A induces B to accept *his* definition of their relationship, and he communicates that desire and emphasizes the differences between himself and B rather than emphasizing equality. (The conventional image of marriage in America is that the "dominant" male earns the living and protects "his" submissive, affectionate wife from the ravages of hunger or other males. Much of the rhetoric of the woman's liberation movement is directed at redefining the symbols of marriage.) In politics a candidate for office normally structures the relationship between himself and his constituents by emphasizing equal status ("I need your help and your votes in this election and you need me in Congress"). Following victory the winner may emphasize status differences with himself acting as the "leader" and his constituents as the "led."

We mentioned earlier that interpersonal communication at some point involves reinforcements or threats to the self-images of participants and their definitions of the desired relationship. John Doe, for example, possessed an image of himself as a candidate acceptable to Jones. In their initial communication Jones seemed to confirm Doe's self-image (the offer of assistance); at least Jones did not reject Doe's self-image (by telling Doe he should not be a candidate for lack of qualifications); but, in the end, Jones disconfirmed Doe's self-image by ignoring his calls. Instead of saying "You are wrong," Jones said, in effect, "You do not exist." In one way or another we see these confirming, rejecting, and disconfirming responses in politics frequently. In his 1971 State of the Union Address, for example, President Richard Nixon listed revenue sharing (a plan to turn federal

[40]Uriel G. Foa, "Convergencies in the Analysis of the Structure of Interpersonal Behavior," *Psychological Review,* Vol. 68 (1961), 341-53.

money back to the states for expenditure to solve local problems rather than have the federal government spend the money) as a major goal. However, in his early development of the revenue-sharing proposal, the President failed to consult adequately with Representative Wilbur Mills, Chairman of the House Ways and Means Committee, through whom the proposal must pass for ultimate House of Representatives approval. Of course, we do not know Representative Mills's self-image, but it is safe to say that he regarded himself as of sufficient power, knowledge, and parliamentary skill in matters of domestic taxing and spending to deserve extensive consultation even though he was a Democrat dealing with a Republican President. He initially reacted to the President's "disconfirmation" of this definition by opposing the measure (although this "rejection" stemmed from substantive as well as relational grounds).

A few summary propositions are appropriate regarding the effects of communication on interpersonal relations: First, in every communication the participants offer definitions of their relationship which they hope will actually structure that relationship; second, they do this through messages that emphasize similarities and/or differences in status and affection; third, each person then confirms, rejects, ignores, or modifies the image of the other; fourth, once relationships are established, *those relationships form the context within which participants define the meaning of the content of messages exchanged;* and therefore, fifth, effective communication (seen as a transaction in which the meaning of messages exchanged is largely the same for all participants) depends upon a *shared definition of both the situations and the symbols* (words, pictures, etc.) *employed.*

Communicating images at the interpersonal level has many characteristics of a game. For one thing, each person involved must anticipate what others will do and how he will adjust to their moves (what transpires in a court of law — the Supreme Court included — between attorneys and judges is but one obvious example from politics). Or, once a relationship between persons has been defined, participants come to expect one another to communicate in certain ways regardless of content areas (as when America's allies expect to be consulted upon major foreign policy decisions by this country as a confirmation of equality of diplomatic status); these expectations become the *rules* of the relationship. We will extend this game analogy below but first let us consider the character of mass communication.

Mass Communication

Mass communication differs from interpersonal communication in that the former is usually directed toward large, diverse, and anonymous audiences; is public, rapid, and transient; transmits messages from a single source to many receivers (jungle drums, smoke signals, radio, television, etc.); and, is generally well organized. Interpersonal communication, in contrast, involves smaller, relatively homogeneous audiences; is more likely to be immediate and private, relying characteristically on intimate face-to-face transmission; and, is more spontaneous.[41] But, in thinking about how leaders communicate political images to mass audiences, we should stress a basic similarity between mass and interpersonal; i.e., both involve social relationships. In the case of mass communication we more accurately label these as *parasocial relationships.*

A parasocial relationship involves people in what *seems* like face-to-face meeting even when they are not in direct contact. Granted the mass media do not bring people together in any physical sense; rather, the mass media stand between people and carry symbols between them. Yet, mass communication often gives the illusion of face-to-face contact between people, even though the receiver and source are not in the physical presence of one another.

We can clarify the nature of a parasocial relationship if we think of television, using as an example the popular television show of the 1960s and 1970s, *The Tonight Show,* starring Johnny Carson. Carson, in the vernacular of television, is a "personality," i.e., a performer who achieves intimacy with mass audiences. The quality of this intimacy differs from face-to-face contact, yet there develops a continuing relationship between performer and audience that is satisfying for the large numbers of viewers who willingly engage and share in it. But, in a relationship such as that between Carson and his audience, the viewer is not simply the target of symbolic messages; rather, he senses himself to be an active participant in the events he observes. This sense of participation is contrived (but no less meaningful) by subtle staging that creates an image of the performer in the viewer's eyes, an "image, while partial, contrived, and penetrated by illusion, is no fantasy or dream; his performance is an objectively perceptible action in which the viewer is implicated imaginatively, but which he does not imagine."[42]

There are several staging tactics, all exemplified on *The Tonight Show.* One employs the informal, conversational style of face-to-face contact; Carson not only does this through easy banter with guests on his "talk" format, but through direct remarks to the television audience as if he were in private, personal conversation with each member. The conversational style bridges, or obscures, the gulf between performer and audience. Carson reinforces this intimacy by calling guests and members of his supporting cast by their first names ("Ed" McMahon, "Zsa Zsa" Gabor, or

[41]Carson, *Interaction Concepts of Personality,* pp. 122-217.

[42]Donald Horton and R. Richard Wohl, "Mass Communication and Para-Social Interaction," *Psychiatry,* Vol. 19 (1956), 215-29; Kurt Lang and Gladys Engel Lang, *Politics and Television* (Chicago: Quadrangle Books, 1968), p. 32.

"Doc" Severinsen) and they call him "Johnny" in return. Carson further blurs the distinction between performer and audience by meandering into the studio audience for more fun and games. Through such devices Carson, and similar television personalities, emerge as sociable, affable, friendly, warm, and intimate.

In a parasocial relationship the viewer is not simply watching a drama unfold, as he might in watching a filmed production; he responds to the cues of the performer, adapts images to those the performer expresses, and supports the artist in efforts to entertain. The appropriate response to the performer is not left wholly to the audience's discretion. Instead, as with Carson, the treatment the performer receives from his supporting cast, guest stars, and members of the studio audience coach the viewer into the proper response — when to laugh or cry, smirk with disdain, agree or disagree, or beam with affection.[43]

In sum, in a parasocial relationship the image people have of the source of a message reflects carefully staged cues. Parasocial relationships, however, are not confined to show business. Politicans eagerly and actively enter into them. Some of Johnny Carson's leading guests have included Mayor John Lindsay, Vice-President Spiro Agnew, and Senator Edward Kennedy. Senator Edmund Muskie, the 1968 Democratic vice-presidential nominee, while seeking the 1972 presidential nomination appeared on a similar program, *Dinah's Place,* to demonstrate his affability and culinary skill by preparing cooked crab before the TV cameras. The formats of many news-interview programs, on which politicians *Face the Nation* or *Meet the Press* promote parasocial relationships. Political candidates use devices for building parasocial relations; recall, for example Richard Nixon's election-eve telethon in 1968 when he sat with the renowned former football coach (now television sportscaster) "Bud" Wilkinson and in a breezy fashion responded to phoned-in questions. Presidents John Kennedy, Lyndon Johnson, and Richard Nixon have all employed "Conversations with the President," a television format in which the President chats with a small number (seldom more than three) of reporters on national issues, always referring to the reporters by their first names.

Just as interpersonal communications resemble games in certain ways, as parasocial relationships mass communications possess game-like qualities, or more precisely mass communications possess *features that resemble play.* *Play* is an activity that, in its pure state, permits a person to see things in a make-believe way (as, for example, when the child uses a cardboard box to represent a house). Play permits a person to insulate himself from his environment — to pretend, to find seclusion, to do what he

---

[43]Kenneth Burke, *Attitudes Toward History,* Vol. 1 (New York: New Republic Publishing Company, 1937), 104.

wants, and to seek temporary satisfaction.[44] Through play a person need not consider *the other* person as something-taken-into-account when communicating. What does this have to do with mass communication? By transmitting symbols, but not physically transporting people, the mass media permit people to imagine themselves with another person without actually taking the other person into account as a real being. The mass media yield the opportunity to play:

> "The media reinstate the opportunity to enjoy the early pattern of taking without deference to the reciprocal needs of the giver. The media offer immediate need gratification without 'paying the piper.' . . . One may weep or laugh or hate or fear and escape the necessity of acknowledging the physical existence and the reciprocal demands of those others who arouse the emotion."[45]

Mass communication, with its parasocial aspects, is a playground. Once the newspaper has been put aside, the radio or television switched off, the stimulus it provided is removed; irritating, threatening, frustrating events can be "turned off." And, newspapers, radio, and television cater to this play need, this popular reluctance to cope with others and instead to take-something-into-account which poses no problems: "It is characteristic of popular media content that it maximizes immediate need gratification, minimizes intellectual effort, and excuses the audience member from acknowledging a substantial other."[46]

Keeping the playlike qualities of mass communication in mind, it is possible to discern three types of mass messages — directive, maintaining, and restorative messages. *Directive* messages emanate from leaders who try to change images — cognitions, effects, and behavior; they exhort, teach, command, or convince. A well-reasoned speech, a teacher's lecture, or a news documentary offer directive messages. Generally, however, in politics directive messages delivered to mass audiences are less successful than interpersonal contact in converting people to new images. *Maintaining* messages are about everyday things that call for little conscious attention; they reinforce learned images rather than change them. A large portion of political messages are of this variety; in political campaigns, for instance, audiences turn to what they believe anyway rather than search for new ideas, evidence, or opinions. *Restorative* messages are play-like in that they release the individual to yield to fantasies and plea-

---

[44]Jean Piaget, *Play, Dreams and Imitation in Childhood* (New York: Norton, 1962), pp. 147-58; Stephenson, *The Play Theory of Mass Communication,* pp. 45-58; Johan Huizinga, *Homo Ludens: A Study of the Play Element in Culture* (Boston: Beacon Press, 1950); Jacques Ehrmann, ed., *Game, Play Literature* (Boston: Beacon Press, 1968).

[45]Gerhart D. Wiebe, "Two Psychological Factors in Media Audience Behavior," *Public Opinion Quarterly,* Vol. 33 (Winter 1969-70), 527.

[46]*Ibid.*

sures. Restorative messages facilitate a desire to escape the values associated with social conformity. In the mass media restorative messages take the form of news about crime, violence, sexual indiscretion, freedom from social restraints — all messages in which *the other,* or victim, is distant and removed. Restorative messages permit a release of inhibitions; if, for instance, stories about public figures involved in tragedy, scandal, or accidents trigger the expression of emotions (as did the story of Senator Edward M. Kennedy's automobile accident in which Mary Jo Kopechne died in Chappaquiddick in 1969) the messages perform restorative functions.

To the extent that a person is predisposed to political activity, directive or maintaining messages often prompt him to take part in a political rally, vote drive, or similar effort. But if the message is restorative, it provides an opportunity for expressive imagery or vicarious participation, but not commitment to join the parade. News accounts of protest demonstrations favoring civil rights or opposing the Vietnam war in the 1960s served as vehicles by which some persons could identify with the protesters and others could vilify them while taking no part in the protests beyond symbolically entering in as a spectators.

We can summarize what we have said about the effects of mass communication on the relations between people by speaking of *general* tendencies. Through the parasocial relationships that mass communications generate, we reduce uncertainty by closing our minds to new data and opening ourselves for the free play of our reigning beliefs, values, and habits. Most of us avoid directive messages, selectively expose ourselves to maintaining ones, and seclude ourselves in restorative images. In parasocial activity we are *engaged* in mass communication, but seldom *involved* in it; that is, the something-taken-into-account is not other people but primarily our own self-images; we assimilate information that reduces our uncertainty by confirming those self-images. In mass imagery we fulfill our desires for *communication-pleasure* (for confirmation, enjoyment, contentment, and serenity) and avoid *communication-pain* (rejection, disconfirmation, work, frustration, and threats). We *consume* mass communication as an end in itself, just as is play an end in itself for the child, or the sound of his voice is for a man who talks with himself. The images we exchange through mass communication are primarily expressive. We pay relatively little attention to the mass media for purposes of acquiring images that help us in gaining tangible goals or reaching judgments, for we find that paying attention to directive messages is hard work, and we sense that our personal values provide us with all we need to make judgments anyway. With these thoughts on the pragmatics of interpersonal and mass communication before us, let us now review our perspective on the communication of political images.

HOW POLITICAL SYMBOLS AFFECT
POLITICAL IMAGES

The burden of much of what we have said in this chapter is that people's political images are fixed, and that messages carrying other images have little impact upon them. To be sure, the game-like and play-like aspects of interpersonal and mass communication reflect strong tendencies of people to preserve their mental pictures of the world against disturbances from external stimuli. Yet, symbolic appeals in communications do change people's images of politics.

The communication of political images between leaders and followers is an intricate process that involves the transmission of a variety of symbols through the media. The meaning of a symbol, as we have seen, consists both of what the source of a message communicates (*his* signs) and what a receiver, responding on the basis of *his own* images, attributes to the message. In political communication there is usually a desire to create shared meaning between leaders and followers whether for tangible, evaluative, or expressive purposes. We label this process of creating shared meaning through communication *persuasion,* "the art of perceiving the weak spots in the images of others and of prying them apart with well-constructed symbolic messages."[47]

Persuasion is a multifaceted process based upon several assumptions about how people relate to one another:[48] first, people relate to one another in ways that appear to them to enhance their self-images; second, when communications threaten a person's self-image, he will oppose symbolic appeals that run counter to his self-image; and, third, if his images are filled with doubt, uncertainty, insecurity, or ambiguity, any symbolic message that helps reduce the uncertainty will influence him.

Assuming these assumptions are correct, we can outline the major steps in persuasion by which symbolic appeals influence citizen's political images.[49] The first step, of course, involves the *selection of a symbol.* As we saw in Chapter One, the symbol may take many forms, but let us focus here on symbolic phrases and use as an example the theme from the 46th presidential inaugural for President Richard M. Nixon — the theme of "Forward Together." Nixon won the 1968 presidential election by a narrow

---

[47]Kenneth Boulding, *The Image,* (Ann Arbor: University of Michigan Press, 1956) p. 134.

[48]Bardin H. Nelson, "Seven Principles in Image Formation," *Journal of Marketing,* Vol. 26 (January 1962), 67-71.

[49]Harold D. Lasswell and Abraham Kaplan, *Power and Society,* (New Haven: Yale University Press, 1950) pp. 112-13; Herbert E. Krugman, "The Impact of Television Advertising: Learning Without Involvement," *Public Opinion Quarterly,* Vol. 29 (Fall 1965), 349-56; Herbert E. Krugman, "Passive Learning from Television," *Public Opinion Quarterly,* Vol. 34 (Summer 1970), 184-90; Herbert E. Krugman, "Brain Wave Measures of Media Involvement," *Journal of Advertising Research,* Vol. 11 (February 1971), 3-9.

margin (43.4 percent of the popular vote). The election was marked by bitter divisions in this country over the Vietnam war, disruptions on college campuses, conditions in urban ghettos, and racial questions. There had been two assassinations of public figures (Martin Luther King and Robert Kennedy), violent demonstrations at the Democratic national convention, and a tumultuous presidential campaign. Nixon's initial problem as President was to restore consensus to a conflict-torn nation. The inaugural was to provide the first effort. At first the President's advisers hit upon the phrase "Bring us together" as a unifying symbol; this phrase was seen upon a banner carried in the presidential campaign by a young girl. While it seemed appropriate, it lacked a sense of direction beyond a restoration of the pre-1968 status quo. But "Forward Together" implied both consensus and progress, important themes to any new administration. Hence, step one in the persuasive process was the selection of a symbol that could, upon emphatic repetition, evoke a desired response.

The selection and repetition of a symbol *directs mass perception to it.* The second step in persuasion is cognitive in nature, namely, *making the symbol understood.* Thus, President-elect Nixon emphasized in public statements his desire for progress through peace and prosperity, reiterating a continuing faith in America and Americans. The third step is affective, *getting the symbolic message to be enjoyed in its own right* because of its aesthetic qualities, style, emotional appeal, structure, and so forth. Thus, banners in patriotic red-white-blue were prepared for the 46th inaugural reading "Forward Together, Welcome 46th Inaugural." In his inauguration speech the President spoke of "lowering our voices" to a moderate, less frenzied, style of public debate. And, in the first months of his presidency he assumed a low profile symbolic of withdrawing the presidency from too much interference in the lives of Americans. The fourth step of the process occurs as *people begin to reconsider their own images* in light of the symbolic message and, if led to do so, change those images and act in keeping with the new symbols. Thus, in the early months of the Nixon administration (at least prior to the invasion of Cambodia in April, 1970), voices did quiet, urban riots became fewer in number, and college administrators spoke of "business as usual."

In sum, harking back to the language of our discussion in Chapter One, when appealing symbols appear in the persuasive process, they guide our perceptions, activate our cognitions, work on our affective outlooks, and produce shifts in our conative ways. Symbols have the meaning we impart to them on the basis of our images, but they influence our images as well — governing what we see and how. And, they help shape our expectations of what will happen. For example, in building up our interest in a major news event such as a national political convention, a presidential election, or a landing on the moon, the news organizations provide us with a context within which events will occur; in reading, hearing, or viewing what happens we interpret the events from the perspective provided us in symbolic form by the media. The New Hampshire Democratic presidential primary in 1972 offers an example of how news organizations structure our expectations about what will happen and thus influence our interpretations of what did. In that primary the relatively unknown Senator George McGovern (among others) challenged what the news media presented as the "front runner" for the Democratic nomination, Senator Edmund Muskie. The news reported the campaign in ways that led interested persons to expect that McGovern could at best make only a token showing. When McGovern received 38 percent of the vote (to 48 percent for Muskie), many news men reported McGovern's "moral" victory as an "upset" of sorts, and the emergence of McGovern as a viable candidate. There was little mention of Muskie's plurality as contrasted with the "momentum" of McGovern. By creating unrealistic expectations of a candidate's strength in a virtual ten-man primary, the media provided a background for interpreting victory as defeat, and vice versa.

The reported news also shapes our expectations and interpretations of events by influencing our imagination of what goes on. Following the assassination of Senator Robert Kennedy in June, 1968, there was widespread public dismay and grief. This was reflected by the crowds that gathered along the route of the funeral train transporting the Senator's body to Washington for burial. As the funeral train passed Baltimore people were softly singing "The Battle Hymn of the Republic." Television reporters remarked on the moving tribute reflected in the apparently spontaneous display. What was not reported was that the singing began because people thought it might appear moving on television, nor that it continued because the crowd heard the praise of television commentators.[50]

To the extent that any mode of communication, interpersonal or mass, creates a set of expectations (from which we draw inferences about the character of events) and dictates our imagination, its symbolic message modifies our images. Communication certainly does this in contemporary politics. By selecting those aspects of events that arouse attention, by emphasizing their dramatic qualities — as with restorative messages about conflicts, personalities, or suspenseful events — and by offering interpretations in ambiguous situations (all of which the news organizations do),[51] the communicators of political messages furnish the symbolic environment from which we acquire our images of politics. How we learn those images is the question we take up in Chapter Three.

[50]Kurt and Gladys Engel Lang, "The Mass Media and Voting," in Eugene Burdick and Arthur J. Brodbeck, *American Voting Behavior* (Glencoe: Free Press, 1959), pp. 217-35; Robert Jervis, *The Logic of Images in International Relations* (Princeton: Princeton University Press, 1970), pp. 63-64.

[51]Doris Graber, "The Press as Opinion Resource During the 1968 Presidential Campaign," *Public Opinion Quarterly,* Vol. 35 (Summer 1971). 168-72; Edith Efron, *The News Twisters* (Los Angeles: Nash Publishing, 1971); Samuel Lubell, *The Hidden Crisis in American Politics* (New York: Norton, 1971), p. 11.

3

adopting
political images

We know that images are mental representations that influence how people see political, as well as other, things; they help people in achieving tangible goals, making judgments, and expressing themselves. We also know that persons exchange images between each other by using symbols in both interpersonal and mass communication. In communicating images people recreate in their minds the content of the messages of others; sometimes they do this successfully, but often they do so only imperfectly. We now want to know how do people acquire images in the first place? We have defined political images as "everything that the organism has heretofore learned"[1] about politics; we shall refer to the way the organism learns, "the process by which the image originates and undergoes modification," as *adoption*.[2] In this chapter we shall first look at a major theory about how people adopt their images; then, we will examine what images people

---

[1]Robert C. Carson, *Interaction Concepts of Personality* (Chicago: Aldine, 1969), p. 83.

[2]John W. Fox, "The Concepts of Image and Adoption in Relation to Interpersonal Behavior," *Journal of Communication*, Vol. 17 (1967), 147-51; in the discussion that follows the concept of adoption will be utilized in preference to image "formation." Generally, our interest is in a learning-developmental process rather than that normally implied by image formation, a notion utilized primarily among psychologists of perception. See Mardi Jon Horowitz, *Image Formation and Cognition* (New York: Appleton-Century-Crofts, 1971).

learn that help them to express themselves in politics, make political judgments, and gain political understanding; we will also see what things influence how people learn images; finally, we will consider some of the problems involved in adapting to politics through images.

HOW PEOPLE ADOPT IMAGES: A DEVELOPMENTAL VIEW

Psychologists and social psychologists employ a variety of theories to describe how people learn.[3] From among these there is one view that is particularly helpful in discussing how people adopt images that are relevant in their political considerations. This theory, which we label a *developmental view,* stems from the research of several people, but in describing it we will rely heavily upon two of its principal formulators, Jean Piaget and Lawrence Kohlberg. Piaget tries to account for how children develop cognitive and affective thinking while Kohlberg emphasizes the development of moral thought.[4] Both emphasize that *learning involves a sequence of adjustments* people make in their perceptions, cognitions, affects, and conations (the principal components of personal images we outlined in Chapter One) in response to their environments. In the life of each individual this sequence is unified, continuous, and unending; i.e., it is developmental.

A fundamental notion of developmental theory is that *a person learns by passing through a series of psychological periods, or stages.* Each stage normally has two aspects: First, as a person passes through each stage he makes progressively finer distinctions between his perceptions, beliefs, values, and proposed courses of action; this is *the process of dif-*

[3]A full review of these approaches can be found in Charles A. Kiesler, Barry E. Collins, and Norman Miller, *Attitude Change* (New York: John Wiley, 1969); see also Daniel Katz, "Attitude Formation and Public Opinion," *The Annals of the American Academy of Political and Social Science* Vol. 367 (September 1966), 150-62; and Robert B. Zajonc, "The Concepts of Balance, Congruity and Dissonance," *Public Opinion Quarterly,* Vol. 24 (1960) 280-96. Anthony G. Greenwald, "On Defining Attitude and Attitude Theory," in Anthony G. Greenwald, Timothy C. Brock, and Thomas M. Ostrom, eds., *Psychological Foundations of Attitudes* (New York: Academic, 1968).

[4]Jean Piaget, *The Origins of Intelligence in Children* (New York: Norton, 1952); Jean Piaget, *The Construction of Reality in the Child* (New York: Basic Books, 1954); Jean Piaget in "The Role of the Concept of Equilibrium in Psychological Explication," *Acta Psychologica,* Vol. 15, 51-62; Jean Piaget, *The Moral Judgment of the Child* (New York: Free Press, 1969); Barbel Inhelder, "Some Aspects of Piaget's Genetic Approach to Cognition," in W. Kessen and C. Kuhlman, eds., *Thought in the Young Child, Monographs of the Society for Research in Child Development,* Vol. 27 (1962), 19-34; Jean Piaget, "A Theory of Development," *International Encyclopedia of the Social Sciences,* Vol. 4 (New York: Macmillan, 1968), 140-47. Note also Bernard N. Meltzer, "Mead's Social Psychology," in Jerome G. Manis and Bernard N. Meltzer, eds., *Symbolic Interaction* (Boston: Allyn & Bacon, 1967), pp. 5-24, and Lawrence Kohlberg, "The Development of Children's Orientations Toward a Moral Order: I. Sequence in the Development of Moral Thought," *Vita Humana,* Vol. 6 (1963), 11-33.

ferentiation between the components of his images. Secondly, he gradually learns to organize these components of his images; this is *the process of integration*. As a person passes through the sequence of intellectual development, each stage involves the progressive growth of images, (i.e., each stage in development incorporates, in a more highly differentiated and integrated synthesis, the images he adopted at earlier stages). This growth is evolutionary in the sense that the images adopted at one stage are the starting points for those acquired in the next; finally, the sequence in the succession of stages is constant, but the ages at which different people attain given stages vary within the limits provided by biological maturation, social experience, and environmental influences.

Stages of Development

Developmental theorists differ on the number and types of stages in learning, but from their works we can speak of four stages that are especially important to our later discussion of how people develop political images. These stages are infancy, assimilation, accommodation, and adaptation. Before describing each, however, it may be useful to think for a moment of a biological metaphor that defines succinctly the major notions underlying these developmental stages of learning. The most fundamental function of living beings is to sustain themselves by on-going transactions with their environments. An organism *adapts* "Whenever a given organism-environment interchange has the effect of modifying the organism in such a way that further interchanges, favorable to its preservation, are enhanced." When the organism acquires food from the environment to meet its own inner requirements, biologists say it *assimilates* the food. But, while assimilating, the organism's digestive structure must adjust to the foodstuffs consumed, a process of *accommodation*. Thus, biological adaptation involves processes in which "every assimilation of an object to the organism simultaneously involves accommodation of the organism to the object: and, conversely, "every accommodation is at the same time an assimilatory modification of the object accommodated to . . ."[5] Keeping these thoughts about adaptation, assimilation, and accommodation before us, let us now consider each of the four stages of development.

[5]J. H. Flavell, *The Developmental Psychology of Jean Piaget* (New York: Van Nostrand, 1963), pp. 45-46. The notion of the "biological metaphor" is that of Albert Mehrabian, *An Analysis of Personality Theories* (Englewood Cliffs, N.J.: Prentice-Hall, 1968), pp. 121-32; for biological approaches in political science see Thomas Landon Thorson, *Biopolitics* (New York: Holt, Rinehart & Winston, 1970) and Peter A. Corning, "The Biological Bases of Behavior and Some Implications for Political Science," *World Politics,* Vol. 23 (April 1971), 321-70.

Infancy

Infancy extends basically from birth to approximately two years of age. It is a stage in which the child relies on adults for the essentials of livelihood. During infancy the child acquires physical skills (eye movement, grasping, sitting, crawling, etc.). Not only that, but he begins to coordinate in his mind the information derived from his physical activity. He acquires a minimal image of his immediate environment as it relates to his actions toward it; or, more accurately he adopts numerous discrete images but each is tied to the content of the specific stimuli provided by his physical actions. In this fashion, "a biological contact is established between the organism and the environment, a previously neutral environmental event becomes a psychological stimulus, and an adaptive response is made."[6] In infancy a subjective viewpoint predominates; for the infant, objects and space (or their symbolic surrogates) simply do not exist independent of his body. Everything in the environment is an extension of his being, and there is a pervasive lack of differentiation (or a prevailing confusion).

Assimilation

The assimilative stage (lasting from approximately two to seven years of age) is a natural progression from infancy. Although the child distinguishes between himself and his environment, he still regards himself as at the center of everything. The major achievement of this period is the emergence of the child's ability to construct mental representations of his environment apart from immediate experience. He develops what psychologists call deferred imitation; that is, he learns to "re-present" something that occurred not in his immediate present, but in the near or distant past. By re-presenting, for example, he constructs a mental image of a parental smile and can imitate it even in the absence of the parent. Reappearance of the parent (smiling or unsmiling) now constitutes a sign to which the child responds by smiling.

Because there is a strong tendency for the child to center upon himself in this stage, he accepts his images of the world as valid pictures for *all* occasions. In short, he is egocentric. Encased in his own world, for example, he ignores the views of others when in an argument and simply reasserts his own position; he rejects evidence; he reasons intuitively and is frequently self-contradictory; and he has great difficulty in cooperating with others. This egocentrism of the child, however, is not the same as the obstinance of the adult; the child in this period *cannot* take the other's viewpoint whereas the obstinate adult *will not*. The child's egocentrism is

⁶Hans G. Furth, *Piaget and Knowledge* (Englewood Cliffs, N.J.: Prentice-Hall, 1969), pp. 44-45.

manifested in symbolic play in which he pretends the world is as he *imagines* it. If he plays "soldier," for instance, his images and not external stimuli provide the cues for his actions; thus a cardboard box *is* a house, a stick *is* a gun. Symbolic play is self-centered and requires no cooperation with others; this contrasts sharply with the playing of games in later life for in game playing the child must obey rules, and "be ready to take the attitude of everyone else involved in that game."[7] In sum, during the ego-centric stage the child assimilates the environment to his images of it, but has difficulty in accommodating those images to unfamiliar stimuli. The period involves the child in differentiating between objects, persons, and events by forming images of them; he integrates those images, however, in a self-centered, assimilative fashion.

Accommodation

From ages of approximately seven to eleven the child goes through an accommodative stage; he loses a bit of the earlier egocentrism, acquires some understanding of the viewpoints of others, and performs mental operations that assist him in accommodating rather than simply assimilat-ing his environment. The earlier periods are characterized by considerable disequilibrium in thought processes but, with decentering, the child ex-hibits relative stability. This stage coincides closely with the beginning of formal education, and there is a decisive shift in mental development. The child learns to order objects by size, classify objects, and deal with equalities and inequalities in number. He acquires mental images of time, space, number, and logic.

Adaptation

Finally, after roughly eleven years of age, the individual enters a period of adaptation extending through adolescence, preadulthood, and adulthood. Ideally, this is a stage when a person is open equally to himself and to his environment and able to adjust to changes in both. In mental development it is a period of learning by formulation of hypotheses, de-ducing outcomes, experimentation, and checking expectations against results. Socially there is adaptation to the rights and obligations of his own and others' behavior. Images during this period become highly differentiated, continually reintegrated, and adaptive. There is, of course, no assurance that all persons move to, let alone through, the period of adaptive imagery. Development for some may halt at an earlier period; some may always be egocentric, and those passing through decentering may regress to earlier modes of behavior. And, there may be differences in the rate of develop-

[7]George H. Mead, *Mind, Self, and Society* (Chicago: University of Chicago Press, 1934), pp. 150-51.

ment of the perceptual, cognitive, affective, and conative components of images. Let us now explore that possibility.

The Development of Image Components

We said earlier that development is a dual process involving the differentiation and integration of image components. Theories of image development provide a few clues as to how this differentiation and integration of image elements gradually evolves.

Perceptual Development

It is impossible to say just which image component develops first, but perception appears early. Initially the child learns to perceive a difference between himself and others (say the mother). We shall see later that this is politically significant for children generalize this initial distinction between self and others in such a way as to influence their adoption of images of groups, the state, the nation, etc. With the self-other differentiation drawn, the child begins to perceive differences between how he actually behaves and the ideal behavior sought by others (as between how he acts and how his parents want him to act). Finally, comes the distinction between seeing himself and others from his own viewpoint or being able to do so from the viewpoint of other people (a difference, for example, between "what I want to do" and "what mother wants me to do"). This last distinction, if developed and generalized into politics in later years, constitutes the capacity of seeing one's own opinions as we think political opponents would see them.

Much of the development of perception during and following infancy contributes to what developmental theorists call figurative, as contrasted with operational, thinking. Operational thought implies the accommodation of a person's existing images to the environment; figurative thinking is also accommodative, or outgoing, but it focuses on the external, figural aspect of an object, person, or event in a static manner.[8] In politics *figurative thought emphasizes appearances and focuses on style to the exclusion of substance,* on the outline rather than internal features. Much of political imagery has this figurative character; we frequently respond to political symbols by perceiving their configurations rather than internal qualities (as, for example, we agonize over the "Threat of Communist Domination" without analyzing how substantial such a threat is).

[8]Furth, *Piaget and Knowledge,* pp. 133-43.

Conative Development

The development of the perceptual components of images is of course, inextricably tied to the acquisition of habits, feelings, and knowledge. Coming equally early in adoption are the conative components, especially as they appear in habits of acceptance or rejection. The distinction between accepting and rejecting may even be the first one made by the child: from birth he learns first to grasp, and then throw objects. Some image of taking and giving apparently precedes, developmentally at least, notions of *whom* he accepts or rejects. In acquiring a sense of social objects as targets of action, as well as simply perceiving them as beings, the child again first distinguishes *himself*, then others. Finally, a mode of accepting or rejecting one's self and others develops; this consists first of an emotional (affective) orientation in liking or disliking, loving or hating and then of status (cognitive) dimension by according superiority-inferiority, dominance-submission to one's self and others.

Affective Development

In the infancy and assimilative periods of development described earlier, it seems clear that the affective components (which are related to moral behavior) of images are integrated in a highly egocentric way. In their earliest years children are unable to view rules, regulations, and moral standards as anything other than "givens," as inherent in the makeup of the environment; those who violate them are guilty. This is virtually a premoral level of development in which children adopt moral standards either to avoid punishment or to win favors and rewards.

From ages seven to eleven, as parental influence diminishes and strong peer bonds appear, a second stage of moral development, built upon mutual respect, begins. Here the individual develops conventional conformity to rules in order to maintain social approval and avoid censure (even though he recognizes that the rules themselves are not inherently correct, but only arbitrarily drawn). Having started out with the view that rules are objectively determined, then moving to an image of subjectively derived rules, the next development is to adopt rules on which there is social consensus.

In the third stage of affective development the individual obeys rules not out of fear of external punishment but in order to avoid self-condemnation; that is, the rules are now *his* rules. To violate them may result not simply in rejection *by* others but in rejection *of* self.

Two points should be kept in mind regarding this development of the moral, affective, component of images. First, it is entirely possible that development may be arrested, or fixed at any period and, hence, a person might go through life ego-centered or simply conforming. Second, affective development is directly related to political questions of obedience to law; that is, it is related to whether persons develop a sense of being able to participate in making laws or regard themselves as mere subjects of laws over which they have no control.[9]

Cognitive Development

As people adopt, differentiate, and organize, perceptual, conative, and affective image components, they also develop cognitions. The child's early efforts to understand his environment are precausal just, as we noted, they are premoral. Precausal thinking appears in a variety of guises. The child begins by accepting the world pretty much as he finds it. He is unaware that he need not accept things imposed upon him. He does not recognize that his own efforts can make a difference. The child attributes "life" to any moving object (such as a ball) by simply equating movement with life; moreover, artificial, supernatural, and unalterable forces play major parts in the child's world; and, as indicated previously, being egocentric he has difficulty distinguishing between himself and the environment. Gradually the child develops the ability to classify, serialize, think sequentially, and order objects. With cognitive growth the child begins to grasp such political phenomena as national identities (classification), law-making (sequential actions), and power (ordering).

Viewed from a developmental perspective, then, the adoption of images is a process that begins in infancy with the construction of a practical environment (perceptions of self-others and the habits of taking-rejecting), unfolds in the assimilative period with the formation of images placing the child at the center of the environment, extends to an affective and cognitive decentering in the accommodative period, and ideally to continuous differentiation and regrouping in adolescence and thereafter.

This general process possesses a basic unity that is exemplified in the adoption of political images. So long as a person's development is not arrested at egocentric (precausal and premoral) periods, his political images promote adaptive behavior; if his development is fixated, however, he may become a captive of these images. For him politics will be either play (the domination of assimilative behavior) or imitation (the dominance of accommodation). There is some reason to suspect that few persons ever make the full passage from infancy to adaptive imagery, particularly in adopting political images. Before examining that problem, let us turn first to the development of political images.

[9]Jean Piaget, "The Mental Development of the Child," in David Elkind, ed., *Six Psychological Studies by Jean Piaget,* (New York: Random House, 1967) pp. 3-73; Richard M. Merelman, "The Development of Political Ideology: A Framework for the Analysis of Political Socialization," *American Political Science Review,* Vol. 63 (September 1969), 750-67; Eleanor E. Maccoby, "The Development of Moral Values and Behavior in Childhood," in John A. Clausen, ed., *Socialization and Society* (Boston: Little, Brown, 1968), pp. 227-69.

DEVELOPING IMAGES OF POLITICS

For several decades political scientists have studied the types of political beliefs, values, and habits that people learn, an area of investigation designated as political socialization. Students of political socialization have found it especially helpful to ask how the political self develops.[10] From this perspective, studies of *the development of self focus on three major areas:* (1) the development of images that assist people in expressing their individual identities — i.e., their identifications as citizens, their loyalties to the community, and their memberships in key political groups, especially political parties; (2) the development of images that aid people in evaluating politics and in responding to government and its policies — i.e., their acceptance of the legitimacy of governmental arrangements, their views of the general nature of "government" and "politics," and their images of authority and compliance; (3) the development of images that assist people in playing political roles (e.g., voter, leader, follower, policymaker, etc.) that influence government and contribute to achieving tangible goals.

In considering the development of political images, then, our focus is the content of images that assist political expression, judgment, and understanding — the three functions of political images introduced in Chapter One (pp. 11-20).

Political learning begins relatively early when children adopt images that help them express identifications and emotional ties with the nation, political parties, and political figures. In later childhood cognitive knowledge combines with affective orientation to permit political evaluation as well as political expression. But the developmental process generally favors assimilation in these early years and the images of expression and evaluation children adopt support their egocentered view of the world. In later childhood, for some, in adolescence and adulthood for others (and perhaps never for many), people begin to accommodate their images to incoming information and to acquire images that assist in voting, influencing officials, and making policies. In sum, people learn affective components of images before they gain cognitive understanding; "the structure of factual knowledge is erected on a foundation of feelings, assessments, and opinions."[11]

[10]Richard E. Dawson and Kenneth Prewitt, *Political Socialization* (Boston: Little, Brown, 1969), pp. 15-24; Jack Dennis, Leon Lindberg, and Donald McCrone, "Support for Nation and Government among English Children," *British Journal of Political Science,* Vol. 1 (January 1971), 25. An excellent review of the literature of political socialization research is contained in Jack Dennis, "Major Problems of Political Socialization Research," *Midwest Journal of Political Science,* Vol. 12 (February 1968), 85-114; David Easton and Jack Dennis, *Children in the Political System* (New York: McGraw-Hill, 1969); Kenneth P. Langton, *Political Socialization* (New York: Oxford University Press, 1969).

[11]Fred I. Greenstein, *Children and Politics* (New Haven: Yale University Press, 1965), p. 35.

Developing Images of Political Expression

One of the first things that occurs in image development is the differentiation a person makes in perceiving himself and others as objects. In the development of political images it is not surprising that *identification of political objects,* becoming aware of them and recognizing them as part of the political realm, is one of the earliest developed perceptions.[12] Moreover, the child learns to distinguish himself as a political being (paralleling the self-other distinction noted above) and to perceive how he acts contrasted with how he should act (the actual-ideal distinction). When the child identifies his political self, it influences both his perceptions of and affective ties to the "nation" or political community. Studies of political socialization in the United States, Great Britain, and Western Europe yield insights into how children adopt images of national identity, a sequence of learning that involves the states of development that we described above.

In infancy (birth to two years of age), of course, there is virtually no adoption of political images. But in the assimilative period of two to seven years of age we detect the origins of a *national identity.* As expected, there is still little cognitive conception of the nation and little familiarity with the characteristics of "nationality" as classifications of people. The child's image of the nation is not defined by geographical boundaries,[13] and, to the extent a child says he is "American," "British," etc., he repeats a learned verbal formula rather than having any grasp of his identity as compared to that of people in other nations (indeed, he has no real knowledge of other nations).[14] Yet, despite the fact that he possesses no knowledge to support it, the affective component of the child's image of his nation at this stage is quite positive. Children are quick to claim their own country and language, for example, as superior.[15] Symbols like the flag, national anthem, or Statue of Liberty are crucial for this emotional attachment. At around five, for instance, the child cannot conceive that other flags than that of his own country even exist, but gradually he develops the sense that there are other countries with their own flags. Then, he tends to think the flags carry the essential qualities of good or evil. Goodness lies *in* the flag and not just in the nation; as one child put it, "God made the flag so they'd know who was the good people."[16]

[12]Robert D. Hess and Judith V. Torney, *The Development of Political Attitudes in Children* (Chicago: Aldine, 1967).

[13]Gustav Jahoda, "Children's Concepts of Nationality: A Critical Study of Piaget's Stages," *Child Development,* Vol. 35 (December 1964), 1081-92.

[14]Jean Piaget and Anne-Marie Weil, "The Development in Children of the Idea of the Homeland and of Relations with Other Countries," *International Social Science Bulletin,* Vol. 3 (1951), 561-78.

[15]Hess and Torney, *Development of Political Attitudes,* p. 29.

[16]Eugene A. Weinstein, "Development of the Concept of Flag and the Sense of National Identity," *Child Development,* Vol. 28 (June 1957), 171.

In this assimilative period the child's egocentrism makes it difficult for him to imagine even his own homeland, let alone others, that extend beyond his family, neighborhood, or town. As he receives information about the larger political community, he assimilates it, but only to his own point of view. In the ensuing accommodative period (seven to eleven years of age) decentering begins to occur and with it a greater cognitive awareness and differentiation in nationality images. By the time he is eight years old, for instance, the child can name his country correctly,[17] provide reasons for being proud of it (such as having the "right to vote"), and classify his homeland as part of a system of nations.[18] As he loses his egocentrism the child subordinates his local community to the larger nation and shifts his awareness from less inclusive to more inclusive communities. Moreover, children grow to understand that the nationals of other countries prefer those countries, i.e., they can *imagine* the images other people have of their own countries.[19] This extends to symbols also. Children from nine through eleven years of age begin to understand that flags stand *for* countries, are not "good" or "bad" in themselves, and that their own flag is not best without qualification — as illustrated by one child's statement that "If I lived in a different country and liked the way things were I probably would think their flag best."[20]

Thus a substantial advance occurs during the accommodative period in the development of the cognitive component of the child's image of national identity. The growing awareness of other countries and the capacity to take the viewpoints of others does not, however, imply a necessary weakening of the affective ties to the homeland. Even after age eleven — into the stage of more adaptive development associated with adolescence and adulthood — there are deep feelings of national pride. In the United States, for example, 64 percent of children ages 8-10 agreed in a survey that the U.S. is the "best country in the world;" and 76 percent of those 14-17 so agreed. A similar study in Great Britain revealed lower levels of national pride (48 percent both of those 8-10 and of those 14-17 agreed Great Britain "is the best country in the world"), but again no significant diminishing of the emotional bond.[21] A plausible interpretation of the continuing strength of the affective ties is that the egocentric view

[17]Dennis, Lindberg, and McCrone, "Support for Nation and Government among English Children," pp. 28-29.

[18]M. Kent Jennings, "Pre-Adult Orientation to Multiple Systems of Government," *Midwest Journal of Political Science,* Vol. 9 (August 1967), 291-317. Hess and Torney, *Development of Political Attitudes,* p. 30.

[19]Margaret R. Middleton, Henri Tajfel, and N. B. Johnson, "Cognitive and Affective Aspects of Children's National Attitudes," *British Journal of Social and Clinical Psychology,* Vol. 9 (1970), 122-34.

[20]Weinstein, 'Development of the Concept of Flag," p. 173.

[21]Dennis, Lindberg, and McCrone, "Support for Nation and Government among English Children," pp. 30-31.

that limits the child to perceiving, knowing, and approving his local community in his early years reemerges "in new guises" as *sociocentrism* or a vague feeling that his nation is "best" whenever compared with others. In this sense national chauvinism reflects the fixation of egocentric images on a larger, yet still maladaptive, scale.[22]

In addition to images of self and homeland serving political expression, the child acquires a sense of *identification with key political groups* that link the political self with the political community. The principal expressive bond is the child's identification with a political party. The degree to which people identify with political parties differs from nation to nation, but in all western nations party identification is a major phenomenon of government. In some nations — the United States, Great Britain, and Uruguay are examples — more than 70 percent of the population are party identifiers and two-thirds identify strongly with their chosen party. Even where the extent and intensity of party identification are much lower, as in Mexico and Italy, from 40-50 percent identify. Other nations, notably Norway and the German Federal Republic, fall somewhere between 50-70 percent in the proportion of citizens who are party identifiers.[23]

The affective component of the partisan self-image develops early in childhood, usually in the assimilative period. At least a majority of children in the United States, for example, acquire a party preference by seven years of age, and in various other nations children do so by the time they complete elementary school.[24] As with conceptions of the nation, however, there is considerable ambiguity in what a political party means to a child. In the assimilative stage children are unable to think in abstract ways; yet they assimilate the highly visible symbols provided by political parties and identify with them. The process of affiliating with partisan symbols assists the egocentric child in identifying the political self and serves as a link for him to his parents (from whom he usually adopts his party loyalty) and to his homeland.

Developing Images of Political Judgment

In addition to his images of self, nation, and party by which the child expresses a political identity, he adopts images he uses as standards of

[22]Piaget and Weil, "Development in Children of the Idea of the Homeland."

[23]Jack Dennis and Donald J. McCrone, "Preadult Development of Political Party Identification in Western Democracies," *Comparative Political Studies,* Vol. 3 (April 1970) 243-63.

[24]*Ibid.,* pp. 249-50; Easton and Dennis, *Children in the Political System,* p. 245; Jon H. Pammett, "The Development of Political Orientations in Canadian School Children," *Canadian Journal of Political Science,* Vol. 4 (March 1971), 132-41. Hess and Torney, *The Development of Political Attitudes in Children,* p. 90, suggests a later development of partisan identification in American children.

right and wrong, desirable and undesirable, good and bad. The development of these evaluative orientations toward government is similar to that outlined earlier regarding moral development generally. The child at age six to eight possesses an implicit trust in the goodness and wisdom of government, accepting laws as sacred and unchangeable, and related only to his egocentered self. At this age he feels that citizenship requires only personal goodness. But at the close of the accommodative stage the child begins to see that passive good is not the whole of citizenship; he begins to realize that being a citizen implies influencing government.

A basic judgment the child makes is whether or not government is a *legitimate* force upon his life, i.e., whether it is morally right for government to affect his life and society. As he becomes aware of governmental and political activities, laws, and authority figures such as the president and police, he adopts images of each. In this process he gradually *shifts from a personal to an institutional outlook.*

Prior to approximately eleven years of age a child takes a purely personal approach to politics. He displays this personalism in the following two characteristics: first, his "disposition to treat institutions and social processes upon the model of person and personal relationships; second, his inability to achieve a sociocentric orientation, that is, his failure to understand that political decisions have social as well as personal consequences."

Between eleven and thirteen years — coinciding with the close of the accommodative stage of development — social outlooks begin to replace personal orientations. The following responses by two boys to the question: "What is the purpose of government?" indicate the shift that occurs between ages 11 and 13:[25]

> An 11-year old: "So everything won't go wrong in the country. They want a government because they respect him and they think he's a good man."
>
> A 13-year old: "Well, I think it is to keep the country happy or keep it going properly. If you don't have it, then it would just be chaos with stealing and things like this. It runs the country better and more efficiently."

"Government," "community," and "society," as abstract notions, are simply beyond the understanding of most young children; representing these vague abstractions in personal terms (such as thinking of "the government" as embodied in a particular president) makes the ideas concrete and within the child's grasp. When, for example, children in one study were presented with several symbols of government — pictures of the flag, Statue of Liberty, a ballot box, George Washington, etc. — and asked to select those "that show best what our government is," the four chosen most

[25]Judith Gallatin and Joseph Adelson, "Individual Rights and the Public Good," *Comparative Political Studies,* Vol. 3 (July 1970), 226-42. Richard Merelman, "Learning and Legitimacy," *American Political Science Review,* Vol. 60 (September 1966), 548.

often were George Washington, voting, Congress, and President Kennedy. Most popular with the youngest children (approximately seven years of age) were two personal figures, Washington and Kennedy. But 13-year olds selected Congress and voting. Similarly, as they develop, children increasingly see Congress as responsible for making laws rather than the President (76 percent of second graders believed the President when asked "Who makes the laws" while 85 percent of eighth graders selected Congress).[26] This depersonalization of the governmental image is not confined to the United States. In Great Britain, for example, the Prime Minister outranks Parliament as the primary symbol of government for 8- to 10-year olds, but for 14- to 17-year olds Parliament predominates; asked "Who has the most to do with making the laws in this country?" younger British children cite the Queen and Prime Minister, adolescents select Parliament and the Cabinet."[27] Cognitively, then, from the beginning to the close of the accommodative, decentering period of development, the child moves from an image of government emphasizing a few visible leaders to one of government as involving competing groups and policy-making institutions.

The affective component of the child's image of government is almost entirely positive, especially in the United States. American fourth-graders, for instance, see government as wise ("almost never" or only "sometimes makes mistakes"), helpful ("would usually want to help me if I needed it"), powerful ("can punish many people"), and important ("makes important decisions a lot of the time"). Although as they grow older they recognize government fallibility (with a higher proportion of children saying government "sometimes" and "often" makes mistakes) and see government as less helpful, the overall image of power, knowledgeability, and leadership is relatively unimpaired.[28] However, this positive affect among children at all stages of development is not so evident in other nations. Increasing disaffection with government in both Britain and Germany, for instance, is higher than in the United States; in Britain during the accommodative period children develop growing feelings that government "sometimes," "often," and "usually" makes mistakes, and is only "sometimes" or "seldom" helpful.[29]

When children think positively about political authority, it is frequently because they have earlier acquired positive feelings for key political figures who represent that authority to them. In the United States, for example, "a young child's image of the national government is confined

[26]Easton and Dennis, *Children in the Political System,* pp. 113-18.

[27]Dennis, Lindberg, and McCrone, "Support for Nation and Government Among English Children," pp. 35-39.

[28]Easton and Dennis, *Children in the Political System,* pp. 128-37; Hess and Torney, *Development of Political Attitudes in Children,* pp. 32-50.

[29]Dennis, Lindberg, and McCrone, "Support for Nation and Government Among English Children," pp. 39-45.

mainly to the President,"[30] while his image of the local policeman represents his early idea of the sacred, immutable character of the law. If the young child thinks well of the President and the policeman, he is likely to think well of government and the law. But, what does he think of such political figures?

Young children attribute to the President the major responsibility for making "sure our country is run well," but what he does to assure it is somewhat obscure beyond being the "top boss." As the cognitive component of images develop children start realizing that the President does not make all laws nor does he give orders to state, county, city, and local officials. Although the cognitive component of the child's image of the President is not clearly delineated, the affective component is, and it is clearly positive. Children see the President, as a person, as trustworthy, likable, benevolent, persistent, and largely infallible. They sense that the President is concerned with their welfare, and they reciprocate his concern by giving him loyalty and affection: "This is the essence of a role relationship, one of the most basic personal attachments: Protection reciprocated by love."[31]

As the child grows older he begins to differentiate the personal characteristics of the President from the abilities needed to perform as a public servant. In the process the President no longer seems so benign. Yet, although there may be some withdrawal of love, the emotional tie is still strong and buttressed by the tendency in older children to attribute even more status to the Presidency if less affection. Among black Americans positive affect toward the President declines more rapidly than it does among whites. Among the oldest black children the President appears as a warm but ineffectual figure who is not particularly hard working, helpful, or powerful. The image for blacks is less the "father" figure developed by whites than the "grandfather" figure.[32]

If we compare images held by American children of the President with those of Canadian children of their Prime Minister, we find some differences. To begin with, Canadian children possess a more sharply defined image of the President than they do of their own Prime Minister. And, Canadian children tend to focus more upon institutions as representing "government" than upon political figures. Hence, even to Canadian children the President is a more highly visible symbol than the Prime Minister, probably reflecting the fact that the American President receives publicity

[30]Hess and Torney, *Development of Political Attitudes in Children,* p. 35 (italics removed from original). See also Easton and Dennis, *Children in the Political System,* pp. 209-42.

[31]Hess and Torney, *Development of Political Attitudes in Children,* p. 42; also see Greenstein, *Children and Politics,* p. 32; Easton and Dennis, *Children in the Political System,* pp. 165-207.

[32]Edward S. Greenberg, "Orientations of Black and White Children to Political Authority Figures," *Social Science Quarterly,* Vol. 51 (December 1970), 561-71.

as a distinct authority in the American system who endeavors to "personalize" his administration, whereas the Prime Minister is part of a parliamentary "team."[33]

The *child's notion of law* (and obedience to laws) owes a great deal to the image he first develops of the local policeman. Like the President the policeman is a highly visible figure in the child's environment. He is portrayed in film and on television, he makes appearances at schools, he is depicted in school texts for the early grades, etc. The uniformed figure is certainly one of the first of which the child becomes politically aware. The young child starts out thinking of policemen as makers of laws, but the older child differentiates the police chiefly as administrative officials who "make people obey the law" or "catch people who break the law" rather than "help people who are in trouble." The policeman does not have the same degree of respect and affection as directed toward the President, but children do regard the police as dependable, trustworthy, and benign. The developmental trend for the affective component of such images is that the child begins with a fairly high level of respect for the policeman which declines, although not substantially, over the years. This generally high respect, however, is more characteristic of American children than of those of other nations.[34]

Children gradually begin to sort out their images of law from their views of the policeman. Seven-year olds, for example, regard laws as helpful and protective, as positive forces in society that keep people safe. Compliance with laws is essential, in the child's mind at least, because failure to comply inevitably means personal punishment. As the children grow older, however, they learn that punishment is not the inevitable consequence of misdemeanor and they generalize this conclusion to the legal system. Yet, this does not portend the development of a sophisticated image of law or of a moral code that the child recognizes as *his* code. Even among high school students in the United States, compliance with the law still results more out of a fear of punishment and from resignation to external, unchangeable rules than from the development of personal standards of right and wrong.[35]

In sum then, children learn early in life to evaluate government, political figures, authority, and laws as legitimate. The child's images develop along two principal dimensions: (1) early adoption is primarily *affective* in orientation, and it is highly positive toward all major, visible

[33]Pammett, "Development of Political Orientations in Candian School Children," pp. 133-36.

[34]Easton and Dennis, *Children in the Political System,* pp. 209-41; Fred I. Greenstein and Sidney Tarrow, *Political Orientations of Children, Comparative Politics Series,* Vol. 1 (Beverly Hills, Calif: Sage Publications, 1970), 520-28.

[35]Hess and Torney, *Development of Political Attitudes in Children,* p. 57; Harrell R. Rogers and George Taylor, "Pre-Adult Attitudes Toward Legal Compliance: Notes Toward a Theory," *Social Science Quarterly,* Vol. 51 (December 1970), 539-51.

political objects, and later development is built upon a firm foundation of support for key aspects of the political system; (2) in later development there is some loosening of the emotional bond and the child begins to distinguish what he *knows* from what he *feels* about politics, at least into early adolescence.

Developing Images of Political Understanding

From our vantage point it is obvious that the development of images that assist expressive and evaluative aims begins very early in childhood. By the close of the assimilative stage the child has some notion of his political identity, his national identity, a party identification, and a judgment of the legitimacy of government, officials, and the law. But, these images are emotion-laden; it is not until the accommodative stage that cognitive differentiation emerges. This cognitive growth is a prerequisite to the development of political images that serve a person as tools in understanding a subtle aspect of democracy — popular control over policy making. The optimum exploitation of political images for influencing government, however, is uncommon. Indeed, "the overwhelming majority of the members of all political systems live out their lives, discover, develop, and express their feelings and aspirations in the intimate groups of the community. It is the rare individual who is fully recruited into the political system and becomes a political man."[36] The relatively late development of a cognitive understanding of government is exemplified in two areas generally associated with achieving tangible goals through politics, i.e., exerting influence through voting, political parties, and pressure groups and knowledge of political ideas and policy alternatives.

During the elementary school years an increasing number of children recognize the importance of *voting*. But, for the vast majority of children, voting in elections is understood as an *obligation* of citizenship performed in conformity with moral principle and in spite of a lack of interest in and/or information about the issue, candidates, and parties involved in the election. Herein lies one reason democratic elections are ritualistic and "largely symbolic and expressive in function."[37] The child's image of elections minimizes the conflict inherent in electoral politics and emphasizes elections as achieving unity and cohesion. Thus, we find 80 percent of children in grades four, six, and eight agreeing that "the man who loses in an election should ask his followers to help the winner."[38]

[36]Gabriel A. Almond and Sidney Verba, *The Civic Culture* (Princeton University Press, 1963), p. 143.

[37]Murray Edelman, *The Symbolic Uses of Politics* (Urbana: University of Illinois Press, 1964), p. 19.

[38]Hess and Torney, *Development of Political Attitudes in Children*, p. 78.

The evaluative side of the child's electoral image is illustrated by his perceptions of candidates. As if drawing upon the parental categorization of children as "good" or "bad" and upon the "good guy" and "bad guy" distinction so commonplace in popular entertainment, the child simply judges candidates as all good or all bad. In contrast to the positive affect felt for government and political officials generally, the child's images of candidates are filled with far more distrust, skepticism, and negativism. Perhaps many an adult would designate children's images as "realistic," but the fact remains that they apparently arise from an intuitive good-bad distinction and not any cognitive appraisal of perceived differences among candidates.

Paralleling the tendency to perceive candidates in affective rather than cognitive ways is a general failure to differentiate between policies. The result is a tendency to see both parties wanting "the same things — just peace and happiness and . . . our country to be free."[39] This image, however, may be more characteristic of American children viewing Democrats and Republicans than of youth in other nations regarding their own parties. In Canada, for example, more than 60 percent of fourth graders and 80 percent of eighth graders perceived sufficient distinctions in the major parties to declare that "it makes much difference which side wins an election."[40]

One of the chief *methods for influencing government* in the United States is through pressure groups. Yet, young children possess only a limited knowledge of the role of pressure groups in making policy, extolling instead the individual citizen's influence over that of the group. Nor does the child seem to develop much of an appreciation for pressure group activity during the accommodative period of 7-11 years; the school's emphasis upon individual obligations (such as voting) and the formal devices of policy making (e.g., Congress) contributes little understanding of group interests and pressures: "Children's evaluation of pressure groups is generally negative, and knowledge of the most efficient channels of influence is limited. They believe in *individual* access to power — an unrealistic viewpoint particularly in a rapidly expanding society."[41]

The foregoing suggests that expressive identifications and evaluative orientations develop during assimilation and accommodation stages whereas cognitive understanding does not. In political areas requiring some sophistication, such as dealing with *political ideas* and policies, development seldom occurs (if it occurs) until adolescence. Take as an example the relatively complex political notion of the "public good" or "public interest." A study comparing children in the United States, Great Britain,

---

[39] *Ibid.,* p. 82.
[40] Pammett, "Development of Political Orientations in School Children," p. 137.
[41] Hess and Torney, *Development of Political Attitudes in Children,* p. 137.

Britain, and West Germany presented boys and girls (10 to 18 years old) with a hypothetical situation describing people attempting to establish a political order after moving to a "Pacific island." They were then given the following problem:

> "A lot of money that was collected by taxes was to go to the public-school system on the island. But the people who did not have children thought it was unfair that they should have to pay taxes to support a school system. What do you think of that argument?"

A majority of both younger and older adolescents objected to the argument, but a markedly larger number of those 15 years and over were in support of the taxing for a public-school system. More significant, however, were the reasons for support. Those under 15-years old fell back on reasons consistent with premoral development such as "because it's the law" or "because they might have children some day." The older groups, however, gave reasons of community welfare for justifying the proposal and emphasized that private interests do not take precedence over the public good. National differences in the sampled children could be noted: German adolescents were more inclined to justify obedience to government policy simply because it is the law, the British emphasized private interests to a slight degree, and American adolescents argued for public welfare. However, the developmental similarities were stronger than national differences.[42]

Just as images that differentiate between abstract political ideas, such as the public interest, develop fairly late in childhood (or even thereafter or not at all) so apparently does understanding of *political issues*. Children take relatively little interest in discussing and taking sides on issues. Prior to adolescence the issues that matter revolve about strikingly presented symbols (e.g., "Communist Russia"), but with cognitive growth issues of unemployment and equal rights become more salient. An ideological stance on political ideas and issues, characterized by a systematic integration of knowledge and values from which stands on issues may be deduced, is almost totally absent among children. It is relatively rare in adolescents (who frequently cannot deal with such ideological concepts as class, capitalism, and competition). In fact, images with ideological overtones may be confined even among adults to less than 5 percent of the population.[43]

The inability of children to think in abstract ways and make critical differentiations means it is virtually impossible for them to deal with *problems of policy*. They are unable to conceptualize the sources of a

[42]Gallatin and Adelson, "Individual Rights and the Public Good," pp. 230-35.

[43]Hess and Torney, *Development of Political Attitudes in Children,* pp. 72-3; Greenstein, *Children and Politics,* pp. 70-71. Philip E. Converse, "The Nature of Belief Systems in Mass Publics," in David E. Apter, ed., *Ideology and Discontent* (New York: Free Press, 1964), pp. 206-62; Richard E. Merelman, "Development of Political Ideology," pp. 750-67.

social problem and visualize the effects of that problem, recognize the social (as distinct from personal) origins of problems, detect the necessity for collective problem solving (as contrasted with individual efforts), visualize alternative solutions, construct arguments contrary to their own preferences, and calculate the effects of inaction and unsolved problems. Their limited moral development impedes policy thought by restricting them to self-centered and hedonistic outlooks. Growing to adolescence contributes to moral thinking, causal thinking, and decentering and at least provides a basis for the development of policy thinking.[44] Whether that development occurs, however, depends upon a number of factors and agencies associated with political socialization.

WHAT INFLUENCES THE DEVELOPMENT OF POLITICAL IMAGES?

Most processes of image adoption consist of the interaction of two sets of forces: (1) factors peculiar to the individual which might conceivably coincide with his intellectual and moral development, and (2) agencies which filter politically related stimuli from the environment and help shape what an individual perceives. Personal factors such as age, sex, social class, and intelligence are in the first category. In the second category are such social agencies as the family, peer groups, school, and the mass media.

Personal Factors

Although the sequence of assimilative, accommodative, and adaptive stages in the development of political images is related roughly to differences in the ages of children, development is not simply a function of physical and/or intellectual maturation. Since we can not say which political stimuli a child may encounter at any given age, we are not able on the basis of chronological age alone to know what images of politics he is likely to hold. So long as the development of images depends upon environmental stimuli acting in combination with maturation (that is, the growth of necessary capacities for learning), *age differences* are significant factors in image development, but not controlling factors.

There are only minor *differences between the sexes* respecting the rates at which political images develop. For instance, the tendency to personalize political authority declines more sharply in the accommodative

[44]Richard E. Merelman, "The Development of Policy Thinking in Adolescence," *American Political Science Review,* Vol. 65 (December 1971), 1033-47.

stage among boys than among girls (the latter still identify government primarily with the President until thirteen or fourteen years of age). But as with age differences, differences in sex are not crucial influences on image development.

The contrast between children from high- and middle-*status backgrounds* vs. those from low-status families is sharper in the development of images that contribute to political interest, participation, discussion, etc. Lower-status children in both the United States and Great Britain, for instance, develop a sense of their own importance in influencing government more slowly and are less inclined to imagine government as involving voting. Because these differences parallel those normally found among adults, it suggests a self-fulfilling process — viz., families and schools in high-status areas provide models imitated by children who, in turn, adopt activist orientations; if those models are absent, as in low-status neighborhoods, children miss the type of political exposure that can interact with maturation to promote cognitive and affective development.[45]

The development of the affective component of images of government, law, and compliance are little influenced by *intelligence* (as measured by IQ tests). But a child's intelligence is one indicator of the capacity for cognitive growth and may act to promote or retard image adoption. There is evidence that intelligence among adolescents is positively correlated with certain cognitive components — knowledge of political facts, an understanding of the political system, an understanding of partisan politics, and a sense of the relevance of government. Moreover, intelligence is a factor in developing the ideological content of images: more intelligent students have been found less likely to hold militaristic, anti-Communist, or superpatriotic views, more likely to have a strong belief in the Bill of Rights, and more likely to be an economic conservative. And, the members of the adult population in the United States who are more proficient in their cognitive skills are more likely to conform to prevailing American beliefs on diverse social and political matters such as those emphasizing the importance of voting, civil liberties, etc. Although IQ and social class standing are generally associated, intelligence is the better predictor of the development of the cognitive side of political images.[46]

[45]Herbert Hirsch, *Poverty and Politicization* (New York: The Free Press, 1971); Middleton, Tajfel, and Johnson, "Cognitive and Affective Aspects of Children's National Attitudes;" Hess and Torney, *Development of Political Attitudes in Children*, pp. 126-71; and Easton and Dennis, *Children in the Political System*, pp. 343-50.

[46]S. K. Harvey and T. G. Harvey, "Adolescent Political Outlooks: The Effects of Intelligence as an Independent Variable," *Midwest Journal of Political Science*, Vol. 14 (November 1970), 565-95. Giuseppe DiPalma and Herbert McClosky, "Personality and Conformity: The Learning of Political Attitudes," *American Political Science Review*, Vol. 64 (December 1970), 1054-73.

Social Factors

Just as we do not explain differences in rates of learning political images solely on the basis of personal factors (such as chronological age) associated with maturation, we do not overemphasize the impact of social experience and social transmission. Only if political stimuli are intense, clearly visible, and unequivocal in their direction do they control the types of political images children develop. Normally this is not the case. Yet, in *conjunction* with maturation, environmental influences play an important part in image development. Generally socializing agencies — the family, peer groups, schools, and mass media — mediate political stimuli, present them to the child as symbols, and act as models for the child's learning.

Socializing agencies influence image development through their role in both direct and indirect learning. In *direct learning* people adopt images by (1) imitating the thoughts, feelings, and behavior of others that they contact directly — as when a small girl dresses like her mother; (2) anticipating what others expect of them in certain situations — as when at some point in professional schooling legal and medical students begin to think, feel, and talk like lawyers and doctors; (3) direct education — as when a student learns from the teacher in the classroom; or (4) direct experience — as when many young Americans learned about politics through direct involvement in Senator George McGovern's 1972 presidential campaign. In contrast, *indirect learning* occurs as a result of experience with symbols that takes the place of direct contact with persons, objects, and events. A person may model his behavior after that of an idealized image of another — as when the small boy learns the behavior of the cowboy, soldier, etc., through their symbolic presentation in books, films, or television.[47]

The importance of the *family* as a socializing agency can not be minimized. By example, direct teaching, and indoctrination the family assists the child in developing his personality, identifying his self, and defining his position in a social and economic hierarchy. Normally, American children adopt the party identification of their parents. So long as both parents express loyalty to the same party, the child has a clear model to follow. In cases of mother-father agreement the mother is usually the principal source for the child's political cues. If there is not agreement between parents, daughters tend to adopt the mother's partisanship while a son's partisan preference is no more likely to be influenced by one parent than the other. The parental influence over partisan learning is strong even in families where relations between children and parents are tense, so long as politics is not salient in the family and, hence, does not become an object

---

[47]A. Bandura and R. H. Walters, *Social Learning and Personality Development* (New York: Holt, Rinehart & Winston, 1963), pp. 48-50.

of child rebellion.[48] But child-rearing methods that lead to frustrations, anxieties, and tense parent-child relations impede the moral and intellectual development necessary to adaptive political imagery. Current studies argue that the optimal child-rearing pattern combines rapid shouldering of responsibility, the use of psychological discipline rather than threats and physical punishment, and sustained parental warmth. Such a combination is difficult to achieve, and its absence in many families may partially explain why so many persons are arrested in their political development (as we note later).[49]

Peer groups play an important role in directly communicating images when ties between childhood friends are close. The child's membership in these groups coincides with the assimilative and accommodative stages of image development. Of course, unless politics is of at least minimal importance among the child's friends, it is unlikely they will influence his views. Members of peer groups normally come from similar social-class backgrounds and, to the extent they do, their political images usually reinforce one another. Where there is diverse membership, lower-class children are frequently more influenced by their upper-class playmates than vice versa.[50]

The school is a source of direct education that intervenes in the child's life when accommodative growth begins. The school introduces images of the homeland and/or reinforces them with patriotic mythology, rituals, and civic indoctrination in the elementary grades — e.g., displaying the flag, reading about "great" historical figures, reciting the pledge of allegiance, singing patriotic songs, celebrating national holidays, discussing major current events, etc. And, even though the words of a pledge of allegiance or the motion of saluting the flag may have no cognitive import, the rituals create an affective bond between child and country. The elementary school teacher is a model for the child to identify with and imitate, particularly in acquiring a conception of legitimate authority, compliance with rules, and a sense of self-competence in influencing decisions. These school influences operate throughout the child's formal education, but diminish somewhat in secondary schools. The impact of the civic curriculum decreases by adolescence in comparison with the more lasting influences of rituals, teachers, and peer groups; the actual content of courses is relatively negligible in building political knowledge and a sense of political effectiveness.[51]

[48]M. Kent Jennings and Richard G. Niemi, "The Division of Political Labor Between Mothers and Fathers," *American Political Science Review,* Vol. 65 (March 1971), 69-82; Langton, *Political Socialization,* pp. 21-83.

[49]Merelman, "Development of Political Ideology," pp. 764-67.

[50]Langton, *Political Socialization,* pp. 120-39.

[51]Dean Jaros, "Transmitting the Political Culture," *Social Science Quarterly,* Vol. 49 (September 1968), 284-95; Hess and Torney, *Development of Political Attitudes in Children,* pp. 101-15; Hirsch, *Poverty and Politicization,* p. 109.

The impact of the *mass media* upon developing political images is difficult to pinpoint, yet clearly present. Certainly in their early years few children pay close attention to political news on radio and television or in newspapers and magazines. Hence, as a source of factual information having a direct effect upon image development, the mass media play no major role. Yet, the mass media present children with dramatic events — a landing on the moon, an inaugural parade, the funeral of a president, etc. The written and pictorial messages of newspapers, film, radio, and television are symbolic models from which children acquire beliefs and feelings. Indeed in some social settings, as in both rural and urban poverty-stricken areas, the media are more important agents of information transmission than parents, peers, or schools. And, in middle-class environments the mass media act as "parents" in communicating images of authority figures, war, political candidates, and violence as a method of obtaining goals. Beyond this, through a variety of entertainment features, the media provide models for childhood emulation — models of the policeman, "foreigners," the "good" and "bad" guys, etc. — and depict the consequences of wrongful action, consequences not lost on the child's development of a moral sense. Finally, whether they be the texts used in elementary civic courses, novels of the lives of great men, or cartoon accounts of the exploits of war heroes, books as mass media provide pictures of the political world from which children obtain a rough image of politics.[52]

THE RESULTS OF IMAGE DEVELOPMENT: ADAPTATION OR FIXATION?

Early in this chapter we introduced the idea that the development of images can be likened to a biological process, such as that occurring when living organisms fulfill their nutritional needs. Ideally, assimilation and accommodation reach a balanced state whereby the organism adapts (that is, it transacts with its environment in such a way as to enhance its preser-

[52]A. Bandura and R. H. Walters, *Social Learning and Personality Development,* (New York: Holt, Rinehart & Winston, 1963), p. 50; Herbert Hirsch, *Poverty and Politicization,* (New York: Free Press, 1971), pp. 118-35; Bradley S. Greenberg and Brenda Dervin, *Use of the Mass Media by the Urban Poor* (New York: Praeger, 1971); Gary C. Byrne, "Mass Media and Political Socialization of Children and Pre-Adults," *Journalism Quarterly,* Vol. 46 (Spring 1969), 140-41; Walter M. Gerson, "Mass Media Socialization Behavior: Negro-White Differences," *Social Forces,* Vol. 45 (September 1970), 40-50; June E. Foster, "Father Images: Television and Ideal," *Journal of Marriage and the Family,* Vol. 26 (August 1964), 353-55; Neil Hollander, "Adolescents and the War: The Sources of Socialization," *Journalism Quarterly,* Vol. 48 (Autumn 1971), 472-79; Steven H. Chaffee, L. Scott Ward, and Leonard P. Tipton, "Mass Communication and Political Socialization," *Journalism Quarterly,* Vol. 47 (Winter 1970), 647-59; Seymour Feshbach and Robert D. Singer, *Television and Aggression* (San Francisco: Jossey-Bass, Inc., 1971); Philip E. Converse, Warren E. Miller, Jerrold G. Rusk, and Arthur Wolfe, "Continuity and Change in American Politics: Parties and Issues in the 1968 Election," *American Political Science Review,* Vol. 63 (December 1969), 1083-1105.

vation). Just as nutritional adaptation depends upon the intake of food, adaptation to our social surroundings requires the intake of information. We must perceive, understand, judge, and respond to information as a prerequisite of social adaptation. That information comes to us in the form of symbolic messages. Symbols are the "foodstuffs" for adaptive processing. And, just as nutritional adaptation involves interchanges between consumed foodstuffs and a biological organism's digestive system, information processing involves transactions between messages and our images.

In adapting to his political milieu, then, a person assimilates political information that is symbolically presented to him and simultaneously accommodates his images of politics to the new information. If he only assimilates information, the perceptive, cognitive, affective, and conative components of images do not change as a result of his experience; he simply processes information and acts without revising his views, feelings, habits, and routines. If he also accommodates information, his images change as a function of his experience; in short, the way he behaves in similar situations in the future will differ because his images of the political world have changed. Through adaptive imagery the individual copes with the problems of living in the political world by simultaneously assimilating symbols and accommodating his images to acquired information.[53]

If our political imagery is *adaptive,* this implies that we *actively participate* in the construction of our political environment. We neither passively accommodate every political symbol nor assimilate information to fixed, unchanging images. If our imagery is adaptive (if our political behavior is minded), we look carefully at the "given" properties of political objects to see if they actually have their origins in our prevailing prejudices, stereotypes, and outlooks rather than in the objects themselves. If, for instance, some Democrats think a Republican officeholder is "surely paranoid," is it because of demonstrable evidence to that effect or because partisans frequently can think only badly of one another? Failure to draw such distinctions may leave us misguided, misinformed, or both. But, adaptive political imagery is not easily achieved. As living organisms we protect our images against perceived challenges. Once an image is adopted, we tend to project it on all things and treat it not as a thought in our minds but as a "property" of a given object.[54] If we believe that politics is corrupt, it is easy to displace that belief on any specific politician and label him corrupt. Thus, we may see a public official as intrinsically "dishonest" when, in fact, it is our stereotype of "dishonesty" which we displace upon him, frequently without any firsthand knowledge or authenticated secondhand reports about him.

[53] Alfred L. Baldwin, *Theories of Child Development* (New York: John Wiley, 1968), pp. 295-97.

[54] David Elkind, "Introduction," *Six Psychological Studies by Jean Piaget,* p. xii.

Although images do change through the sequence of development we have described in this chapter, we have implied that the process of development does not always unfold smoothly. There are at least two things that commonly occur to disrupt the process, thereby resulting in images that do not help us much in political adaptation. To begin with, it is entirely possible that a person might progressively develop images of politics in the stated sequence; first, he acquires affective orientations providing him with images useful in expressing his political self and national identity; second, he expands those affective feelings to a positive evaluation of government, political leaders, the law, and compliance; and, third, he develops a cognitive understanding and sufficient political knowledge to allow him to become an influential participant in the politics of his local, state, and federal community. But, having progressed to the adaptive imagery we associate with adult citizenship something may happen to make him *regress* to earlier ways of thinking. For instance, people revert to personalizing political phenomena when a topic of political discussion becomes too advanced or difficult to follow, when it reveals an area of ignorance or uncertainty, when it exposes intensely held beliefs and resentments, or when they fear a loss of control over the outcome of political controversies. Think, for instance, of the common tendency of persons to label highly controversial public figures as *solely* responsible for disagreeable states of affairs — to blame Lyndon Johnson for a war in Vietnam, Richard Nixon for sending troops into Cambodia, "permissive" college administrators for campus riots, Herbert Hoover for the Great Depression, the "Establishment" for repression, and *THEM* (who make us pay taxes, foul our air, pollute our waters, and enslave our minds).

But, there is a second possibility; i.e., most people *never even reach* the stage of adaptive political development. To be sure, they adopt an initial stock of affective images. Then, however, something happens. Instead of accommodating their expressive-evaluative feelings through an increasing cognitive differentiation, they continue to assimilate political stimuli to emotionally laden, childhood images. Instead of outgrowing earlier egocentric, self-centered orientations, they remain oblivious of the viewpoint of others. Instead of internalizing a moral code of equity, charity, tolerance, and compassion, they take the view that if they are wronged others should be wronged in return. And, instead of processing and ordering information about their political environment and responding adaptively, they remain cheerfully ignorant of all phases of politics. The person who never outgrows his childlike faith, for instance, that the President can do no wrong, questioning neither the President's judgments nor motives, is not likely to be interested in, let alone dissuaded, by information to the contrary. To such people information does not provide the function we discussed in Chapter Two; that is, information does not reduce uncertainty but rather produces it. Hence, like children in the assimilative stage, they encase themselves in the secure world of previously adopted images, ignoring information and simply reasserting their own views. For these people the development of political images has been fixated at a precausal and/or premoral phase of childhood; the requisite intellectual and moral development contributing to adaptive political imagery may then never occur.

There is ample evidence that such fixation, or at least something similar, is all too common. Studies of the cognitive content of adult political images reveal low information levels, only moderate differentiation, inability to look beyond the immediate political present, and the absence of political involvement among large segments of the population. Studies of the affective, evaluative content of political images reveal that there is frequently only token support for even the most central values deemed essential to democratic government.[55]

The possibility that the progressive development of adaptive political imagery can be fixated as well as enhanced raises the question of precisely what political images adults do hold. We will consider this question in the next two chapters in a discussion of the distribution of political images in mass society.

---

[55]John H. Kessel, "Cognitive Dimensions and Political Activity," *Public Opinion Quarterly,* Vol. 29 (Fall 1965), 377-89; Herbert McClosky, "Consensus and Ideology in American Politics," *American Political Science Review,* Vol. 58 (June 1964), 361-82.

4

political images in a mass society: popular supports

Having looked at what political images are, their basic characteristics, how they are communicated, and how they are learned, it is now appropriate to ask how they are *distributed;* what we mean by this is (1) what do people believe, feel, and propose to do about politics that gives popular support to their government and its policies; and (2) what political images — serving as tools for tangible gains, evaluation, and self-expression — do people use in stating their concerns to governors? In this chapter we shall investigate the images of popular support, and in Chapter Five we will look at images that assist in making popular demands.

POLITICAL IMAGES IN MASS SOCIETY

A characteristic of contemporary societies is mass participation in political life.[1] By *mass* we refer to a collection of people who come together in a relatively spontaneous way. The mass displays certain features, as follows: (1) mass membership is highly diverse and comes from all social strata, and thus the mass consists of persons of different ethnic groups,

[1]Gabriel A. Almond and Sidney Verba, *The Civic Culture* (Princeton: Princeton University Press, 1963), p. 3.

occupations, educational levels, incomes, ages, religions, etc.; (2) the mass consists of persons who seldom meet and are relatively anonymous to one another; (3) the mass is only loosely organized in the pursuit of collective goals; (4) the members of the mass are attracted to political objects that transcend parochial concerns; and (5) the collective decisions of the mass are relatively free from social control, but rather they reflect the *convergence of voluntary individual choices.* The mass consists, therefore, of "an aggregation of individuals who are separate, detached, anonymous, and thus, homogeneous" and the behavior of the mass "is not made by pre-established rule or expectation, is spontaneous, indigenous, and elementary."[2]

Elites and nonelites play significantly contrasting roles with respect to their images of politics in a mass society; i.e., the former supply symbols to which the latter assign meaning. Just as mass behavior reflects the convergence of individual choices, images in mass politics consist of the convergence of individual political images in response to political symbols normally manipulated by elites. By supplying symbols that help fulfill the needs and wants of followers, leaders (when successful) mobilize nonelites in at least three ways.

For one, leaders frequently seek popular support for programs that provide material gains for some groups at the expense of others; to win support they employ symbols they deem persuasive to all followers. Think, for example, of President Richard Nixon's appeal to self-sacrifice in his second inaugural address. Preparing the way for some future programs of his Administration that would reduce federal expenditures to various groups and even to the states, Nixon condemned "paternalism" and the notion that "Washington knows best." Instead, individuals should be encouraged "to do more for themselves"; we must "measure what we will do for others by what they will do for themselves." Thus did symbols of self-sacrifice and self-sufficiency serve as persuasive tools in the President's appeals for popular support of policies with potentially unpopular tangible consequences.

Second, leaders respond to popular strivings for social and moral status by manipulating symbols with evaluative overtones. Apparently many Americans in the late 1960s and early 1970s, especially in the South but also in other regions, felt that Washington lawmakers were ignoring their wishes in sensitive domestic policies. For instance, on civil rights issues, particularly the ever touchy question of school integration, many whites expressed the notion that politicians no longer cared about them. In campaigning for the 1972 presidential nomination Governor George Wallace responded to those who felt they had lost status in the eyes of

---

[2]Herbert Blumer, "The Mass, the Public, and Public Opinion" in Bernard Berelson and Morris Janowitz, eds., *Reader in Public Opinion and Communication* (New York: Free Press, 1966), p. 44.

Washington lawmakers by urging them to "Send Them a Message," i.e., to vote for him as a statement of disapproval of the way the country was being run. Wallace became a symbol many could rally around in an evaluative way; by supporting him they pronounced judgment on "the government in Washington" and sought to reinstate what they perceived as a lost sociopolitical position vis-à-vis more favored ruling interests.

Finally, leaders reinforce popular loyalties and identifications with the nation by patriotic appeals, taking part in ceremonies, and identifying with revered national symbols. Few patriotic appeals have been as moving as that made by Great Britain's Prime Minister Winston Churchill when, early in World War II, his nation and its inhabitants were threatened by the forces of Nazi Germany. Urging that he had "nothing to offer but blood, toil, tears and sweat" he rallied his countrymen to "survival for the British Empire" through "Victory — victory at all costs, victory in spite of all terror; victory no matter however long and hard the road may be." Harkening to the imagery of blood, toil, tears and sweat, victory, and the survival of the British Empire, the beleaguered British expressed reaffirmation of themselves and the nation.

To accomplish these ends elites need some idea of both the fixed and shifting beliefs, values, and tendencies that comprise popular images of politics; to the extent that elites adapt their symbolic appeals to their perceptions of popular thoughts and feelings, the elites are thus influenced by the political images of nonelites.[3]

There are key differences in the images of politics elites and nonelites hold in a mass society. Elite images are rich, articulate, and quasi-logical in content when contrasted with the poorly organized, disconnected, undifferentiated, inarticulate, and largely amorphous images of the mass. To the extent that popular images take on a more organized character, it is due to exposure to the "forensic" beliefs of elites, that is, to the symbolic cues elites provide the mass.[4]

Of course, elites are primarily responsible for policy making, and nonelites are not. This contributes to the fact that in their role as policy makers elites are more concerned with using images as tools to communicate with one another about tangible matters, exchanging messages to promote immediate and long-range material goals. But in communicating with nonelites they are more apt to use vague rather than concrete images to foster a positive popular evaluation of their performance (as moral men of status, success, and distinction worthy of admiration) or to permit a mass display of support (as when political orators stimulate patriotic fervor).[5] In contrast

[3]William Kornhouser, *The Politics of Mass Society* (Glencoe: Free Press, 1959), Chapter 2.

[4]Giovanni Sartori, "Politics, Ideology, and Belief Systems," *American Political Science Review*, Vol. 63 (June 1969), 398-411.

[5]Suzanne Keller, *Beyond the Ruling Class* (New York: Random House, 1963), pp. 154-55.

nonelites in communicating among themselves and with elites debate issues in more emotional language bearing evaluative and expressive overtones that may have little to do with the specific decisions made by policy makers.

We find, therefore, ". . . meanings conveyed to mass publics are consistently different from those reflected in the responses of small, immediately involved groups; . . . the mass public progressively disappears as a factor as policy definition moves toward the allocation of tangible values."[6] The debate over "law and order", for example, occurs at two levels — the mass level of emotional concern with making it "safe for our wives and daughters to be out alone at night" and the elite level of raising sufficient revenue to augment the police force, correct the underlying conditions which promote crime, and preserve basic civil liberties. However, saying that elites are more prone to communicate images that advance material interests while nonelites use images for judgmental and expressive ends, does not imply that popular concerns are any less "real" simply because they are couched in different symbols. To those who have them, emotionally charged concerns are every bit as politically meaningful, if not more so, as material issues, and politicians recognize this by responding to them.[7]

Such a distinction in the political images of elites and nonelites should not be taken to mean that elitist images are always accurate or that there is consensus in elite images. There have been countless instances of erroneous images of elites (even the leaders of the world's societies at one time thought the earth to be flat!). The images that political elites have of nations in foreign affairs are frequently inaccurate. Take as an example the misperception of American leaders that the Chinese People's Republic would not enter the Korean War in 1951 or the inaccuracies in the images held by Egyptian leaders of Israeli strength prior to the Six Day War of 1967. Many political conflicts are illustrative of lack of agreement in elitist images (as, for example, the marked differences in the images of Richard Nixon and George McGovern in 1972 over how best to end the Vietnam war).

The differing emphasis in the images of elites and nonelites in mass societies suggests a political hierarchy.[8] At the top in each mass society is a *policy-making elite* composed of a relatively small number of elective and appointive officials and influential private citizens. In

[6]Murray Edelman, *The Symbolic Uses of Politics* (Urbana: University of Illinois Press, 1964), p. 149.

[7]Joyce M. Mitchell and William C. Mitchell, *Political Analysis and Public Policy* (Chicago: Rand McNally, 1969), pp. 135-64.

[8]Gabriel A. Almond, *The American People and Foreign Policy* (New York: Praeger, 1960), p. 139; V. O. Key, Jr., *Public Opinion and American Democracy* (New York: Knopf, 1961), pp. 536-43; James N. Rosenau, *Public Opinion and Foreign Policy* (New York: Random House, 1961), pp. 39-41; Donald J. Devine, *The Attentive Public* (Chicago: Rand McNally and Company, 1970).

America we would include the President and his advisers, congressmen, bureaucrats, the courts, governors, legislators, and influential
businessmen, labor leaders, journalists, etc. in this elite group. In
politics this policy-making elite usually exchanges images as tools for
internal communication about tangible issues, but is more inclined to
use evaluative-expressive imagery with outsiders. Below this elite is a
larger circle of people, the *attentives,* who are not directly involved in
policy-making, but who keep informed on policy issues, debate them,
judge them, and make their judgments known. These people do not
hold government positions but are civic-minded citizens who are members of a wide variety of voluntary organizations, interested in politics,
talk about it, read about it, and engage in political activity. The judgmental proclivities of the attentives reflect that they employ images
primarily to evaluate politics, although they are sometimes privy to
images of elites concerning material issues, and they also use politics
for self-expression as does the mass. Finally, there is the *mass* who
take part in politics much more sporadically than either of the two
other groups, are more apathetic and more passive. Their political participation is generally expressive; even the most sacred institutions of
democracy such as elections are approached as a spectator sport from
which members of the mass seek reassurance, a reduction of anxieties,
and a confirmation of self.[9]

In the remainder of this and the next chapter we will explore the
political images held at the mass level about a variety of political objects. As noted in introducing this chapter, we will look at two major
categories of mass images, popular supports and concerns. Starting
with the assumption that governments are only as strong as the imagi-
nations of their supporters permit, we will consider in this chapter
the political images that lend mass support to three major sets of
political objects in society: (1) *the political community,* i.e., that collection of persons who have agreed to live together by regulating disputes that arise between them; (2) *the political regime,* or the rules
that include the constitutional order, policy-making institutions, and
governmental processes; and (3) *the political leaders* — people who
govern the society or who influence the   policy-making elites or
rulers.[10]

Even though people may support the political community, its
regime, and its authorities, they also have concerns which are manifested in political ways. In Chapter Five we will examine the political

[9]Giuseppe Di Palma, *Apathy and Participation* (New York: Free Press, 1970), p. 201;
Edelman, *The Symbolic Uses of Politics,* pp. 1-21.

[10]David Easton, *A Systems Analysis of Political Life* (New York: John Wiley, 1965),
pp. 171-219.

images associated with popular concerns in five areas; viz., popular aspirations, social movements, ideologies, elections, and policy issues.

In Figure 4-1 we suggest that there is a ranking of the political objects related to images of mass support and mass concern, a ranking from most abstract, diffuse objects (political communities) to the most specific objects, policies. We suggest that as we move down the listing of political objects depicted in Figure 4-1, the imagery associated with objects moves from expressive to evaluative to instrumental. Why this may be so should become more apparent as we consider each object of political imagery.

	Political Objects	*Types of Imagery*
Mass Supports	Political Communities Political Regimes Political Authorities	Expressive
Mass Concerns	Popular Aspirations Social Movements Ideologies Elections Policy Issues	Evaluative Instrumental

FIGURE 4-1 The Relationship of Political Objects and Types of Political Imagery

Cognitive and Affective Components of Supporting Political Images

Whether or not a population proposes actively to support its political community, regime, and authorities (the conative component of their images) depends largely upon the cognitive and affective aspect of those images, expecially how much people know and how they feel about politics. There is considerable evidence to indicate that citizens in our mass society are relatively uninformed about a variety of governmental areas: only about one in five Americans can correctly name the three branches of the federal government or know anything about the Bill of Rights; the Electoral College is known to only one-third of Americans; in 1967 only 28 percent of respondents in a Gallup poll could name their state senator and only 24 percent could name their representative in the lower house of their state legislature; fewer than 20 percent of those polled by Gallup could state correctly the position held by their Congressman on Vietnam, civil rights, or labor matters; and in 1970 only a bare majority in a Gallup survey could even name their Congressman. On specific policy questions and current events Americans also do not score well: in 1967 42 percent did not know the meaning of "open housing" when it was being widely debated in the press;

in the same year only 34 percent could estimate the number of American troops in Vietnam within 150,000 of the correct troop strength.[11]

Compared to other national populations, however, the level of political information of Americans fares well. For example, a significant study of political cognitions in five countries (the United States, Great Britain, West Germany, Italy, and Mexico) asked respondents to name the leaders of the political parties in their respective nations. In the United States 16 percent could name no party leader but 65 percent could name four or more. This display of information was superior to all nations except West Germany (where 12 percent could name no party leader and 69 percent could name four or more). Americans also compared well in the degree of attention paid to political campaigns and the regularity of following news about public affairs.[12]

Moreover, there is evidence that levels of political information are increasing in this country. The majority of Americans who could name their congressman in 1970 was a slight increase over the percentage who could do so in 1966 and a substantial improvement over 1947 when only 38 percent correctly identified their congressman in a Gallup survey. As educational, occupational, and income levels for Americans rise, there is a general tendency for their political images to become better informed.[13]

Americans, then, have better informed political images than people in some other nations, but in mass societies generally, America included, information levels are not high. If support for governments and their policies were solely dependent upon cognitive awareness of the specific things governments do, given mass ignorance of such matters, levels of support probably would be low and governmental instability high. Governments, however, persist even in the face of mass ignorance (and perhaps because of it!). They do so if there is a "reservoir of favorable attitudes or good will that helps members to accept or tolerate outputs to which they are opposed or the effects of which they see damaging to their wants."[14] This reservoir of positive affect in political images is what political scientists refer to as *diffuse support*. As we noted in Chapter Three, people frequently develop

[11]Norval D. Glenn, "The Distribution of Political Knowledge in the United States," in Dan Nimmo and Charles M. Bonjean, eds., *Political Attitudes and Public Opinion* (New York: McKay, 1972); Lloyd A. Free and Hadley Cantril, *The Political Beliefs of Americans* (New Brunswick, N.J.: Rutgers University Press, 1967), p. 61; John Kessel, "Cognitive Dimensions and Political Activity," *Public Opinion Quarterly*, Vol. 29 (Fall 1965), 377-89.

[12]Almond and Verba, *The Civic Culture*, pp. 88-94.

[13]Don D. Smith, " 'Dark Areas of Ignorance' Revisited," *Social Science Quarterly*, Vol. 51 (December 1970), 668-73.

[14]Easton, *A Systems Analysis of Political Life*, Chapter 10; Edward N. Muller, "Correlates and Consequences of Beliefs in the Legitimacy of Regime Structures," *Midwest Journal of Political Science*, Vol. 14 (August 1970), 392-412.

political images that generate diffuse support (such as favorable images of the American presidency or the local policeman) early in life. Let us then consider the images that reflect the presence or absence of diffuse support for political communities, regimes, and authorities.

Images of Political Community

Nations spend a great deal of money on symbols that are intended to build mass support for the political community, a diffuse support expressed through national identifications, patriotism, and pride. Flags, official uniforms and attire, national holidays, seals of office, capitol buildings, courthouses, civics courses in schools, public ceremonies and funerals — all are symbolic expressions of the political community, and each generation of citizens normally respects what they represent. If some people do not appear to respect these symbols, more fervent citizens question their loyalty (as illustrated in Chapter One by the furor over lack of respect for the American flag in recent years).

In many nations a sense of communal loyalty finds expression in the homage paid to a monarch or other symbolic figure. A leading example is the coronation of a new monarch in Great Britain, a ritual that provides an opportunity for citizens to reaffirm the moral values of their society and renew their devotion to them. Several parts of the coronation ceremony serve these purposes: the Administration of the Oath acknowledges that the moral standards of British law and custom are superior to the individual will of the monarch; the Presentation of the Bible represents the idea that God's intentions are passed to the monarch, and he or she becomes the earthly source of the inspiration for the morals of society; the Presentation of Sword and Orb symbolizes the monarch as the vessel through which virtues flow from God to society. Through reaffirmation of mass values a symbolic Crown commands the devotion of large numbers of Britishers, while political conflicts are the province of the Prime Minister and Parliament. The result is an "effective segregation of love and hatred." Despite criticism of the Crown as an expensive luxury in recent years by several Britishers, it remains as a focal point for the expression of a collective identity.[15]

Different people have different images of a nation's monarch. After World War II various military and political leaders of the victorious allies wanted to hang the Japanese Emperor to symbolize that

[15]Edward Shils and Michael Young, "The Meaning of the Coronation," *Sociological Review*, Vol. 1 (December 1953), 63-81.

the world had been freed of imperialism. Others, more conscious of the image the Japanese had of their Emperor, advised against execution. The widespread belief of the Japanese was that when men die they become deities who watch over their descendants. The more important the man the more important a deity he would become on death. Execution might have had the unintended effect of elevating the importance of the Emperor and his imperial majesty in the eyes of his followers. Thus, the Emperor remained alive and became a symbol affiliated with the new Japanese parliamentary democracy.[16]

National monuments and parks also are symbols stimulating and strengthening expressions of collective loyalty. In the United States the Federal Government has set aside over 10 million acres of land to accommodate national historic monuments, parks, and shrines.[17] Where the sentiments for the creation of such memorials are powerful and persistent, the usual practice is to build a physical structure — such as the Washington or Lincoln memorials — and to combine the expressive function of the memorial with certain esthetic features. In recent years there has been a tendency to combine symbolic and esthetic features with utilitarian functions; hence, for example, in 1971 the Kennedy Center for the Performing Arts opened in Washington, D.C., and became a "living" memorial to the assassinated President John F. Kennedy.[18] Political conflicts frequently arise over the types of memorials intended to commemorate cherished values. How to preserve the memory of John Kennedy gave rise to such a conflict in 1971 when an investor purchased the Texas School Book Depository building in Dallas, Texas. The investor sought to place a museum honoring Kennedy in the building. Since the building was allegedly the structure from which the Kennedy assassin fired the fatal shots, some Texans insisted that it was inappropriate to preserve the building at all, let alone convert it into a museum that might become a commercial venture in the future.

Certain symbols not only reaffirm and strengthen images of community loyalty; they can be used to create it. In Germany in the 1930s, for example, Nazi leaders sought to replace the family with the state as the primary unit of society. The Nazi elite symbolically purged the traditional heads of the family, i.e., the father and mother. In Nazi leaflets, pictures, movies, etc. the child, instead of being raised and nurtured by the family, appeared to represent the state to the family rather than to represent the family to the state. Moreover, women were portrayed as warriors, cooks, or innocent maidens, but not as wives.

[16]William Stephenson, *Quantal Analysis of Communication* (forthcoming).

[17]Donald J. Devine, *The Political Culture of the United States* (Boston: Little, Brown, 1972), p. 123.

[18]Bernard Barber, "Place, Symbol, and Utilitarian Function in War Memorials," *Social Forces,* Vol. 28 (October 1949), 64-68.

Fathers became objects of distrust and scapegoats for the pre-Nazi breakdown of Germany. In large measure the traditional role of father was deleted from the Nazi conception of society. Men were portrayed not as fathers but as knights (who repel attacks but are never at home) or grandfathers: "In sum, the German version of this drama makes the state the symbol for the family rather than the converse, the family a symbol of the state."[19]

Whether made by democratic or totalitarian regimes, efforts to mobilize images on behalf of community traditions meet with variable success. In some nations (as in the United States) as many as 85 percent of those surveyed in a cross-national study mentioned some feature of their political tradition when asked, "Speaking generally, what are the things about this country that you are most proud of?" But in West Germany and Italy, fewer than 10 percent responded to that question by referring to the political heritage. A simple expression of national pride contributes to higher rates of political participation by citizens, indicating perhaps that images of political expression promote images that people use to evaluate politics and even to act on material issues.[20]

The use of unifying symbols for building a sense of community among the mass is sufficiently important that it is possible to measure the growth of cognitive and affective awareness of political community by noting the frequency with which such symbols are employed in communication. For instance, one study examines the rate of integration of the American community by looking at the frequency and distribution of certain political symbols in the press from 1735 to 1775. Among these symbols were place-name symbols (such as "British colonies," "English colonies," or "British North America"), symbols identifying the population as American ("Americans," "North American"), symbols of local communities (such as New York City or Newport), and similar references. Generally, over the 40-year period there was a slow increase in symbols referring to American place-names, with a dramatic shift of attention to America in 1763. The colonists gradually symbolized the colonies as a single unit ("British colonies" or "America") rather than as separate political entities, but it was not until the close of the period that "Americans" began to refer to themselves by that name.[21]

[19]William Kinser and Neil Kleinman, *The Dream That Was No More: A Search for Aesthetic Reality in Germany, 1890-1945* (New York: Harper & Row, 1969), p. 18.

[20]Almond and Verba, *The Civic Culture*, p. 102; Di Palma, *Apathy and Participation*, p. 54.

[21]Richard L. Merritt, *Symbols of American Community, 1735-1775* (New Haven: Yale University Press, 1966). For the presence of symbolism in the integration of other communities, see Manuel Servin, "Religious Aspects of Symbolic Acts of Sovereignty," *Americas,* Vol. 13 (January 1957), 255-67, and Louis C. Faron, "Symbolic Values and the Integration of Society Among the Mapuche of Chile," *American Anthropology,* Vol. 64 (December 1962), 1151-64.

The consolidation of a mass population means that they not only begin to have a common image of themselves as a political community, but people in other nations regard them as such. Thus, each nation acquires over time an image in international affairs, and the way it is treated by other nations may depend upon that image. In 1962, for example, leaders of the Soviet Union apparently regarded the United States as unwilling to take serious risks to protect itself from foreign threats. In part because of that image the U.S.S.R. began to build surface-to-surface missile bases in Cuba. The response of the Kennedy administration, however, demanding withdrawal of the missiles forced the Russians to change their estimate of the United States; the Soviet Union complied with Kennedy's demand, and "A major change in Soviet policy resulted from this change of image."[22]

Political communities emerge as people converge upon a set of cherished beliefs, values, and ways of behaving. Political symbols not only reflect this convergence of images, but in turn they help foster community identifications, loyalties, and pride.

Images of the Political Regime

The political regime consists of the constitutional order, institutions, and procedures by which a community resolves its disputes. The legitimacy of any regime, i.e., the view by the mass that the regime is morally acceptable to govern, depends upon a relatively stable distribution of diffuse support among the population.[23] That distribution is determined in part by an appropriate manipulation of political symbols.

Legitimacy of the Constitutional Order

Diffuse support for the constitutional order appears as *political trust,* the general images that people have about the quality of treatment they expect from a government and accordingly the degree of confidence they place in the regime. Feelings of trust involve using political images to evaluate events more than employing them to gain tangible rewards through public policy or to express individual identities. Political trust relates simply to whether government is judged

---

[22]Robert Jervis, *The Logic of Images in International Relations* (Princeton: Princeton University Press, 1970), p. 5.

[23]Easton, *A Systems Analysis of Political Life,* Chapter 18.

as generally "good" or "bad."[24] If a person trusts the constitutional order, that is "the government," and has confidence in its general ability to improve things, he may yet be dissatisfied with specific policies of government but is not disaffected: "Dissatisfaction means simply a general dislike for anything that falls short of one's wishes; it may be manageable and temporary. Disaffection is an alienation of feelings and so involves remoteness and estrangement: it can be permanent."[25]

Political trust can be measured in a variety of ways. One technique relies upon responses from sample surveys of mass populations to indicate political efficacy, political proximity, commitment to the political order, satisfaction with government performance. These four factors are defined as follows: *Political efficacy* — a feeling that government cares about the individual combined with the view that a person can really understand and influence what government does; *political proximity* — the individual's sense of how close government is to him, how much it affects his day-to-day life; *commitment* to the political order — a sense of obligation to one's country and government; and *satisfaction* with government performance — assessments of whether government improves conditions or makes them worse. Such survey data from the United States, Germany, Italy, and England indicates a greater frequency of trusting images of politics in the United States, although not always strikingly so. The measure which taps simple dissatisfaction with governmental performance does little to explain differences in the rates of political participation in the four countries, but measures of political efficacy, proximity, and commitment indicate that a *loss of trust in government ("disaffection") decreases participation.* A person dissatisfied with his government is not likely to reduce his political activity; but the *estranged* person who has lost confidence in government is likely to be apathetic.[26]

A few observers, notably pollsters George Gallup and Louis Harris, have suggested that the low turnout of voters in the 1972 presidential election (only about half of those of voting age cast ballots) was due to an apathy fostered by growing alienation. Gallup found more than one-fourth of a nationwide sample of Americans "not interested in politics."[27] Harris in another 1972 survey revealed a sharp rise in feelings of alienation over the preceding year, from 40 to 47

[24]William A. Gamson, *Power and Discontent* (Homewood, Ill.: The Dorsey Press, 1968); Donald E. Stokes, "Popular Evaluations of Government: An Empirical Assessment," in Harlan Cleveland and Harold D. Lasswell, eds., *Ethics and Bigness: Scientific, Academic, Religious, Political and Military* (New York: Harper & Row, 1962), p. 67.

[25]Di Palma, *Apathy and Participation,* p. 30.

[26]*Ibid.,* pp. 32-73.

[27]*The Gallup Opinion Index,* Report #90, December 1972, p. 11.

percent, as measured by agreement with such statements as "the rich get richer and the poor get poorer," "the people running the country don't really care what happens to people like yourself," "what you think doesn't count very much," "people who have the power are out to take advantage of you," and "you feel left out of things around you."[28]

In general, the images of government of people of higher education, income, and occupational status are more trusting than those of lower social and economic status. Studies of differences in levels of political trust among whites and blacks in the United States also indicate ethnic differences. Blacks are generally less trusting of the constitutional order. Among whites, the source of the political distrust that does exist often lies on what whites perceive as a worsening racial situation spawned by granting black demands at white expense. A 1967 survey in Detroit, Michigan, even suggests that blacks are less likely than whites to lose faith in government simply because of racial policies. But for many blacks, particularly lower-status blacks, a feeling of deprivation (of not being able to accomplish personal goals in life) triggers political distrust. This sense of frustration also exists among middle-class blacks (where the highest political distrust was encountered in the 1967 survey). Middle-class blacks have an image of a black community which they identify with so strongly that they feel their own private aspirations depend upon winning respect for all blacks. While expressing identification with that black community, they look to government for policies that symbolize a recognition of their black status and identity. Their expression of loyalty to the black community carries with it a desire for status which in some respects means more to them than material gain. Not receiving status recognition, they tend to be distrustful even in the face of tangible benefits.[29]

Trusting images of politics stem in part from tangible gains such as higher educational, occupational, and income levels for people. But trust is also related to how governments manipulate the symbols people use to define their station in life. To obtain mass compliance with their decisions, policy makers associate themselves with symbols that have widespread popular appeal. If the decisions to be presented will actually mean an immediate material cost for people (such as the mandatory 90-day wage-price freeze decreed by the Nixon administration in 1971), then leaders try to convince the populace that material loss will be compensated by a rise in self-respect, social status, or moral

[28] *The Harris Survey,* June 19, 1972.

[29] Joel D. Aberbach and Jack L. Walker, "Political Trust and Racial Ideology," *American Political Science Review,* Vol. 64 (December 1970), 1199-1219; Milton Rokeach and Seymour Parker, "Values as Social Indicators of Poverty and Race in America," *The Annals of the American Academy of Political and Social Science,* Vol. 388 (March 1970), pp. 97-111.

betterment. As we described in Chapter Two, the Nixon administration attempted to meet this difficulty by an appeal to Americans' sense of self-sacrifice and the work ethic as justifying symbols.

The manipulation of symbols in order to promote the legitimacy of a political regime is not restricted to the United States. Indonesia in the 1950s and early 1960s was a striking example of the use of symbols to try to mobilize diffuse support. A relatively small elite composed of President Sukarno and army leaders ruled Indonesia. The Sukarno regime was beset with a variety of problems — low food production, inflation, low levels of compliance with laws, corruption, dissension and the opposition resulting from the overthrow of a previous parliamentary order. Both to detract from and to alleviate these difficulties, the Sukarno government embarked upon a major symbolic campaign to promote a popular image of solidarity and leadership, radical changes, response to the demands of the people, national strength, and national identity. We have no way of knowing that the symbolic themes had the intended effects in Indonesia, but the campaign for popular support provides an excellent case study of how some governments approach symbol manipulation. The symbol "Guided Democracy" became the focal point of the campaign. "Democracy with leadership" replaced a parliamentary regime of "liberal democracy" or "50 percent plus one democracy," and signified the solidarity and leadership theme. In line with the idea that the regime must and would foster radical changes to meet existing social and economic problems, Sukarno called for a "National Revolution" to remove the vestiges of the earlier colonial and parliamentary periods. His speeches reiterated the symbols of a "just and prosperous society" and "retooling." To create the impression of a regime built upon national strength with a national personality that would respond to the demands of the people, Sukarno labeled the revolution a "People's Revolution" that would carry into effect the "Mandate of the People's Suffering." A continuing struggle against imperialism, colonialism, and neocolonialism would assure national strength, and this struggle took cultural as well as military form. Sukarno railed against rock-and-roll and cha-cha-cha dances and called for reaffirmation of traditional village values. The Indonesian regime resorted to a variety of devices to reiterate its symbolic themes. These included speech-making by public figures, special days and ceremonies ("National Awakening Day" and "Electricity and Gas Day"), conferral of badges and medals to enthusiastic supporters, renaming of streets, movie houses, mountains, etc. with national names (including the renaming of the Indian Ocean to the Indonesian Ocean).

As stated above, the success of such a symbolic campaign (or of similar efforts in Nazi Germany in the 1930s, the Soviet Union in the

1920s, and in all nations in all times to some degree) is hard to assess. The manipulations sometimes create an atmosphere which directs mass attention away from material problems. From the standpoint of policy makers, political images are tools for ensuring political control. Viewed from the perspective of the mass, however, the images serve evaluative and expressive purposes. In Indonesia the symbolic themes employed by the Sukarno regime evoked among some people a sense of moral superiority over imperialists and neoimperialists; moreover, by identifying with Sukarno, Indonesians heightened their status as a people, and the more important a world leader he became, the more prestige they too acquired.[30]

Images of Political Institutions

The popular images of the institutions of a political regime contribute to the legitimacy of the constitutional order, be it democratic or despotic. Indeed when people think of "government," they usually think of legislatures, presidents, prime ministers, or other such institutions. We shall confine ourselves in this section to considering those types of institutions (primarily in the United States) on which there is sufficient data relating to mass images — i.e., executives, legislatures, courts, political parties, and elections.

We know from our discussion in the preceding chapter that children develop supportive images of certain executive agents in America, especially the presidency and police. In so far as the presidency is concerned, that diffuse support persists through adulthood. Regardless of the specific occupant of that office, Americans display greater confidence in the presidency than in other governmental institutions. For example, when asked in a nationwide survey to rate their degree of confidence in the presidency, the Congress, and the judiciary in 1964, the mean response of all ratings for the presidency was higher than for either of the other institutions.[31]

The *presidency* is the most visible symbol of government for most Americans. Headed by a single individual, the presidency provides a cognitive "handle" Americans can grasp to gain an understanding of political goings on. The presidency is also a focus for emotional responses to American government.[32] It is, by and large, the

[30]Herbert Feith, "Indonesia's Political Symbols and Their Wielders," *World Politics* (October 1963), pp. 79-97.

[31]Free and Cantril, *The Political Beliefs of Americans*, p. 118.

[32]Fred I. Greenstein, "The Psychological Functions of the Presidency for Citizens," in Elmer E. Cornwell, *The American Presidency: Vital Center* (Chicago: Scott, Foresman, 1966), pp. 30-36; Merlin Gustafson, "The Religious Role of the President," *Midwest Journal of Political Science*, Vol. 14 (November 1970), 708-22; Richard E. Donley and David G. Winter, "Measuring the Motives of Public Officials at a Distance: An Exploratory Study of American Presidents," *Behavioral Science*, Vol. 15 (May 1970), 227-36.

center of ceremonial activity, and in that symbolic capacity it performs very much as does the English monarchy. The expressive symbolism of the presidency is augmented by its religious role. The President issues proclamations for national religious observances, communicates with religious groups and leaders (as demonstrated, for example, by the presence of Reverend Billy Graham at so many governmental functions during the Nixon administration), and engages in religious activity himself. Finally, the presidency is the unifying symbol of our relations with other nations. Thus, in 1972, it was through trips by President Richard Nixon to China and the Soviet Union that an image of a "thaw" in affairs with those nations began to emerge.

From highly publicized confrontations between police and civil rights, antiwar, and other demonstrators in the 1960s (and because of such names as "fascist pig" used for policemen), it is easy to assume that images of the police, which are positive in early childhood, erode as people get older. This, however, is not the case. National surveys in 1970, for example, revealed generally favorable views of *law enforcement officials;* over 60 percent rated federal, state, and local officials favorably. Asked what terms best describe law-enforcement officers, respondents most frequently selected "dedicated," "hard working," "interested in helping fellow man," and "intelligent," virtually avoiding such labels as "sadistic," "violent," "corrupt," or "lazy."[33]

A third major executive institution about which we know something of mass images is the *federal bureaucracy* in the United States. Nationwide surveys of the general public, students, teachers, and persons in private business reveal popular images of the civil service. Among the general public, favorable images of civil servants outnumber unfavorable references by five to one; students and teachers also hold favorable images of federal civil servants; business executives, natural scientists, social scientists, and engineers have more negative images. However, surveys reveal that in no group outside the federally employed do civil servants have a more favorable image than employees of private business.[34]

With respect to both the police and bureaucrats the crucial images are *how people expect to be treated* by officials; that is, do they expect to be taken seriously and treated equally? If so, people generally have sufficient trust in their governing institutions to constitute diffuse support. The available evidence indicates that these expecta-

---

[33]Louis Harris, *The Harris Survey Yearbook of Public Opinion: 1970,* (New York: Louis Harris and Associates, Inc., 1971) pp. 70-72; David Easton and Jack Dennis, *Children in the Political System* (New York: McGraw-Hill, 1969), pp. 294-97.

[34]Franklin P. Kilpatrick, Milton C. Cummings, Jr., and M. Kent Jennings, *The Image of the Federal Service* (Washington, D.C.: The Brookings Institution, 1964), Chapter 10.

tions vary considerably from country to country. Surveys conducted in 1960 indicated that 83 and 85 percent of Americans respectively would expect to be treated equally by bureaucrats and by the police. Approximately the same proportion of persons in a British sample indicated they also expected equality of treatment. In both Germany and Italy a majority of respondents expected equal treatment from each institution, but in Mexico a majority of respondents said they would not expect equal treatment from either bureaucrats or police. In Britain and Germany majorities expected "serious consideration" for their point of view from both bureaucracies and police, but in the United States only 48 percent of respondents expected serious consideration from bureaucrats whereas 56 percent thought they would receive it from police. In Italy and Mexico far smaller percentages expected serious consideration and in Mexico three of every ten respondents expected "to be ignored."[35]

The average man's image of government probably extends less to administrative functions than legislative ones; he "thinks of making policy, not enforcing it, of stating aims and goals, as well as codes of behavior."[36] Popular images of *legislatures* have two facets, i.e., public support for legislatures as governing bodies and images of individual legislators. A 1966 survey in Iowa revealed that large portions of that state's residents held favorable images of the legislature as an institution; fewer than 3 percent agreed that it was all right to disobey a law passed by the legislature and 78 percent opposed the proposal that the legislature should be abolished if it persistently passed disagreeable laws. But, support for the legislature was not uniformly high on all matters. One-fourth of the sample agreed that "there are times when it would almost seem better for the governor to take the law into his own hands rather than wait for the state legislature to act." Nearly one-sixth agreed that there were times when it might be better if citizens would take the law into their own hands rather than wait for the legislature to act.[37]

As far as images of what characteristics the individual legislator should possess, Iowans ranked honesty, industry in studying problems, knowledge of the will of his district, hard work, and interest in serving others highly. They generally thought "half" to "most" legislators had these qualities, but not "all." All of these qualities are consistent with a "Tribune" image of a legislator; that is, a legislator should place uppermost

[35]Almond and Verba, *The Civic Culture,* pp. 101-14.

[36]Robert E. Lane, *Political Ideology* (New York: Free Press, 1962), p. 146.

[37]Samuel C. Patterson, G. R. Boynton, and Ronald D. Hedlund, "Perceptions and Expectations of the Legislature and Support for It," *American Journal of Sociology,* Vol. 75 (July 1969), 62-76; G. R. Boynton, Samuel C. Patterson, and Ronald D. Hedlund, "The Structure of Public Support for Legislative Institutions," *Midwest Journal of Political Science,* Vol. 12 (May 1968), 163-80.

in his work the opinions of his constituents. Evidence from a nationwide survey in 1968 demonstrates that the tribune image extends beyond any single state; two-thirds of those asked to describe the job of a member of the House of Representatives in Washington gave responses indicating a tribune image. Only a minority of citizens, particularly those with lower levels of education,[38] had an "Inventor" image, the view that a congressman should be free to act upon his own initiative without closely checking with constituents' opinions.

Evidence about popular images of the *courts* as governmental institutions is limited primarily to the Supreme Court of the United States. Research suggests two major characteristics of mass images of the Court. First, decisions of the Court are seldom known by more than a minority of the people and, therefore, images pertaining to areas of specific support have little cognitive content. When asked to list their likes and dislikes about court decisions, a majority in both 1964 and 1966 samples could not even specify anything. Second, diffused support for the Supreme Court is much more widely distributed than specific support. Four times as many Americans have positive images of the Court in *general* than they do of specific decisions. It is primarily attentive persons rather than the mass that have supportive images of the Court; indeed, in a 1966 survey 73 percent of the populace could not even be classified as having definable images of the Court, favorable or unfavorable.[39]

The majority of persons surveyed in nationwide samples in 1970 do have clear images about the relationship of the judiciary to one problem in America, that of crime. Americans generally link judicial leniency with rising crime rates. Of these surveyed, two-thirds believed the courts "too lenient (too easy) in dealing with criminals," 19 percent believed court treatment fair and only 3 percent found it "too severe." (The remainder responded "it varies" or "not sure.") Americans are also critical of the courts on another score, i.e., the amount of time it takes to bring a person arrested for a crime to trial. In 1970 78 percent thought it took "too long a time."[40]

Political parties are also major institutions of most political regimes, and mass populations have supportive or non-supportive images of them. Here we are looking not at the images of specific political parties (we shall do that later) but at the degree of support for partisan competition for control of government. The most pertinent evidence on the degree of diffuse support for parties as institutions comes from a 1964 study conducted in

[38]Roger H. Davidson, "Public Prescriptions for the Job of Congressman," *Midwest Journal of Political Science,* Vol. 14 (November 1970), 648-67.

[39]Walter F. Murphy and Joseph Tanenhaus, "Public Opinion and the United States Supreme Court," in Joel Grossman and Joseph Tanenhaus, eds., *Frontiers of Judicial Research* (New York: John Wiley, 1969), pp. 272-303.

[40]Harris, *The Harris Survey Yearbook of Public Opinion: 1970,* pp. 66-67.

Wisconsin, indicating an "ambivalent and irresolute state of diffuse support for the party system." Whereas two-thirds of those surveyed rejected the ideal of making all elections nonpartisan, almost a majority still agreed that "the conflicts and controversies between the parties hurt our country more than they help it." Only 10 percent disagreed with the proposition that "The best rule in voting is to pick the man regardless of his party label." At best the mass image of the party system is lukewarm, sufficiently positive to tolerate party competition but anti-party enough to indicate that an increased role for parties in the political regime might be rejected.[41]

The 1964 Wisconsin study also furnishes us with relevant data for estimating the content of popular images of *elections* as political institutions.[42] There are three aspects to that content. First, mass images of elections are positive to the extent that people believe they have an obligation to vote in them. Second, the public has a negative view of political campaigns and related aspects of elections. A majority of respondents felt that money is wasted in campaigns. (Similarly, a 1960 nationwide survey revealed that 58 percent of Americans "sometimes find campaigns silly or ridiculous."[43]) Finally, a slim majority hold the belief that elections are an effective way for people to influence government. Overall, the public image of elections is more supportive than the image of political parties, but there is a gap between the view that one *should* vote and the perception of the *value* of elections as instruments of popular influence. This gap contributes to a tendency to respond to elections as obligatory rituals rather than as effective devices for making decisions.

Images of the Rules of the Game

Any democratic political regime has certain procedures to preserve basic human rights and liberties. These "rules of the game" include fair play, majority rule, minority rights, freedom (of thought, conscience, expression, and opposition), equal protection, and due process of the laws. Research in American politics indicates the mass is more committed to the principles of underlying democratic rules than to behavior required to put those rules into practice. For example, a noted study in the 1950s revealed several things about mass images typical of other studies: Support for general statements of the principles of free speech and equality are relatively high among both attentive people and the mass; for instance, a majority of both groups agreed that "People who hate our way of life should still have a chance to talk and be heard," "Freedom of conscience should

[41]Jack Dennis, "Support for the Party System by the Mass Public," *American Political Science Review*, Vol. 60 (September 1966), 600-615.

[42]Jack Dennis, "Support for the Institution of Elections by the Mass Public," *American Political Science Review*, Vol. 64 (September 1970), 819-35.

[43]Almond and Verba, *The Civic Culture*, p. 146.

mean freedom to be an atheist as well as freedom to worship in the church of one's choice," and disagreed that "Most people don't have enough sense to pick their own leaders wisely." But, when stated as specific actions, support of the rules fell off among both attentives and the mass but more sharply among the latter; thus, only 17 percent of attentives agreed that "A book that contains wrong political views cannot be a good book and does not deserve to be published" but a majority of the mass agreed. Finally, consensus on both principles and practices relating to free speech and opinion is much higher for both attentives and the mass than consensus of the tenets and implications of political, social, ethnic, and economic equality.[44]

Images of Political Leaders

A final object of supportive images meriting consideration is a nation's political leaders. To most people the very word "image" probably suggests political leaders, because journalists regularly publicize such notions as "image candidates," "image merchants," and "image projection." There is some reason for emphasizing the images of political leaders. After all, one way leaders advance their causes is by manipulating symbols to influence mass perceptions. How political leaders behave also influences how citizens react toward the political regime; depending upon what they think of the people who lead them, people are trusting or suspicious of politics.

There is both an organizational and symbolic character about political leadership, but popular images of leaders respond more to the symbolic.[45] A politician is an organization leader to the extent that he relies upon a hierarchy of superior-subordinant relations and formal designations of authority to govern. The politician's symbolic leadership "works on masses and audiences prior to, without, and in spite of organization," and people respond to the leader by identifying with him (either loving or hating him) and imitating him. Through symbolic ways leaders persuade people to follow them by identifying with the images their potential followers have of themselves or with the images those same people have of an "ideal" president, congressman, senator, governor, mayor, or other public official. But governmental position is not essential to political leadership — a businessman, a labor union organizer, or any popular celebrity can be a political figure so long as he has an impact in politics. For example, mass reactions to the conviction of Lieutenant William Calley, the army officer court mar-

[44]Herbert McClosky, "Consensus and Ideology in American Politics," *American Political Science Review,* Vol. 58 (June 1964), 361-82.

[45]Orrin E. Klapp, *Symbolic Leaders* (Chicago: Minerva Press, 1964), pp. 22-23; Douglas K. Stewart and Ted C. Smith, "Celebrity Structure of the Far Right," *Western Political Quarterly,* Vol. 17 (June 1964), 349-55.

tialed in 1971 for allegedly murdering Vietnamese civilians, made him, for at least a short time, a symbolic leader of a segment of popular opinion (for those who claimed he was a "scapegoat").

Most political leaders, both governmental and nongovernmental, combine symbolic and organizational activities (as for example, the late Martin Luther King). If we look at the names of the ten men Americans listed in a 1971 Gallup poll as those they "most admired" we find only one, comedian Bob Hope who was ranked ninth, whom we might say is almost exclusively a "symbolic leader." Others — Richard M. Nixon, Billy Graham, Edward Kennedy, consumer advocate Ralph Nader, Pope Paul VI, or George Wallace — are certainly symbolic leaders, but men who buttress their symbolic appeals with organizational support.[46]

Research into symbolic leadership consists of examining the techniques used by political leaders to establish themselves as popular symbols and the popular images of symbolic leaders, confined basically to the images of political candidates or major public officials such as the President. We will summarize the relevant research pertaining to images of political candidates in Chapter Five. Here we will first consider the popular images of the occupant of the presidential office, then turn to the techniques symbolic leaders use.

We observed earlier that the image of the presidency as an institution is generally positive. The same cannot be said of the images of specific presidents. Some past occupants of the presidency have, of course, become legendary figures (George Washington, Thomas Jefferson, and Abraham Lincoln) although at the time they served their popularity probably fluctuated a great deal. One of the few measures we have of the affective content of mass images toward American presidents lies in the regular opinion polls conducted by the American Institute of Public Opinion (the Gallup Poll). For almost a quarter of a century, the Gallup organization has asked cross-sections of the American public the question, "Do you approve or disapprove of the way (name of the incumbent) is handling his job as President?" Table 4-1 reports the high, low, and average levels of public approval for Presidents Truman, Eisenhower, Kennedy, Johnson, and Nixon (the last-named through the autumn of 1973). The figures indicate considerable variability of popular support ranging from a low of 23 percent for President Harry Truman to a high of 87 percent, also for Truman.

There are various explanations for this fluctuation in the popularity of American Presidents, but four factors are especially relevant.[47] The first lies in the tendency for the popularity of a President to decline over the length of his incumbency. A man is elected President largely through

[46]News Release, American Institute of Public Opinion, January 2, 1972.

[47]John E. Mueller, "Presidential Popularity from Truman to Johnson," *American Political Science Review*, Vol. 64 (March 1970), 18-34.

TABLE 4-1 Presidential Popularity: 1948 - 1973			
President	*Percentage Approval*		
	High	Low	Average
Truman	87	23	46
Eisenhower	79	49	66
Kennedy	83	57	70
Johnson	80	35	54
Nixon	68	30	53

Source: Gallup Opinion Index, October 1973.

his ability to forge a coalition of various interests. The longer in office the more likely he is to take positions that please some elements of this diverse coalition but displease others. This was a principal factor in the sharp decline of popularity of both Presidents Truman and Johnson during their incumbencies. Dwight Eisenhower was an exception; his popularity rose slightly during his first term and declined little thereafter in his second. The more normal pattern was displayed in Nixon's gradual decline in popularity in his first three years in office — slipping annually from an average approval rate of 62 percent to 57 percent to 50 percent. Economic conditions are a second factor related to presidential popularity. Economic well-being is a major concern of most Americans (see Chapter Five). One indicator of that well-being is the rate of unemployment. When correlated with shifts in presidential popularity, there has been about a three-percentage-point decline in approval of a president for each 1 percent rise in unemployment in America (a drop in unemployment, however, does not seem to portend a rise in presidential popularity). A third factor lies in presidential appeals for support in time of domestic or foreign crisis. Truman, for example, appealed for popular support upon entering into the Korean conflict in 1950; Kennedy made an appeal for such support when endeavoring to force removal of Soviet missile bases from Cuba in 1962. Evidence is that there is generally a rallying around the President at these times, but a 5 or 6 percent decline in popularity for every year following the last "rally point." Finally, war affects popular images of the President. President Truman's popularity declined as American involvement in Korea persisted, but the Vietnam war had little *independent* impact on the decline of President Johnson's popularity.

Presidential popularity, as with the popular image of many governmental leaders, is influenced in part by the fact that he symbolizes the aspirations of citizens in matters of social justice, the economy, war, etc. The president is thus credited with national victories (Nixon's popularity, for example rose slightly following man's first landing on the moon in 1969 in spite of the fact that the decisions to make the effort had been made in the Kennedy administration), and the president suffers from national defeats. But, the president or any political leader can employ certain techniques that contribute to defining his symbolic image. These techniques pertain to his leadership style, the way he personifies events and issues, his identification with political phenomena and his use of dramatic encounter.

As with *rhetorical style* discussed in Chapter Two, there are various things that enter into the leadership style of a public figure. One lies in his choice of being an active or passive political leader; if he is active, he purposely raises political issues and ideas (or "trial balloons") to promote controversy and focus attention upon himself, and takes definite policy positions. If passive, he is more cautious, deliberate, and ambiguous (see Chapter Two) in his approach to defining public issues. Many of President Lyndon Johnson's actions (the "war on poverty," for example) reflect an activist style whereas President Eisenhower was more passive, waiting for issues to arise before risking presidential prestige (as in the case of controversies over school desegregation in the 1950s). Related to the active vs. passive style is that of consensual vs. conflict politics; i.e., whether a politician consistently employs symbols with widespread public appeal (such as national pride, justice, equality, etc.) or makes appeals through specific interests against others. We commented earlier on the propaganda of President Sukarno of Indonesia, an example of a consensual style. In contrast we could point to a leader such as Ralph Nader who directs his attacks on a variety of sacred and profane cows — automobile manufacturers, insurance companies, doctors, pharmaceutical companies, universities, and others.

Personification refers to the efforts of leaders to play definite roles in political conflicts. They become social types, i.e., amalgams of traits that characterize a person in societies — the "little man," the "playboy," the "ward heeler," the "nice guy," etc. J. Edgar Hoover, first director of the Federal Bureau of Investigation, had an image of America's "Number One Crime Fighter." Adlai Stevenson, Democratic nominee for President in 1952 and 1956, was an "egghead" to many people because of his highly literate approach to politics (an image that Stevenson attempted to rebut with his typical brand of humor by urging "Eggheads Unite, you have nothing to lose but your yokes!") Prior to his second term President Richard Nixon had gone through several personifications during his political career: as a congressman from California he wore the mantle of fighter of Communism; as Vice-President he was "Ike's Hatchet Man"; after defeats in the presidential election of 1960 and the California gubernatorial contest in 1962 he personified the "loser," and later some regarded his managerial approach to the presidency as that of a "Superpresident."

Following revelations in his second term connected with the Watergate scandal, Nixon's image took on the character of one "more wrong than wronged." Harris surveys in 1973 revealed that 40 percent of respondents thought Nixon knew in advance of the break-in of Democratic headquarters in 1972; 58 percent thought he knew of the effort to cover-up White House involvement. When Nixon refused to testify before the Select Senate Committee Investigating the Watergate affair, by a 51-37 majority of those having an opinion, Nixon was thought "more wrong" than right in refusing to appear.[48]

A political leader usually tries to appear as a hero rather than acquire a reputation as villain or fool.[49] A single politician, of course, can personify all three roles, depending upon his relationship to specific interests; e.g., Vice-President Spiro T. Agnew was a hero to many Republican partisans because of his tireless efforts in speaking at party fund-raising dinners and his unrelenting attacks on the opposition, but a villain to many network news broadcasters because of his charges against them that they are biased and represent the "liberal establishment," and a fool or villain to those who find humor in his ineptness at golf or who take offense at his use of such ringing phrases as "effete intellectual snob" or the reasons for his resignation.

Through *identification* a political leader seeks to symbolize what he believes are the principal aspirations of the mass.[50] If he senses a resentment against governmental decisions, a growing frustration among people, etc. he may identify with it. George Wallace in 1968 and 1972 made specific appeals to capitalize on what he believed to be a resentment against the growing role of the federal government, bureaucracy and courts, the rich and affluent, and the black. In 1972 George McGovern ran for the presidency by identifying with those whom he regarded as the alienated people in this country, those he believed demanded political and social change.

Dramatic encounter refers to the efforts of a political leader to place himself in selected settings that demonstrate he is virtuous, trustworthy, forceful, decisive, and the authentic leader of the forces of good. There are numerous techniques of dramatic encounter, and it is impossible to review them all. A few examples indicate the variety.[51] (We will consider the dramatistic character of political imagery in greater detail in Chapter Six.)

Leaders employ rituals, ceremonies, or the trappings of office for dramatic effects. For example, politicians aspiring to the presidency often embark on "around-the-world fact-finding trips" which bring them into contact with the heads of various states. Pictures in newspapers and on television of the aspirant shaking hands with the Prime Minister of India, Israel, or the Premier of the Soviet Union help build the impression that he

[48] *The Harris Survey,* June 25, 1973; July 24, 1973.

[49] Klapp, *Symbolic Leaders,* p. 21.

[50] Richard H. Merelman, "The Dramaturgy of Politics," *Sociological Quarterly,* Vol. 10 (Spring 1969), 216-41.

[51] Klapp, *Symbolic Leaders,* pp. 77-96.

is known by world leaders and, more importantly, that he *is* one himself. Or, take the example of President Richard Nixon's dramatic telephone call in 1969 to Neil Armstrong and "Buzz" Aldrin, America's first men to land on the moon; the President, before an international television audience, spoke with the men as they stood on the moon's surface, and thus he not only honored them but built a closer identification between himself and the monumental achievement.

A politician can also use dramatic confrontations with his opposition, his chief rival, or some other well-known figure. A relative unknown, for example, running for political office against a widely known public figure may challenge his opponent to a debate and the opponent, by accepting the challenge, conveys the impression that he regards his lesser-known challenger's threat as worthy of recognition; the challenger, of course, in appearing with the better-known opponent publicizes his own candidacy (the debates between Senator John F. Kennedy and Vice President Richard Nixon in the presidential campaign of 1960 helped the Senator gain broader acceptability as a serious contender against his more experienced and more visible opponent).

Public denunciation is a favorite tactic of symbolic leaders. Senator Joseph McCarthy in the 1950s attacked a variety of public figures and governmental employees, denouncing them as communists, fellow travelers, and conspirators. Senator Estes Kefauver of Tennessee was one of the first to use television for purposes of dramatic encounter as he conducted televised congressional hearings in the 1950s investigating the activities of a variety of persons allegedly connected with organized crime. Senator William Fulbright, Chairman of the Senate Committee on Foreign Affairs, conducted hearings into America's Vietnam policies, and several senators engaged in encounters and denunciations with the Secretary of State and Secretary of Defense in the Johnson administration.[52]

These techniques of symbolic leadership are not always successful. Nor do political leaders simply change images at will. We have stressed repeatedly that popular images have a durability that is not easily changed by symbolic appeals. And, in spite of their best efforts to manipulate symbols, political leaders can suffer image trouble for a variety of reasons not under their control. For instance, following Senator Edward Kennedy's automobile accident on Cape Cod in 1970 that resulted in the death of Mary Jo Kopechne, 43 percent of Americans in a national survey reported that they had less respect for the Senator because of the episode.[53] Symbolic leaders live in a world of risks; mass support may result as much from chance as from calculation.

[52]Harold Garfinkel, "Conditions of Successful Degradation Ceremonies," *American Journal of Sociology,* Vol. 61 (March 1956), 420-24.

[53]Harris, *The Harris Survey Yearbook of Public Opinion: 1970,* pp. 26-29.

TRUST IN CONTEMPORARY POLITICS

Supportive images of political communities, regimes, and leaders are a product of how well governments improve the material conditions of people and, very importantly, of how successful they are in giving people a sense that leaders care about them. If the people *imagine* that they have social and moral status in the eyes of political leaders (if, as discussed in Chapter Two, they think they are something-taken-into-account in government), then images of political trust are more likely. If, however, they believe the political regime does not care about them and the constitutional order, institutions, and processes are closed to them (if, to use again the notions developed in Chapter Two, governments *disconfirm* the self-images of the mass), then disaffection is likely. However, the jury is surely out on the question of how widespread diffuse support must be for a regime or its leaders to survive. We suspect that identification with and loyalty for the political community must be extensive among the mass, but the research we have reviewed indicates that even in the face of only moderate levels of mass support the positive images of the attentives help preserve the constitutional order, keep institutions operating, and protect democratic procedures.

As the decade of the 1960s closed many Americans expressed the fear that support for the political community, the regime, and its leaders had dropped below critical levels. Although contemporary politics are less frenzied (i.e., on the surface there has been a return to "normalcy" in the 1970s), there are indications that in recent years popular trust in politics has diminished. Nationwide surveys report that almost two-thirds of Americans believe that "only a few men are dedicated public servants" (58 percent agreed in a similar survey in 1967). In 1946 47 percent agreed that "most politicians are in politics to make money for themselves;" by 1971 the percentage had climbed to 63. Whereas in 1967 54 percent believed that "most politicians take graft," 59 percent thought so four years later. To be sure, Americans have always been skeptical of politicians, but that skepticism is growing; 35 percent of those surveyed in 1971 expressed the view that "politics today is more corrupt" than it was ten years earlier.[54] Perhaps the increase in mass skepticism does not threaten the viability of the community; yet, the erosion of mass trust warrants concern.

[54]News Release, *The Harris Survey,* December 4, 1971.

5

political images in a mass society: popular concerns

In Chapter Four we concentrated on popular images of politics under-lying specific and diffuse supports. Now we examine the political images connected with voicing and channeling popular concerns. After reviewing research into the content of popular aspirations and fears, we will illustrate the relationship between political images and popular concerns by looking at three particular forms of collective behavior where that relationship exists — social movements, ideologies, and voting. Finally we will discuss the influence of mass images upon public policy.

POLITICAL IMAGES AND POPULAR CONCERNS

We have made the point in earlier chapters that people have images of themselves as individuals, as well as of political objects. Each person has a self-image of what he is and what he would like to be; he acquires a self-image through the development of his personality. Having a self-image means that a person can act toward himself just as he might act toward another; i.e., he can perceive himself, communicate with himself, and confirm, disconfirm, or reject himself. These acts may be purely inner experiences. But it is also possible for a person's self-images to be socially involved with others. Social involvement occurs when a person, wittingly or not, *projects* his self-image upon other persons and objects in his environment, including political objects. In this way he sees in other people and objects the same qualities he *imagines* himself to have. The self-image is thereby a background against which a person "imagines" the qualities of political objects in his environment, sometimes confirming his imagination and sometimes rejecting it.[1]

As we noted in the last chapter, when people imagine that governments take seriously their aspirations and fears (or concerns), they are more likely to trust government. They also may imagine that mass movements, ideologies, voting, policies, and other political means either reflect their concerns or fail to do so. Put slightly differently, mass politics is partly a function of the way people express popular concerns. Hence, to understand popular images of politics, we need to have some idea of what people regard as politically relevant aspirations and fears.

Images of the Good Life

A comprehensive study of the aspirations and fears of mass populations throughout the world appeared in 1965.[2] Investigators interviewed representative samples of the populations of twelve nations (a total sample of nearly 20,000 people) about their personal hopes and fears and the concerns they held for their nations. In any such massive undertaking there may be problems associated with selecting representative samples, asking comparable questions in various nations, and otherwise getting valid data. Despite such problems, however, the study provides some gross indications of popular concerns in various parts of the world. The relevant results appear in Tables 5-1 and 5-2. Table 5-1 displays the percentages of persons sampled in each nation who expressed personal hopes and fears in response to two questions; viz., "When you think about what really matters in your own life, what are your wishes and hopes for the future?" and "Now, taking the other side of the picture, what are your fears and worries about the future?" There are eight major categories of concerns: (1) *Economic* — references to a decent standard of living, an individual's own business, own land or farm, own house, wealth, employment, social security, etc.;

[1]See Bernard N. Meltzer, "Mead's Social Psychology," in Jerome G. Manis and Bernard N. Meltzer, eds., *Symbolic Interaction* (Boston: Allyn & Bacon, 1967), pp. 5-24; Harold D. Lasswell, *Psychopathology and Politics* (New York: Viking, 1960); Murray Edelman, *Politics as Symbolic Action* (Chicago: Markham, 1971); Richard S. Brooks, "The Self and Political Role: A Symbolic Interactionist Approach to Political Ideology," *Sociological Quarterly,* Vol. 10 (Winter 1969), 22-32; Al E. Birdwell, "A Study of the Influence of Image Congruence on Consumer Choice," *Journal of Business,* Vol. 41 (January 1968), 76-88; Franklin B. Evans, "The Brand Image Myth," *Business Horizons,* Vol. 4 (Fall 1961), 19-28.

[2]Hadley Cantril, *The Pattern of Human Concerns* (New Brunswick, N.J.: Rutgers University Press, 1965); see also a more recent study, George Katona, Burkhard Strumpel, Ernest Zahn, *Aspirations and Affluence* (New York: McGraw-Hill, 1971).

(2) *Family* — references to happiness or worries about relatives, children, or general family life; (3) *Health* — concerns about good or bad health for one's self or family; (4) *Values and Character* — references to emotional stability or instability, acceptance or rejection by others, sense of personal worth, etc.; (5) *Job or Work Situation* — concerns over success or failure in work, congenial fellow workers, aspirations or fears of quality of work performed; (6) *Social* — references to matters of social justice, religious questions, morality, etc.; (7) *International* — concerns with war and peace, aggression, militarism, and communism; and (8) *Political* — references to freedom or loss of freedom, political stability, and performance of government.

Table 5-1 reveals that the people in the nations under study were primarily concerned with economic, health, and family matters rather than with social, international, and political affairs. Economic aspirations and fears are particularly dominant personal concerns; ranked in the order of the number of people represented in the world by the percentage who named a particular concern, *hoping for an improved or decent standard of living* was the chief concern of the world's population.

People were also asked in this study "What are your wishes and hopes for the future of our country?" And "What about your fears and worries for the future of our country?" There were five chief categories of response: (1) *Economic* — References to economic stability, housing, etc.; (2) *Political* — concerns with honest government, efficient government, freedom, law and order, political stability, etc.; (3) *International* — references to peace and war, disarmament, friendly relations with all nations, etc.; (4) *Social* — references to social justice, elimination of discrimination, education, population growth, etc.; and (5) *Independent Status* — concerns that the country be militarily strong, a world power, exert leadership, etc. People again ranked economic matters as uppermost concerns. However when their thinking was directed to concerns for their nation, people were more likely to take international and political affairs into account. The top ranked fear of people for their country throughout the sample was the fear of war; the number one ranked hope of respondents for their nation was an improved or decent standard of living.

The concern for a decent standard of living, both as a personal and national aspiration, is uppermost in the minds of mass populations. There is, however, considerable difference in the image of what a decent living standard is as expressed from country to country. To an Indian a decent living standard may mean the opportunity for his children just to read and write while to an American it may conjure up the desire to send children through college. What is important in the image is the hope for *improvement in the status quo*. The fulfillment, or failure to fulfill, that aspiration influences mass images in politics.

TABLE 5-1 Personal Hopes and Fears By Country

(Figures represent % of those interviewed who expressed personal concern for each category of hope or fear)

						Country						
Hopes	Brazil	Cuba	Dominican Republic	Egypt	India	Israel	Nigeria	Panama	Philippines	United States	West Germany	Yugoslavia
Economic	68%	73%	95%	70%	70%	80%	90%	90%	60%	65%	85%	83%
Family	28	52	39	53	39	76	76	53	52	47	27	60
Health	34	47	17	24	4	47	45	43	6	48	46	41
Values & Character	14	30	15	39	14	29	42	26	9	20	11	18
Job or Work	8	14	25	42	22	35	19	26	11	10	10	20
Social	1	4	2	9	8	10	14	3	5	5	3	4
International	1	3	—	2	—	12	—	—	—	10	15	8
Political	—	15	9	4	—	2	—	1	—	2	1	—
Fears												
Economic	30	47	82	46	51	55	65	57	38	46	51	33
Family	17	24	25	30	19	44	27	37	30	25	14	26
Health	42	42	29	42	23	58	64	64	25	56	51	60
Values & Character	7	23	4	23	5	10	17	7	2	3	3	5
Job or Work	2	4	10	20	6	10	2	6	7	5	2	2
Social	2	3	1	2	2	4	14	1	1	3	2	2
International	3	5	1	4	—	27	1	3	23	24	50	27
Political	1	15	9	4	—	2	5	2	1	5	8	—

Source: Tabulated from data in Hadley Cantril, The Pattern of Human Concerns, pp. 169-70. (1965)

TABLE 5-2 National Hopes and Fears By Country
(Figures represent % of respondents expressing concern for their country for each category of hope or fear)

Hopes	*Brazil*	*Cuba*	*Dominican Republic*	*Egypt*	*India*	*Israel*	*Nigeria*	*Panama*	*Philippines*	*United States*	*West Germany*	*Yugoslavia*
Economic	58%	75%	84%	58%	70%	79%	81%	74%	52%	45%	69%	81%
Political	16	18	78	26	9	35	50	22	37	13	49	47
International	5	7	2	29	3	69	12	7	10	59	42	31
Social	19	21	14	36	19	70	66	31	13	33	16	31
Independent Status	4	13	1	44	9	37	24	3	9	4	11	6
Fears												
Economic	34	24	42	29	24	44	43	33	13	29	44	12
Political	24	59	74	26	20	23	69	41	34	23	27	19
International	19	10	9	35	25	72	11	23	45	57	70	79
Social	8	8	4	19	14	30	37	15	8	21	15	2
Independent Status	3	11	8	37	8	16	7	6	17	11	19	5

Source: Compiled from data in Hadley Cantril, The Pattern of Human Concerns, pp. 180-81.

There are other noteworthy observations about the data in Tables 5-1 and 5-2. Politics is a relatively low-ranked concern for most people in the world. There are few countries where politics of their nation is a concern of a majority of people. This is consistent with the general lack of information about politics displayed by the mass, as indicated in Chapter Four. Finally, note that higher percentages of persons generally express hopes of various kinds both for themselves and for their nations than express fears.

The personal emphasis on economic hopes and fears combined with a concern for the threat of war has been fairly stable over the course of the last two decades. For example, nationwide samplings of the American adult population in recent years indicate that personal economic or living conditions and employment concerns are primary categories of hopes and fears of Americans. And, in the 1970s opinion surveys indicate that Americans rank economic problems, the Vietnam war, and crime as the most important problems facing the country.[3] Moreover, there is evidence that both the political elites and the attentives in various nations share the concerns expressed by the mass of their populations. In the twelve-nation study referred to above, samples of legislators from the United States, West Germany, Brazil, Nigeria, India, and the Philippines were asked the same basic questions as the representative samplings of the adult population. They too placed general economic affairs uppermost, followed closely by concerns over war and peace. In contrast to the general citizenry legislators are more cognizant of their nation's position in the world and express greater sensitivity to the necessity for stable government. Additional evidence on the images of attentives comes from a 1971 survey of statesmen, scientists, business executives, and others representing seventy nations asking each person to name the five most important problems facing the world. Inflation, crime, inadequate housing, air and water pollution, and unemployment were the five ranked most highly.[4]

Although popular concerns are primarily economic, popular images of economic questions are not the same as the hard-headed, concrete, images people use to reach tangible aspirations of wealth and well-being. Rather, mass images of a "decent standard of living" are far more expressive and evaluative than instrumental. Such images are ends in themselves; they express and evaluate the good life people want, but they say nothing of how to obtain it. The promise of an improved standard of living, success, happiness, or health can thus be used as symbols by political elites to advance their own self-serving or altruistic causes. This symbolic use of popular images can be illustrated in the symbols surrounding social movements.

[3]News Release, American Institute of Public Opinion, September 23, 1971; News Release, *The Harris Survey,* January 4, 1971.

[4]News Release, American Institute of Public Opinion, May 2, 1971.

Political Images and Social Movements

A *social movement* consists of large numbers of people organized to support *or* resist changes in social institutions.[5] Examples include the French Revolution, the agrarian movement in the United States in the last century, the prohibition movement in this country, the civil rights movement of the 1960s, and the anti-war movement at the close of that decade; some contemporary analysts would also label current discontent by youth with the "establishment" of American politics, business, labor, and education as the beginnings of another long-term social movement.[6]

We consider social movements in our discussion of political images because the success of such movements often depends upon symbolic appeals. Most people take part in social movements informally and indirectly; they identify with the movement without joining formal organizations connected with it. The imagery of the movement facilitates or inhibits mass identification with the movement's goals, leaders, and organization. Frequently at stake in social movements *is not simply the redistribution of material goods between classes, but the redistribution of prestige between status groups.* While "class politics is political conflict over the allocation of material resources," status politics "is political conflict over the allocation of prestige." Status politics "is an effort to control the status of a group by acts which function to raise, lower, or maintain the social status of the acting group vis-a-vis others in society."[7]

The contemporary struggle over school desegregation is a case in point. A measure proposed to achieve racial balance in public schools is to transport students in buses from their areas of residence to distant, formerly segregated schools; this calls for busing blacks to schools that once had only whites and vice versa. "Busing" has become a salient symbol of the civil rights movement; proponents of busing identify with it as the only measure to achieve more than "token" integration while opponents argue that it will destroy the "neighborhood school" and "freedom of choice." The issue divides both leaders and followers. Opponents of busing include President Richard Nixon and George Wallace of Alabama, while such presidential aspirants as Senator George McGovern and Senator Edmund Muskie have favored it. A 1971 Gallup survey revealed that 76 percent of a

[5]For descriptions of the nature of social movements see Herbert Blumer, "Collective Behavior," in A. M. Lee, ed., *New Outline of the Principles of Sociology* (New York: Barnes & Noble, 1946), pp. 167-222; George A. Theodorson and Achilles G. Theodorson, *A Modern Dictionary of Sociology* (New York: Thomas Y. Crowell, 1969), p. 390; and Preston Valien, "Social Movement," in Julius Gould and William L. Kolb, eds., *A Dictionary of the Social Sciences* (New York: Free Press, 1964), p. 658.

[6]Louis Galambos, "The Agrarian Image of the Large Corporation, 1879-1920: A Study in Social Accommodation," *Journal of Economic History,* Vol. 28 (September 1968), 341-62; Theodore J. Lowi, *The Politics of Disorder* (New York: Basic Books, 1971).

[7]Joseph R. Gusfield, *Symbolic Crusade* (Urbana, Ill.: University of Illinois Press, 1966), pp. 18-19.

nationwide sample opposed busing, 18 percent favored it and 6 percent were without opinion. Whites opposed busing by a 79-15 percent margin, but blacks opposed it by a scant 47-45 percent.[8] Although part of the debate over busing includes arguments over whether the plan will actually result in better education for whites and blacks, also at issue is the relative prestige of being white in American life. This prestige extends to living in select neighborhoods with separate schools, recreational facilities, and conveniences. It also extends to the status that goes with preserving the "understanding" (image) that whites, for all their racial tolerance, still control decision making in society. In this context whether busing achieves equality in education or not is less important to many than whether it threatens the image of a dominant white society.

The slogan "Black Power" also illustrates the evaluative overtones in the imagery associated with social movements. In 1967 a survey of whites and blacks in Detroit sought to discover what Black Power symbolized to the two groups.[9] More than 80 percent of whites interviewed held an unfavorable image of the slogan; of those, almost one-half imagined that it meant blacks would rule whites. Almost one-half of blacks also responded unfavorably to the slogan (but 22.3 percent of blacks with unfavorable images said, in effect, the slogan meant "nothing"). Of those blacks with positive notions of the slogan, almost equal proportions viewed it as an instrument to promote black unity and as an evaluative standard symbolizing a fair share for black people. In sum, for both blacks and whites Black Power symbolized a status loss or gain; for whites "the slogan presents an unmistakeable challenge to the country's prevailing racial customs and social norms; for precisely this reason it seems exciting and attractive to many blacks."[10]

However, the images American whites hold of "busing" and "Black Power" are not simply blatantly racist. The point is rather that the political images associated with social movements often symbolize prestige and status for various interests. For these interests it is vital to preserve or enhance social status; this goal may even be more important to them than to achieve material gains. Actually, research regarding white images of blacks indicates that many whites are neither vindictively racists nor wholly equalitarian. For example, a significant study explicitly examines the cognitive, affective, and conative content of white images of blacks in fifteen major cities. The cognitive component of such images consists of the awareness of whites of discrimination against blacks; the affective content involves levels of white sympathy for black protests; and, the

[8]News Release, American Institute of Public Opinion, November 1, 1971.

[9]Joel D. Aberbach and Jack L. Walker, "The Meanings of Black Power: A Comparison of White and Black Interpretations of a Political Slogan," *American Political Science Review*, Vol. 64 (June 1970), 367-88.

[10]*Ibid.*, p. 373.

conative aspect includes predispositions of whites to enter into interracial contact with blacks — by having them as friends, working with them, and working under their supervision. On the equalitarian side 68 percent of respondents believed blacks were victims of discrimination in housing, 67 percent favor laws against discrimination in hiring and promotion, 49 percent would not mind living next to a black of equal income and education and 86 percent would not mind having a qualified black as a supervisor on their job. On the racist side 56 percent believe blacks create their own problems in jobs, education, and housing; 51 percent oppose laws to remove housing discrimination; and 33 percent say that if they had small children they would rather they have only white friends. Comparing white and black images of one another there seems little evidence that two separate societies exist, one black and one white. While ". . . the data at hand had the great virtue of closely bracketing the riot period of 1965-1968 . . . they do not show the events of this period brought about a deterioration or widening of relationships between the races." On the contrary, "within its limits, the evidence shows that on many questions of principle and policy white and black attitudes moved closer together."[11]

We have said that political leaders employ symbols as tools to achieve specific ends, but that from the viewpoint of the mass these symbols serve evaluative functions rather than instrumental purposes. The symbols used by Mahatma Gandhi in India prior to independence in 1947 exemplify this leader-follower difference in a social movement. For Gandhi symbols supplied the link between the values he espoused and the politics he practiced; for his followers those symbols provided a sense of ethical commitment and of moral worth to those who voluntarily adopted them.

Gandhi espoused a nonviolent politics resting on chastity, poverty, truth, and fortitude. To represent poverty, truth, and fortitude Gandhi chose a most important symbol of the movement, the spinning wheel or *Khadi*. Through spinning, taught Gandhi, India could achieve economic self-sufficiency. Since India was not prepared for industrialization and industrialization was not prepared for rural India, spinning could supply Indians with a means for providing their own goods. But the *Khadi* symbolized more than self-sufficiency. By using the wheel man could be master over the machine. Since the spinning wheel could provide his necessities, he would not need superfluous material goods nor the machinery required to produce them — machinery which could enslave him. The spinning wheel also symbolized a status harmony between rich and poor and between urban and rural classes. Gandhi organized compulsory spinning for his rich, urbane followers so that they could remind themselves of the hardships of the poor and the monotony of manual labor. Finally, the spinning

---

[11]Angus Campbell, *White Attitudes Toward Black People* (Ann Arbor, Mich.: Institute for Social Research, University of Michigan, 1971), p. 154.

wheel was a symbol peculiar to India and thus represented the idea of national independence.

Associated with the *Khadi* were other major symbols. Fasting, for example, represented chastity, truth, and fortitude; followers were to fast for purposes of atonement, vicarious suffering, purification, and enlightenment. Gandhi fasted to restore harmony between Hindus and Muslims and publicized that fact through press conferences, meetings, mass petitions, general strikes, and renunciations of public honors. The cow was also a Gandhian symbol. Long a sacred religious symbol of Hindus, Gandhi attempted to associate secular images with it, but he ran into difficulty since for Muslims the sacrifice of the cow was part of their most prestigious religious festival. The contradiction contained in the cow symbol (as sacred for one group and as sacrificial for another) made it impossible for Gandhi to convert the cow into an unifying political symbol. Finally, the caste-system supplied a status symbol around which Gandhi rallied support for social reform. Gandhi symbolized the outcasts as *harijan* ("God's people") with rights no human institution such as the caste-system could violate. In addition to the spinning wheel, fasting, the cow, and the harijan, *Gandhi himself* became a symbol and the rallying point for a movement for national independence from the British.[12]

There are numerous other examples of social movements wherein emotional aspects are just as important to the participants as material goals. No example, however, would hit so close to home to many contemporary Americans as the symbolic struggle generally labeled the "generation gap." Despite the emphasis given in the nation's press to the differences between adults and adolescents in aspirations, outlooks, and preferences, there is significantly less difference between adults and adolescents in fundamental values. By and large, American youth accepts many ideals of its parents' generation. Note the findings reported in Table 5-3 from nationwide cross-sections of American youth between the ages of 15 and 21 in 1970. On most matters a large percentage of respondents perceived their views to be very similar to those of their parents. The major exception is the feeling that parents do not approve of the way youth expresses values and ideals. What is at issue in the "generation gap" is not major differences of principle so much as differences in status. Again, the desire to be taken seriously, to have self-images as something-taken-into-account and confirmed or rejected rather than ignored and disconfirmed by adults (see Chapter Two, p. 42), is basic. In the endeavor to be taken seriously youths use modes of expression that they think their parents will disapprove of at least enough to take notice of them.

A desire for prestige and respect is but one source of the "generation

[12]Anthony Parel, "Symbolism in Gandhian Politics," *Canadian Journal of Politics,* Vol. 2 (December 1969), 513-27.

TABLE 5-3   Perceptions of American Youth of Differences With Parents

Question	Yes	No	Not Sure
"Do you for the most part accept and agree with the ideals and values of your parents?"	73%	23%	4%
"Do you think in general your parents have lived up to their own ideals?"	80	14	6
"Do you feel that your parents generally approve of your own ideals and values, or not?"	65	29	6
"Many people have said that hard work leads to success and wealth in America. Do you think this is still really true today or not?"	61	34	5
"Do you feel that success, in the sense of achieving wealth and status, is worth striving for?"	66	28	6
"Would you say that your parents generally approve of the manner in which you and other members of your generation express your ideals and values?"	33	55	12

Source: Compiled from data in Louis Harris, The Harris Survey Yearbook of Public Opinion: 1970 *(New York: Louis Harris and Association, Inc., 1971), pp. 362-69.*

gap." Note that in Table 5-3 there is a significant minority ranging from one-fourth to one-third of respondents who could be classified as perceiving disagreement with parental principles. The 1970 population of the United States was around 203 million; the total of youths between the ages of 15 and 21 was approximately 26 million, or roughly one-eighth of America's population. If the poll data are representative, 6 to 9 million young Americans believe they disagree with their parents. However, the sheer increase in numbers of potentially dissatisfied youth, some of whom do voice grievances, has given an impression that most youth are alienated enough to clash with their elders. If there is a distinctive youth movement implied by the survey results it would appear to be a larger-than-expected mass of youth accepting the status quo and attempting to find a respected position in society rather than a major movement of younger Americans toward social revolution.

Political Images and Ideologies

There are at least two distinguishable views of the relationship of ideology and politics. The first defines an ideology as an integrated, interdependent set of ideas of a social group or society which reflects, rationalizes, and defends the political community, its regime, leaders, and programs. Specific interest groups use ideological appeals in a struggle for political advantage. In this perspective, for example, Communism is a set of ideas, or an ideology, that assists regimes such as the Soviet Union in explaining and justifying authority and aids such specific interests as the Communist Party winning electoral support in democratic regimes. For the individual the function of the ideology is to aid him, on the basis of the integrated body of beliefs, values, and principles, in reaching sound political judgments. Thus, ideologies are directive communications (see Chapter Two, p. 46) used to achieve political unity and facilitate political decision.

A second view of ideology emphasizes restorative (see p. 46) rather than directive functions.[13] Instead of being a body of well-reasoned, logically structured ideas, an ideology consists of any set of notions (no matter how loosely knit or even contradictory) manifested in symbols and slogans with strong emotional appeal. These symbols and slogans evoke popular images that enable people to make quick judgments (the evaluative aspect of images) or to express their national and group loyalties (the expressive aspect). For instance, people who are unhappy with their lot often seek symbolic scapegoats to blame for their perceived misery; thus "The Jews" symbolized for many Nazis in the 1920s a set of notions about "race" that could at one and the same time judge Germans to be inherently of superior social and moral status, yet rationalize Germany's defeat in World War I (a defeat, it was argued, caused in part by "the Jews"). Or, consider "The Establishment," a symbol evoking the image to some Americans of a political system controlled by a relatively small socioeconomic class in its own interests to the detriment of the nonaffluent; the policies of such a government, since made by "The Establishment," are labeled *bad* regardless of content and consequences. The slogan "Better Dead than Red" provides a means for expressing loyalties to the political system. Implied in it is the notion that communism represents a way of life so intolerable that it is better to die, perhaps, to preserve the "American way."

Both the directive and restorative views of ideologies take account of the political images inherent in ideologies. The directive view emphasizes how political leaders use those images to mobilize mass support and how followers use their images to judge political issues. The restorative view stresses how the images evoked by ideologies can be expressive outlets for personal concerns. The first view implies that the mass hold integrated sets of beliefs, values, and predispositions from which they can deduce positions on specific political matters. The second view implies that popular ideologies are far less systematic.

[13]Clifford Geertz, "Ideology as a Cultural System," in David Apter, ed., *Ideology and Discontent* (New York: Free Press, 1964), pp. 47-76; see also Ben Halpern, " 'Myth' and 'Ideology' in Modern Usage," *History and Theory*, Vol. 1 (1971), 129-49.

In Chapter Four we contrasted in a general way the differences between the images held by political elites and the mass (p. 80). Elite
images have a richer cognitive content, covering a wider range of political
objects, and are more integrated than images of persons constituting mass
society. This contrast is apparent in a study using a nationwide sampling
that endeavored to determine the extent of ideological thinking among
adult Americans.[14] Five distinctive ways people think about politics were apparent; it is fair to treat these five ways as separate sets of popular images
of politics. In the first set were people characterized as "Ideologues."
These respondents utilized fairly elaborate, abstract, and well-organized
sets of images (generally along a liberal-conservative continuum) as yard-
sticks for evaluating political objects. Only 2.5 percent of the total sample
had "ideologies." The second set consisted of "near-ideologues." These
people had an integrated ideology but used it less frequently for evaluative
purposes; 9 percent of respondents were classified as holding near-
ideologies. Third, were people evaluating politics on grounds of group
interest — that is, people who regarded politics as a clash between groups,
perceived their own group interests, and evaluated issues accordingly.
These people used symbols such as "big business," "the working man,"
or "rich people," to express their judgments. This category of political
images has the character of restorative ideology sketched above; 42 percent
of respondents thought about politics in this way. The fourth set (with
24 percent of respondents) consisted of people who evaluated parties and
candidates on the basis of the "nature of the times," i.e., expressing concerns about economic prosperity or depression, war or peace. The remainder of the sample (22.5 percent) were people who had little or no idea of
what the political parties stood for, paid little attention to politics at all,
and thought only of personal qualities of candidates.

Americans are not unique in evaluating politics on the basis of
emotion-based ideologies rather than from the perspective of an integrated
set of ideas. Opinion surveys conducted in conjunction with the 1964
British elections discerned the extent to which Britishers employ the concepts "left" and "right" to organize their images of politics.[15] As in the
earlier American study five sets of images appeared. The first involved well-
elaborated and well-organized ideas used by respondents to distinguish
left and right in politics; only 2 percent of those sampled fell into this
category. The second consisted of persons who distinguished social classes

[14]Angus Campbell, Philip E. Converse, Warren E. Miller, and Donald E. Stokes, *The
American Voter* (New York: John Wiley, 1960), Chapter 10. See also Philip E. Converse, "The
Nature of Belief Systems in Mass Publics," in Apter, *Ideology and Discontent,* pp. 206-56. For
evidence that ideological orientations among the mass of voters is a function of issues raised
in campaigns, see John Osgood Field and Ronald E. Anderson, "Ideology in the Public's Conception of the 1964 Election." *Public Opinion Quarterly,* Vol. 33 (Fall 1969), 380-98.

[15]David Butler and Donald Stokes, *Political Change in Britain* (New York: St. Martin's,
1969). pp. 206-14.

on a political continuum of left and right and believed the Conservative Party the right and the Labor Party the left in British politics; 14 percent of the sample were in this category. The third group (4 percent) could attribute no meaning to "left" and "right" beyond remembering that one political party seemed on one side and the other party seemed on another side, but there was no left-right continuum of any sort underlying their thinking. The fourth set (20 percent of the sample) were merely able to designate which party, Conservative or Labor, was right or left, and the fifth group (60 percent) recognized no left-right distinction.

Do popular images of politics reflect an underlying liberal-conservative, or left-right, continuum? The evidence is strong that few do so. People *do* possess ideological self-images; that is, they think of themselves as liberal or conservative, but these self-images are not central to their evaluations of political objects. In 1970 a Gallup Poll asked, "Suppose you had to classify yourself as either a liberal or conservative, which would you say you are?" Of the sample, 52 percent said conservative, 34 percent said liberal, and 14 percent had no opinion. Asked to describe a conservative, the public's image ranged from "a person who looks before he leaps," who "saves, doesn't throw things away," and a "decent sort of guy" to "a penny pincher," "closed minded, self-centered, and intolerant," and a "square." The sample imagined a liberal to be "someone who looks at all sides of a problem," "a person who believes in mankind," and who "wants change," or "someone who is generous with other people's money," and "a drug addict."[16]

Although many Americans are willing to label themselves as liberal or conservative, their ideological self-images are of little help to us in predicting their feelings about government. In 1964 a nationwide, representative sampling of Americans classified respondents as liberal, conservative, or middle-of-the-road on two bases.[17] First, each person was simply asked which ideological label best described him. The result was that 26 percent called themselves liberal, 30 percent responded conservative, and 34 percent said middle-of-the-road. Second, the researchers classified members of the sample in one of the three ideological categories on the basis of how respondents answered six questions: (1) was the federal government interfering too much in state and local matters; (2) should government attempt to solve social problems or leave their solution to people in local communities; (3) was government going too far in regulating business and the free enterprise system; (4) was government interfering too much with property rights; (5) was there too much communist and left-wing influence in government; and (6) was there a definite trend toward socialism in the country? On the basis of how people answered these questions

[16]News Release, American Institute of Public Opinion, April 4, 1970.
[17]Free and Cantril, *The Political Beliefs of Americans,* pp. 23-50.

16 percent were classified as liberal, 34 percent middle-of-the-road, and 50 percent conservative. As Table 5-4 illustrates, how people thought of themselves did not always match how they could be classified on the basis of their feelings about government. The self-images of conservatives were most consistent with their views about government (70 percent of those calling themselves conservative were categorized as such on the basis of answers to the six questions) but even among this group 23 percent had "middle-of-the-road" views and 7 percent even expressed "liberal" views about the role and scope of government.

TABLE 5-4 **A Comparison of Americans' Ideological Self-Images with How They Feel About Government**

Classification of Respondents on Basis of How They Feel About Government	How Respondents Classified Themselves		
	Liberal	Middle-of-the-Road	Conservative
Liberal	28%	16%	7%
Middle-of-the-Road	46	38	23
Conservative	26	46	70
	100%	100%	100%

Source: *Adapted from data reported in Lloyd Free and Hadley Cantril,* The Political Beliefs of Americans *(New Brunswick, N.J.: Rutgers University Press, 1967), p. 47.*

In general the bulk of research offers the verdict that the mass of political participants relate to ideologies in expressive, but nonetheless important, ways. Although the images that make up popular ideologies are illogical, diffuse, poorly articulated, and uninformed to observers, from the standpoint of those who hold them those images help people identify who they are and which groups they find meaningful: "The great difficulty with one observer standing as critic of another's beliefs is that the first may not be able to see the logic of the other's thought processes, that is, one's explanation of why he believes as he does may not be comprehensible to the other."[18] The ideologies of mass men, inconsistent and uninformed though they appear, often work for them in expressing their identities, aspirations, and fears.

Political Images and Mass Voting

Election campaigns change the political images of relatively few voters, because people pay attention to campaign appeals in a selective

[18]Steven R. Brown, "Consistency and the Persistence of Ideology: Some Experimental Results," *Public Opinion Quarterly,* Vol. 34 (Spring 1970), 68; see also Robert E. Lane, *Political Ideology* (New York: Free Press, 1962); Brooks, "The Self and Political Role."

way, filtering out messages contrary to acquired images. Yet, a sufficient number of voters make up their minds on the basis of campaign messages to influence the outcome in close elections. Since the pictures in voters' heads are not easily changed, campaigners try to get the electorate to perceive their efforts favorably within the limits set by existing voter images. Politicians use symbols in campaign rhetoric channeled through party platforms, party followers, the press, radio, television, and other media. We shall examine three major sets of voter images that figure in election campaigns. These are images of the political parties, images of campaign issues, and images of political candidates.

Party Images

In Chapter Four we described the relatively low levels of diffuse support of Americans for party politics. We now examine two other types of images involving political parties that influence mass voting, namely, *the images people have of specific parties,* such as Republicans and Democrats, and *the partisan self-images of voters.*

Political parties are organizations of people competing for authority to govern. They vie for government control by nominating candidates and mobilizing support for them in elections. In elections party symbols assist voters in understanding the various conflicting issues, programs, and personalities: ". . . to each citizen, living as he does in the infinite stream of things, only a few of his million fellow-citizens could exist as separate objects of political thought or feeling, even if each one of them held only one opinion on one subject without change during life. Something is required simpler and more permanent, something which can be loved and trusted, and which can be recognized at successive elections as being the same thing that was loved and trusted before; and a party is such a thing."[19] In America the Republican Party is symbolized by the elephant, "rather old, rather dignified, a little slow, not perhaps terribly bright, but with a good deal of wisdom, hard working, full of integrity, rather conservative, a little isolated from the world around him, patient, thick-skinned, but capable of occasional inarticulate squeals of rage." And, the Democratic Party is imagined as a donkey, "active, agile, clever, a little unsure of himself, a bit of an upstart, quick, sensitive, a little vulgar, and cheerfully absurd."[20]

Asked in opinion surveys to describe the properties they associate with specific political parties, people define their party images. The affective content of party images consists of positive or negative comments about a political party; the cognitive content includes the properties

[19]Graham Wallas, *Human Nature in Politics* (Lincoln: University of Nebraska Press, Bison Book Edition, 1962), pp. 103-4.

[20]Kenneth E. Boulding, *The Image* (Ann Arbor, Mich.: University of Michigan Press, 1956), p. 110.

themselves — associations with particular people (Lincoln, Roosevelt, Eisenhower, etc.), groups, governing styles, or policies. American surveys reveal that the number of favorable comments made about each of the two major political parties generally exceeds unfavorable references. There was an exception in 1964 when the Republican Party was unfavorably viewed, largely because of an unfavorable image of its presidential nominee, Senator Barry Goldwater. The favorable public side of the image of the Republican Party associates it with former President Eisenhower, conservatism, fiscal responsibility, peace, and efficiency in government; the negative aspect of the image links Republicans to bad times, favoritism for big business and rich people over "common people," and a lack of concern for civil rights and welfare programs. The positive aspects of the Democratic Party image are associations with former President Kennedy, a liberal philosophy, welfare programs, medical care, full employment, civil rights, and good times for the "common people"; negative aspects are scattered remarks linking the party to former Presidents Truman and Johnson and references to dishonesty in government, spending too much money, too much for civil rights, the party of war, and leanings toward socialism.[21] Surveys among 18-21 year olds suggest that their images of our two major parties are approximately the same as for older voters. Asked what first comes to mind when thinking of the Republican Party, younger voters mention conservatism, big business, unemployment, high prices and taxes, Richard Nixon, and the failure to keep campaign promises; overall unfavorable responses outweigh favorable ones by 2-1, but the majority (59 percent) of younger voters are neutral or have no opinion. The Democratic Party to younger voters stands "for the people," liberalism, responsibility for the Vietnam war, and Hubert Humphrey, Edmund Muskie, George McGovern, and Franklin Roosevelt. The overall image of the Democratic Party is slightly favorable among 18-21 year olds, but two-thirds are neutral or without opinion.[22]

A person's image of a political party is likely to reflect his partisan self-image, that is, whether he identifies himself psychologically as Republican, Democrat, or other. We saw in Chapter Three that learning a partisan self-image comes fairly early in the lives of most people. In some nations such as the United States, Great Britain, and Uruguay as high as 70 percent of the populations identify with political parties; in others, Italy and Mexico for example, less than half the population have partisan self-images; in still others, such as West Germany and Norway, there are intermediate

[21]Angus Campbell, "Interpreting the Presidential Victory," in Milton C. Cummings, Jr., ed., *The National Election of 1964* (Washington, D. C.: Brookings Institution, 1966), pp. 256-81; Donald R. Matthews and James W. Prothro, "Southern Images of Political Parties: An Analysis of White and Negro Attitudes," *The Journal of Politics,* Vol. 26 (February 1964), 82-111; Butler and Stokes, *Political Change in Britain,* pp. 359-72.

[22]News Release, American Institute of Public Opinion, August 15, 1971.

levels of partisan identification.[23] For some persons the partisan self-image is intensely held, for others the identification is relatively weak. The distribution and intensity of partisan self-images in the United States in recent years is depicted in Table 5-5.

Once developed most people's partisan self-images are quite durable, and the distribution of those images among the mass is fairly stable. These partisan self-images influence voting decisions: "Identification with a party raises a perceptual screen through which the individual tends to see what is favorable to his partisan orientation. The stronger the party bond, the more exaggerated the process of selection and perceptual distortion will be. Without this psychological tie, or perhaps with commitments to symbols of another kind, the Independent is less likely to develop consistent partisan attitudes."[24] A man may not always vote for the party with which he identifies, but his partisan self-image is an affective bond that nonetheless guides what he sees in the political parties, issues, and candidates.

The stability of the distribution of partisan self-images among people provides a clue to the impact of such images compared to other factors on the outcome of an election. Taking into account the fact that Democratic identifiers vote less frequently than do Republicans in elections, students of voting behavior estimate that if each person voted strictly for the party dictated by his self-image the nationwide vote in American elections would normally be 56 percent Democrat and 44 percent Republican. This "normal vote" is rarely attained in presidential elections (although it is more frequently attained in congressional elections). This indicates that there are other factors besides partisan self-images at work on the electorate.[25] These are factors specific to each election and include the images people have of the parties themselves (discussed earlier), salient issues, and political candidates.

Images of Issues

Let us define an issue simply as a matter on which social interests disagree (as, say, workers and businessmen disagreeing over wages, or a dispute between "hawks" and "doves" over the legality of a war). In presidential elections many issues generally are important, or *salient,* to various social interests. For the specific interests involved, there is conflict over the issue in question. The result is that in any single election differing

[23]Jack Dennis and Donald J. McCrone, "Preadult Development of Political Party Identification in Western Democracies," *Comparative Political Studies,* Vol. 3 (July 1970), 243-63; Philip E. Converse, "Of Time and Partisan Stability," *Comparative Political Studies,* Vol. 2 (July 1969), 139-71.

[24]Campbell *et al., The American Voter,* p. 133.

[25]Angus Campbell, Philip E. Converse, Warren E. Miller, and Donald E. Stokes, *Elections and the Political Order* (New York: John Wiley, 1966), Chapter 2.

TABLE 5-5 The Distribution of Partisan Self-Images in the United States, 1952-1970

Question: "Generally speaking, do you usually think of yourself as a Republican, a Democrat, an Independent, or what? IF REPUBLICAN OR DEMOCRAT: Would you call yourself a strong (R) (D) or a not very strong (R) (D)? IF INDEPENDENT: Do you think of yourself as closer to the Republican or Democratic Party?"

	Oct. 1952	Oct. 1954	Oct. 1956	Oct. 1958	Oct. 1960	Nov. 1962	Oct. 1964	Nov. 1966	Nov. 1968	Nov. 1970
Democrat										
Strong	22%	22%	21%	23%	21%	23%	26%	18%	20%	20%
Weak	25	25	23	24	25	23	25	27	25	23
Independent										
Democrat	10	9	7	7	8	8	9	9	10	10
Independent	5	7	9	8	8	8	8	12	11	13
Republican	7	6	8	4	7	6	6	7	9	8
Republican										
Weak	14	14	14	16	13	16	13	15	14	15
Strong	13	13	15	13	14	12	11	10	10	10
Apolitical, Don't Know	4	4	3	5	4	4	2	2	1	1
Total	100%	100%	100%	100%	100%	100%	100%	100%	100%	100%
Number of Cases	1614	1139	1772	1269	3021	1289	1571	1291	1553	1802

Source: Interuniversity Consortium for Political Research, November, 1970.

issues touch differing groups so that we have a pluralist, fragmented series of issues rather than major divisions over one or two highly publicized issues. To be sure, people who are not members of the various groups contesting an issue may still be aware of the conflict. For example, surveys conducted in 1960 and 1964 revealed that on three-fourths of the more than two dozen issues that were salient to specific social interests, a majority of respondents generally were aware of the issues and could detect differences between the positions of the two major political parties on those issues.[26] Other research strongly suggests that the images Americans have of the issues that divide key social interests and the political parties are becoming increasingly important in shaping how citizens vote.[27]

Although the general rule for most elections is that rarely do one or two issues result in fundamental cleavages between voters, in presidential elections certain issues do become highly salient to virtually all voters. In the last four presidential elections the "normal vote" of 56-44 Democratic vs. Republican was never achieved. The fact that people took issues more seriously than party identification, in part, accounted for this. The most salient issue in 1960, for example, was the question of John F. Kennedy's Catholic religion; Kennedy won a narrow victory over Richard Nixon (Kennedy received 49 percent of the vote) explained in large measure by defections of Protestant Democrats to the Republican candidate. In 1964 the Democratic candidate Lyndon Johnson received 61 percent of the vote — a victory in part attributable to his opponent Barry Goldwater's capacity for taking many heretofore accepted items (such as widespread support for federal programs for social security) and treating them as relevant issues on which he was perceived as opposing the prevailing consensus. In Richard Nixon's scant victory in 1968 (43 percent of the vote), the salient issues of the Vietnam war and "law and order" worked to Hubert Humphrey's disadvantage, while in Nixon's 1972 landslide re-election many voters of both parties simply perceived George McGovern as on the wrong side of issues they thought important.

One issue voters respond to is whether current conditions are "good" or "bad." The popular image of the nature of the times can produce de-

[26]David E. RePass, "Issue Salience and Party Choice," *American Political Science Review,* Vol. 65 (June 1971), 389-400; see also Ruth S. Jones and E. Terrence Jones, "Issue Saliency, Opinion-Holding, and Party Preference," *Western Political Quarterly,* Vol. 24 (September 1971), 501-9; Samuel A. Kirkpatrick, "Issue Orientation and Voter Choice in 1964," *Social Science Quarterly,* Vol. 51 (December 1970), 689-705; Philip E. Converse, Angus Campbell, Warren E. Miller, and Donald E. Stokes, "Stability and Change in 1960: A Reinstating Election," *American Political Science Review,* Vol. 55 (June 1961), 269-80; Ithiel de Sola Pool, Robert P. Abelson, and Samuel Popkin, *Candidates, Issues, and Strategies* (Cambridge: M.I.T. Press, 1964); The American Institute for Political Communication, *Anatomy of a Crucial Election* (Washington, D.C.: American Institute for Political Communication, 1970).

[27]Gerald M. Pomper, "From Confusion to Clarity: Issues and American Voters, 1956-1968," *American Political Science Review,* Vol. 66 (June 1972), 415-28.

fections from the party of one's self-image. In 1952, for example, uneasiness over the Korean war and inflation made it much easier for many lifelong Democrats to defect to the candidacy of the already popular Republican Dwight Eisenhower. Similarly concern in 1968 over Vietnam, inflation, and law and order added up to a negative image for many of what the times were like and they shifted their support from the "ins" to the "outs." In these instances the nature of the times provided a symbol of a growing discontent, wariness, and time for change.

Candidate Images

There are contrasting views regarding how voters form impressions of candidates in political campaigns. One is that popular impressions are *candidate-determined;* that is, what voters see in a candidate depends upon what the candidate deliberately conveys in his speeches, radio and television appearances, political advertising, personal contacts, etc. This view contends that even though the voter's image of one candidate may be modified by his perception of that candidate's opponent, all candidates are free to make their own images. If properly packaged, a candidate can be marketed and sold to the mass just as can any consumer product.[28]

A contrasting view argues that the images of candidates are *voter-determined,* and a candidate "projects" an image only within very narrow confines. Those limits exist because the voter's party allegiance leads him to perceive the good qualities of his party's candidate and the negative qualities of the rival party's candidate. In this view voters make up their minds very early in the campaign, if not before the campaign begins, and there is little that candidates can do to change them.

There is evidence in support of both theses, and neither view tells the whole story of how members of the electorate form images of competing leaders.[29] The formation of images of candidates is a subtle transaction between the symbols candidates project to demonstrate their capacity to govern, on the one hand, and the images voters use to evaluate candidates, on the other. Voter images are multifaceted constellations of beliefs, values, and predispositions in two major areas.

First, the voter has an impression of the way a candidate plays a *political role.* This includes what people think of his public leadership:

---

[28]Joe McGinniss, *The Selling of the President 1968* (New York: Trident, 1969).

[29]Roberta S. Sigel, "Effect of Partisanship on the Perception of Political Candidates," *Public Opinion Quarterly,* Vol. 28 (Fall 1964), 483-96; Joseph E. McGrath and Marion F. McGrath, "Effects of Partisanship on Perceptions of Political Figures," *Public Opinion Quarterly* (Summer 1962), 236-48; Bertram H. Raven and Philip S. Gallo, "The Effects of Nominating Conventions, Elections, and Reference Group Identification upon the Perception of Political Figures," *Human Relations,* Vol. 18 (August 1965), 217-29; Donn Byrne, Michael H. Bond, and Michael J. Diamond, "Response to Political Candidates as a Function of Attitude Similarity-Dissimilarity," *Human Relations,* Vol. 22 (June 1969), 251-62.

(1) his record and experience, (2) his qualifications and abilities — whether he is a good leader, knows how to handle people, is a good administrator, is strong, decisive, educated, and knowledgeable; (3) his position on issues and policies; (4) his philosophy — perhaps as liberal or conservative; and (5) his group associations — with the "common people," special interests, "big business," "labor," etc. The voter's impression of political role of the candidate also involves what people see in the candidate as a "party" politician: (1) his political strength, connections, and dynamism; (2) what political party he represents; and (3) his political aspirations.

Second, people have an impression of the candidate's *political style.* This includes perceptions of his personal qualities — appearance, traits (such as integrity, impulsiveness, sincerity, maturity, etc.), personality, and background (age, wealth, education, etc.) — and of his performance capabilities as a campaigner (as a good or poor speaker, cool or hot television performer, comfortable or ill at ease, formal or informal, etc.).

Not only do voters have impressions of the *actual* candidates in each of these areas, they also have images of their *ideal* official, that is, what political role he should play and what political style he should display. These conceptions of the ideal combined with the voter's partisan self-image and his preferences on issues comprise the cognitive-affective-conative background against which he imagines what competing candidates are like.[30]

Political candidates have enough hold on mass awareness and are, by nature of the fact that they usually lead political parties, sharply enough set apart from one another so that popular images of them influence election outcomes. There has been sufficient research into the images of political candidates competing for national office in various political regimes to make it possible for us to chart the general outlines of the affective and cognitive content of candidate images.

In American presidential elections from 1952-1972 the mass has generally responded favorably to all the candidates (as measured by responses to questions asking them to name the qualities they like and dislike in the candidates). In both successful presidential campaigns Democrats and Republicans alike perceived Dwight Eisenhower favorably (the ratio of favorable to unfavorable comments about "Ike" in both 1952 and 1956 was better than 2-1). Eisenhower wore the mantle of "national hero" and "victorious general," an image that has impact in nations other than America as testified to by the fact that General Charles De Gaulle's image in France in 1958 reflected marked similarities to Eisenhower's popularity in

[30]Dan Nimmo and Robert L. Savage, "Political Images and Political Perception," *Experimental Study of Politics,* Vol. 1 (July 1971), 1-37; Charles N. Brownstein, "Communication Strategies and the Electoral Decision Making Process: Some Results from Experimentation," *Experimental Study of Politics,* Vol. 1 (July 1971), 37-50.

the United States.[31] Voters also perceived Eisenhower's opponent favorably in 1952, Adlai Stevenson (the ratio of favorable to unfavorable comments was also about 2-1), but in 1956 positive and negative comments among a nationwide sample concerning Stevenson were about balanced. In 1960 neither Richard Nixon nor John Kennedy held much of an "image" advantage over the other. However, in 1964 the ratio of favorable to unfavorable responses about Lyndon Johnson (2.5-1) far exceeded the generally negative image of his opponent Barry Goldwater (with a ratio of 1-2 positive to negative references); in 1964 positive references to Republican Barry Goldwater were primarily to personal qualities, but Lyndon Johnson's stands on policies and his political experience accounted for the bulk of his favorable image. Again in 1968 neither Richard Nixon nor Hubert Humphrey had a significant image advantage with other than their own party supporters, although both were generally more favorably perceived than George Wallace, candidate of the American Independent Party.[32] In 1972 Nixon's image was markedly more favorable than that of his opponent, George McGovern.[33]

The tendency of Americans to respond favorably to candidates of both major parties is not necessarily matched by voters in other political regimes. In Great Britain, for example, over the period 1963-1966 the leader of the Labor Party, Harold Wilson, attracted almost two and a half times as many favorable as unfavorable references in opinion surveys; his Conservative Party rivals, however, were not so fortunate. In 1963 Harold Macmillan attracted as many unfavorable as favorable responses. Images of party leaders in the 1968 federal elections in Canada reflected that voters there reacted more to personal qualities than political experience in evaluating Liberal leader Pierre Trudeau, Conservative Robert Stanfield, and the NDP's Tommy Douglas. In the case of Trudeau voters mentioned his policies and ideas, but 60 percent of all references were to personality; in the case of Stanfield personal references were equally high, and only for Douglas did qualities of experience, leadership, ability, etc. outweigh personality.[34]

In American presidential elections approximately one-third of voters

[31]Philip E. Converse and Georges Dupeux, "De Gaulle and Eisenhower: The Public Image of the Victorious General," in Campbell et al., *Elections and the Political Order*, pp. 292-345.

[32]Campbell et al., *The American Voter*, pp. 52-63; American Institute for Political Communication, *Anatomy of a Crucial Election*, Chapter II; Herbert F. Weisberg and Jerrold G. Rusk, "Dimensions of Candidate Evaluation," *American Political Science Review*, Vol. 64 (December 1970), 1167-85.

[33]The Gallup Opinion Index (Report No. 88), October 1972, pp. 5-14.

[34]Butler and Stokes, *Political Change in Britain*, pp. 373-88; Gilbert R. Winham and Robert B. Cunningham, "Party Leader Images in the 1968 Federal Election," *Canadian Journal of Political Science*, Vol. 3 (March 1970), 37-55.

make up their minds during the campaigns, the remainder having decided before or during the national nominating conventions. In the 1964 and 1966 British general elections only 11 percent of those surveyed had made their voting decisions during the campaigns.[35] This raises the question of the relative impact of candidate images upon mass voting behavior. There are important reasons for insisting that the impact is considerable. First, for the vast bulk of voters the long-term image of a politician is more influential in shaping voting decisions than the "packaged" image in a given campaign; but even the short-term image is significant. Studies measuring the relative effect of party, issue, and candidate images upon the decisions of voters to defect from their traditional party loyalties indicate that images of competing candidates are the major statistical explanation of defection from party.[36]

Second, a sufficiently large minority of voters do arrive at their choices during campaigns to determine the outcome in close elections. Voters who decide on candidates during a campaign are likely to be people with weak partisan self-images or none at all. There is evidence that the symbols employed by a candidate do shift the perceptions of these voters of the candidate's political strength and personal qualities, but because of lesser involvement in politics generally, these are also voters who pay less attention to campaign appeals.[37]

Third, in forming both their long-term and short-term images of politicians, the mass responds to both substantive and stylistic traits of candidates, with a tendency to emphasize personal style over political experience; popular images of political leaders are an amalgam of both role and style considerations, and in attempting to "build" his image no politician can run simply as a governmental "technician" or as a popular "celebrity."

Fourth, political candidates perform three major functions for the electorate during campaigns; first, they play a symbolic *cognitive* part by informing voters about political events, issues, and problems; second, they perform a symbolic *moral* function by appealing to the party faithful, reinstilling enthusiasm, and urging judgments upon the electorate; finally,

[35]William H. Flanigan, *Political Behavior of the American Electorate,* 2nd ed. (Boston: Allyn & Bacon, 1972), p. 110; Butler and Stokes, *Political Change in Britain,* p. 428.

[36]Richard W. Boyd, "Presidential Elections: An Explanation of Voting Defection," *American Political Science Review,* Vol. 63 (June 1969), 498-514; Donald E. Stokes, "Some Dynamic Elements of Contests for the Presidency," *American Political Science Review,* Vol. 60 (March 1966), 19-28.

[37]Jay G. Blumler and Denis McQuail, *Television in Politics* (Chicago: University of Chicago Press, 1969), Chapter 12; Kurt Lang and Gladys Engel Lang, *Politics and Television* (Chicago: Quadrangle, 1968); Philip E. Converse, "Information Flow and the Stability of Partisan Attitudes," in Campbell et al., *Elections and the Political Order,* pp. 136-160; Angus Campbell, "Surge and Decline: A Study of Electoral Change" in Campbell et al., pp. 40-62.

they perform a *cathartic* function by arousing emotional responses, serving as the targets for both praise and abuse, hope and fear, admiration and hatred.[38]

In sum there are at least three levels to any political campaign — an instrumental campaign involving the candidate's symbolic appeals, or propaganda, to activate wavering and latent followers, reinforce the faithful, convert the independent, and neutralize the opposition; an evaluative campaign to permit voters with fixed partisan self-images to stand fast or defect on the basis of their subjective appraisals of how closely party, issue, and candidate images match their own loyalties; and an expressive level in which people enter into the drama, ritual, and mythology of the democratic election to enjoy the spectacle of the contest and reveal their innermost aspirations and anxieties.

POLITICAL IMAGES AND PUBLIC POLICY

In this and the preceding chapter we have described a variety of ways that popular images of politics enter into support for political communities, regimes, and leaders; we have also examined what people imagine as their most fundamental hopes and fears and the way popular images enter into social movements, ideologies, and mass voting behavior. We have emphasized that, for the mass, political images serve very real psychological needs. In this sense mass politics is a process through which people make moral and social judgments (evaluative imagery) and find outlets for their self-images and identifications (expressive imagery). But politics is concerned with the tangible as well as psychic needs of mass society and that too involves imagery.

Political images enter into policy making in a variety of ways, but they are not the political images manifested in mass support for the political community, regime, and its leaders nor those common to social movements, ideologies, and mass voting. Popular images of political parties, issues, and candidates, for example, determine whom voters elect to public office, but they hardly provide officials with a clear, detailed policy mandate; although democratic elections provide outlets for public judgment and emotion, they are not devices for articulating mass concerns and translating them directly into policy.

Elective and appointive policy makers represent various interests competing with one another for material advantage. As such they perceive (rightly or wrongly) what their constituencies seek as well as what rival

---

[38]Suzanne Keller, *Beyond the Ruling Class* (New York: Random House, 1963), pp. 156-57; Steven R. Brown and John D. Ellithorp, "Emotional Experiences in Political Groups: The Case of the McCarthy Phenomenon," *American Political Science Review,* Vol. 64 (June 1970), 349-66.

interests demand. They also have some conception of broader interests that transcend the desires of specific groups, classes, and interests (images of what is "good for the people" or "good for the nation"). Politicians communicate to each other through symbolic messages that reflect the special demands of their constituents and the general interests of the community. The mutal exchange of and response to these symbols constitutes the give-and-take by which policy makers debate, make charges and countercharges, and reach compromises or stalemate.

For policy makers political images are thus the currency for negotiating acceptable allocations of material resources that meet the demands of powerful interests. Political elites, as with the mass populace, achieve social, political, and moral prestige and boosts to the ego by responding to symbolic cues, but *the principal function of symbols* and their associated images for policy makers is instrumental, i.e., they serve to facilitate a satisfactory division of tangible goods.

Yet, political leaders must relate to the mass as well as to one another; they must demonstrate that material allocations that benefit only a few actually work to the interest of all. For this purpose political images are also employed as instruments to appease people into believing that their interests are being served and to arouse popular expectations of tangible gains in the future. A primary example of the use of political imagery to appease popular concerns rather than accommodate them lies in policies surrounding taxes upon personal wealth in this country. Taxes are rarely popular. Nonetheless governments finance their various programs through tax levies. The question is who shall be taxed and how much?

In the United States the answer has been to establish a "graduated" or progressive" income tax, a tax on personal incomes in accordance with a person's "ability to pay." Those with low incomes allegedly pay a smaller proportion of their total income in taxes than do those with higher incomes. The "progressive income tax" thus symbolizes a redistribution of economic resources; it taxes more highly the incomes of the prosperous and spends the money upon educational, welfare, health, transportation, and other projects which benefit people with low and moderate income. However, the image of the desirability of what such a tax structure is supposed to accomplish does not reflect actual conditions. For one thing, the federal income tax structure is only slightly progressive; viz., many loopholes permit those with higher incomes to protect portions of them from taxation, including provisions for writing off business losses, averaging incomes over several years in order to take advantage of lower tax rates, deferring income earned in one year for payment at a later time, depletion allowances, and others. Moreover, whereas the direct tax upon personal income provides more than one-third of all tax revenues for all levels of government in this country, there are also a host of indirect taxes that contribute revenue (those levied on one set of citizens but later passed on to others to pay — as in the case of sales and excise taxes). When indirect taxes at federal, state, and local levels are added to the direct tax structure, the overall tax burden is not progressive at all but falls out of proportion upon those with lesser incomes.[39]

In employing such symbols as "progressive income tax" and "ability to pay" policy makers arouse public expectations that there will actually be a redistribution of wealth on the basis of these formulas. People expect that their life will be better because of it. But, as the gap between what is symbolically promised and what is actually received widens, the end product of this policy making imagery is more than mere popular dissatisfaction with policies; public distrust of leaders and disaffection with the regime is also likely to develop. The "taxpayers' revolt" in this country (that is, the growing refusal of citizens to vote higher taxes for the support of schools and other services) is an example of dissatisfaction (indeed, 60 percent of Americans surveyed in 1970 said the "breaking point" had been reached in the amount of taxes they could pay).[40] Unfortunately there are already too many cases where the gap between popular expectations and actual conditions has contributed to violent reactions against the regime (as in riots in urban ghettos in the 1960s).[41]

In the face of disparities between what official pronouncements say and what people perceive (a variation on the "credibility gap" of which we hear so much in contemporary politics), astute political leaders in democratic regimes promise reforms — sometimes sincerely and sometimes hypocritically. In so doing they raise even higher the popular expectations that their most fundamental hopes for an improved and decent standard of living and for peace (as we observed earlier in this chapter) will be realized. Whether or not policy makers are successful in rebuilding diffuse support for themselves, the community, and the regime depends upon the degree of substantial improvement their policies make in the lives of the deprived, as well as upon the impression they convey as politicians that they are committed to enhancing the dignity and identities of citizens — the haves and have-nots, the contented and discontented, the trusting and distrustful, the merely dissatisfied and the sadly disaffected. No policy allocates solely material or psychic benefits; the most efficacious policy distributes a blend of both that responds to the basic welfare and deference needs of humanity.

[39]Joyce M. Mitchell and William C. Mitchell, *Political Analysis and Public Policy* (Skokie, Ill.: Rand McNally, 1969), pp. 169-75; Murray Edelman, *The Symbolic Uses of Politics* (Urbana, Ill.: University of Illinois Press, 1964), p. 28.

[40]Louis Harris, *The Harris Survey Yearbook of Public Opinion,* 1970 (New York: Louis Harris and Associates, Inc., 1971), p. 152.

[41]Edelman, *Politics as Symbolic Action.*

6

the drama, illusion
and reality
of political images

People have subjective knowledge of political objects. On the basis of such knowledge, which we have called *images,* they give meaning to political signs. These signs are *symbols* representing their environment. We have reviewed several aspects of this symbolic-subjective activity including the instrumental, evaluative, and expressive functions of political images; the communication of political images; the development of personal images; and the distribution of important political images in mass society. In order to put these various aspects of our topic into a single focus, we will conclude by discussing the dramatic character of political imagery. Looking at the dramatic, illusionary, and realistic aspects of political images will afford us an opportunity to recall and summarize the major points made in previous chapters as well as to offer our own images of politics.

THE DRAMATIC QUALITIES OF POLITICAL IMAGERY

The view that human behavior is dramatic action has a long and rich tradition.[1] By probing that tradition, one can isolate the principal qualities of dramatic action relevant for dealing with political images.

[1]The view dates back prior to the ancient Greeks but is put most clearly by Shakespeare in Act II, Scene VII, of *As You Like It* in the oft-quoted passage,

The Dramatistic Perspective

There is a simple but crucial distinction made in dramatistic theories of behavior — the distinction between motion and action. *Motion* consists of the mere physical movement of any object or being, as when a rock rolls or dust blows. *Action,* however, differs from motion in that an act consists both of physical movement and of the subjective significance of the movement for the person committing it, or for some observer. *Action* is motion plus subjective significance, but "action cannot be reduced to motion:"

> "The man who designs a computer is acting. The computer that he designs can but move. Though the processes of the computer can throw light upon its designer, they do not provide a terminology adequate for the defining of its makers. That's the crux of the Dramatistic position."[2]

In politics we find an example of the motion-action distinction in voting. Pulling the lever on a voting machine is motion; the voter's sense of why he is moving that lever makes it an act: "insofar as a vote is cast without adequate knowledge of its consequences, one might even question whether it should be classed as an activity at all; one might rather call it passive, or perhaps sheer motion (what the behaviorists would call a Response to a Stimulus)."[3] The automatic obligation some Americans feel regarding voting, while thinking that elections have little or no effect upon policy making (see Chapter Four, p. 96), is evidence that voting is sometimes motion rather than action. Yet, so long as discharging a civic duty gives meaning to voting, it is an act beyond mere motion.

But how do we give meaning to the things we do? How do we make actions of our motions? As argued in Chapters One and Two, we represent objects through our images and by communicating images through symbols. By symbols we communicate what objects and events mean to us. Since those symbols do mean something to us, a meaning that rests upon our images of the world, the symbols we use to achieve material gain, make judgments, and express ourselves are actions in themselves (i.e., these

---

"All the world's a stage
And all the men and women merely players;
They have their exits and their entrances;
And one man in his time plays many parts."
The tradition is most apparent in the following: George Herbert Mead, *Mind, Self, and Society* (Chicago: University of Chicago Press, 1934); Kenneth Burke, *A Grammar of Motives* (Englewood Cliffs, N.J.: Prentice-Hall, 1945); an example of an explicit attempt to employ dramaturgical analysis in political studies is Joseph R. Gusfield, *Symbolic Crusade* (Urbana: University of Illinois Press, 1966); a critique of the approach can be found in Patricke Johns Heine, *Personality in Social Theory* (Chicago: Aldine Publishing, 1971), pp. 58-66.

[2]Kenneth Burke, "Dramatism," in Lee Thayer, ed., *Communication: Concepts and Perspectives* (Washington: Spartan Books, 1967), p. 329.

[3]Burke, *A Grammar of Motives,* p. xx; see also Harold D. Lasswell and Abraham Kaplan, *Power and Society* (New Haven: Yale University Press, 1950), p. 10.

symbols are meaningful in themselves), as well as means to an end. Put in the language of the dramatistic view, human behavior consists of symbolic acts that make up theatrical performances, that is, people presenting themselves to each other to influence their mutual impressions of one another and their joint expectations of what must be done to sustain the performance.

To get a better picture of the nature of dramatic performance consider the words of heavyweight boxer Muhammad Ali (then Cassius Clay), on the eve of his 1964 bout with the reigning champion, Sonny Liston:

"This fight with Liston is truly a command performance. And that's exactly the way I planned it. . . . Where do you think I would be next week if I didn't know how to shout and holler and make the public sit up and take notice? I would be poor, for one thing, and I would probably be down in Louisville, Ky., my home town, washing windows and saying 'yes suh' and 'no suh' and knowing my place. . . . When I walk into a room where he [Liston] is and see him staring at me with that mean, hateful look, I want to laugh, but then I think maybe it's not so funny. I'm pretty sure the way he acts is just a pose, the same way I have a pose, but that look of his still shakes me. I wonder what's really going on in that head of his. . . ."[4]

The relationship between images and performances is circular: our performances define our self- and public images; those definitions set the conditions and expectations of others' performances toward us; our impressions of their performances and what they think of us helps us confirm, reject, or disconfirm our self-images; and this, in turn, establishes the limits of our return performance before them (the verbal and nonverbal messages we transmit and the settings in which we transmit them). In other words, what a person does toward others restricts or enhances what he can and will choose to do in the future. Life and politics, in this sense, is drama. People do not relate toward one another *as if* engaged in dramatic performances. They are caught up in a drama: "the proposition 'things move, persons act,' is literal."[5]

Dramatistic theory, then, conceives of the individual as a performer who manages the impressions people have of him by playing various roles. Moreover, from the dramatistic perspective all of us are members of the cast. We are "on-stage"; i.e., through motivated role performances we present images for audiences to observe, interpret, and respond to. Our performances take place in particular settings, and we use several media and props to convey the impressions appropriate to our roles. In theatrical parlance the key elements of any performance are the act (or acts), actor, motive, role, scene, and vehicle for addressing an audience.[6]

---

[4]Cassius Clay, "I'm a Little Special," *Sports Illustrated,* February 24, 1964, p. 14; a detailed account of the dramatic performances in everyday living can be found in Erving Goffman, *The Presentation of Self in Everyday Life* (New York: Doubleday, 1959), pp. 1-76.

[5]Burke, "Dramatism," p. 331.

[6]Compare Burke, *A Grammar of Motives,* p. xv.

Two recent Presidents of the United States presenting policies toward the war in Vietnam illustrate the dramatic elements in political action. In the 1964 presidential campaign (the scene) Lyndon Johnson (the actor) performing in the role of a campaigner seeking reelection (motive) promised in campaign speeches (vehicle) that his administration sought "no wider war" (symbolic act). He raised the public (audience) expectation that there would be no massive commitment of American ground forces in Southeast Asia. Yet, from his perspective as President once reelected (a different role), he deemed that practical conditions made such a commitment necessary. Hence, to sustain his performance, now as President rather than campaigner, he sent troops to Vietnam to "contain" the war (symbolic act), not to widen it. In 1968 another actor in the role of capaigner, Richard Nixon, proclaimed a desire to extricate the United States from Vietnam by a "plan" to bring "peace with honor" and without surrender (symbolic act). Upon occupying the Presidency (his new role) he announced graduated troop withdrawals (symbolic act) and "Vietnamization" of the war to replace the United States in a fighting role with South Vietnamese forces. Later, in keeping with this performance, the President said the 1970 invasion of Cambodia was undertaken to shorten rather than prolong the war by destroying enemy supply bases; similarly resumption of bombing of North Vietnam in 1971-72 was necessary to "hasten" the day of American withdrawal. Then, in the dual role of President as Campaigner in 1972, Nixon created the expectation of a cease fire in Vietnam either before or shortly after election day. In both cases the Presidents' declarations of peaceful intentions heightened demands from other actors (members of the U.S. Senate, antiwar groups, the North Vietnamese, and others) for quick withdrawal.

There are a number of ways to look at these two performances. One can attribute error to both Presidents and say that they were overly optimistic about the possibilities for peace. Or one can say that both presidential candidates purposely misled the American People. The dramatistic analyst, however, would argue that these performances illustrate how political images evoked in one dramatic setting and for one dramatic purpose ("we seek no wider war" and "peace with honor" as campaign messages) affect political action by shaping what an audience expects about goals and, what is of equal importance, by structuring the rhetorical context within which politicians reach and publicize political decisions.[7] In the dramatistic perspective neither Johnson nor Nixon could be charged with deliberate deceit. Rather, the very *drama* of running for President constitutes a framework of popular expectations that a politician should have peaceful intentions which, given his image of an ethical performance

[7]Hugh Dalziel Duncan, *Symbols in Society* (New York: Oxford University Press, 1968), p. 48.

in the role of presidential contender, he sincerely declares. Once President the dramatic scene, role, and motives change even though other dramatic elements (actor, media, and audience) remain. In short, there is a logic for each dramatic performance; the logic of campaigning for the presidency is not the logic of being president. Yet the images a candidate commits himself to in one role carry over to influence his role performance in the presidential drama.

Dramatic performances therefore are not inherently deceitful, pretentious, faked, or acted out by charlatans. In studying "life as theatre" the dramaturgic analyst "seeks to describe the ways in which 'impressions' are created, sustained, and ruptured under the condition that the actor is 'unconscious' or only dimly 'conscious' that this is part of the business he is in."[8] A dramatistic approach does not assert that politics is deception or that politicians are confidence men. This approach is merely a device to emphasize that the *images* people have of politics, politicians, and the mass are, in themselves, *actions* that establish the contours of leader-follower relationships; they are actions that stem from *and* determine motives, but the motives themselves are inherently neither good nor bad, conscious nor unconscious. But the subtleties of politics make it hard to be precise about who is on stage and who is in the audience. As an example take President Nixon's historic visit to China, a drama in which it was especially hard to tell who was performing for whom. Wrote one thoughtful journalist:

"There are so many performers and audiences in this spectacle it is impossible to sort them out.

There is the mammoth American television audience, apparently off on another international romance, and not to be deterred by a Presidential party that warns of only minimal results from a week that started in such high spirits and multiple toasts to the Communist leaders.

There is the vast population of China, which remained obediently aloof when the Nixons drove into town but which tied up the sidewalks straining for the newspapers and pictures when the government let on that there was a big show in town for all.

There are the Russians, whom the Chinese want to make uncomfortable — and worse — by this Peking display of cameraderie, and whom the Americans want to make uncomfortable — only not too much so — in hopes of softening them up for major agreements later this year.

And . . . there are multiple audiences right inside the secret summit conferences. Both Nixon and his hosts were thought to be preparing fairly formal statements on their many differences, so as to reassure nervous allies — in Tokyo or Hanoi — and to leave a record about which they could honestly say that no deals were made at anyone else's expense. But they were also

[8]Sheldon L. Messinger et al., "Life as Theater: Some Notes on the Dramaturgic Approach to Social Reality," *Sociometry*, Vol. 25 (1962), 106.

expecting to address each other more flexibly and informally, by gesture, in-
nuendo, implication and perhaps even only by omission.

This particular part of the drama will be played out not only this week but
for many months, with speeches, made and not made, with emissaries sent,
with background briefings in Washington and with seasonally adjusted new
slogans in Peking's Square of the Gate of the Heavenly Peace."[9]

To be sure, the performers we see when we go to the theatre do
several things to remind us that we are witnessing a play. They use exaggerated gestures, take bows, and appear in public outside their stage roles.
But in political dramas we seldom get such clues. If politicians have characters different from those they portray on stage, we are rarely privy to
the back stage where they appear. As members of the mass audience, as
Shakespeare wrote, "the play's the thing"; and participation in politics for
most of us is limited to being members of that mass audience.[10]

In sum, the dramatistic viewpoint regards all social relationships as
dramatic action. A person in a social drama (be he in a political setting,
religious ceremony, business-labor negotiation, marital contract, or even in
the bedroom) performs in accordance with the impression he wishes to
leave on his audience. While on-stage the logic of the dramatic performance
guides and controls his relations to other performers and spectators.

The Political Uses of Drama

In earlier chapters we alluded to the use of various dramatic devices
in shaping political images. In discussing political leadership we spoke of
how symbolic leaders use personification, identification, ceremonies,
public denunciation, and dramatic confrontation (Chapter Four, pp. 99-
102); and in Chapter Two we considered style, rhetoric, parasocial interaction, and play — all aspects of image communication with dramatic overtones. Which ones of many possible dramatic devices people use in politics
depends upon several factors, but principally upon the actors, audience,
issues, setting, and media.

Two considerations affect the *political actor's* choice of dramatic
mechanisms. One is whether a politician can adapt his political style
to certain performances. Can a leader take advantage of his appearance and
forensic abilities to capitalize on the opportunities afforded by unfolding
political dramas? President Franklin Roosevelt was one politician who
could. Although confined to a wheel chair by poliomyelitis, he stood when

[9]Max Frankel, "Actors, Audience Interchangeable in Peking Drama," *New York
Times* News Service, February 23, 1972. © 1972 by the New York Times Company. Reprinted
by permission.

[10]James N. Rosenau, *The Dramas of Politics* (Boston: Little, Brown, 1973).

making a public address, thus giving the impression of a man with indom-
itable strength and courage who could lead America out of the Great
Depression and through World War II. Moreover, his speeches were even
prepared by a dramatist, Robert E. Sherwood (the writer of a successful
1930s drama, *Abe Lincoln in Illinois*). In his "fireside chats" (radio addresses to the American public from the informal setting of his White House
study), Roosevelt employed many of the devices conducive to cementing
a parasocial relationship with his audience.

In addition to possessing an advantageous political style, the politician's penchant for performing leads to his use of certain dramatic
devices. In the 1964 Democratic national convention President Lyndon
Johnson employed suspense as a dramatic mechanism. In what was basically a cut-and-dried nominating convention he played cat-and-mouse with
the press and hinted at several possibilities regarding the selection of a
running mate; the President contrived to wait until the last minute to
announce personally to delegates that Hubert Humphrey was his vice-
presidential preference.

The *spectators* to a dramatic performance are not a passive audience.
Since they read meanings into the performance, their expectations help
determine the expressions an actor uses to influence the audience's impressions of him. If audience expectations permit, reinforce, or even demand it, an actor can deliberately "play" to his audience. On the night of
an election, for example, candidates who know they have been soundly
defeated maintain an optimistic front, go to their campaign headquarters
and assure supporters that things will change when the "late returns are
in," and withhold any concession statement until all hopes for victory are
lost. The electoral winner in the drama goes through "rites of passage"
by following a definite scenario to demonstrate to one and all that he is
exchanging the role of partisan contender for that of public official. He
makes a gracious acceptance speech, praises the gentlemanly conduct of
his opponent, asks both his supporters and opponents for help, and dedi-
cates himself to public service. He takes the oath of office in a formal
inaugural ceremony; usually the more important his role is to the governmental drama, the more elaborate the ritual (compare, for example, the
inauguration of a President or Governor with the swearing in of a city
councilman). Finally, he addresses his entire constituency in his inaugural
speech, no longer as a divisive partisan but as a unifying political authority.
This marks the end of his passage from partisan to winner to public servant.
Both victor and vanquished perform as the audience expects regardless of
what may be their private feelings: "Whether an honest performer wishes
to convey the truth or whether a dishonest performer wishes to convey a
falsehood, both must take care to enliven their performances with appropriate expressions, exclude from their performances expressions that

might discredit the impressions being fostered, and take care lest the audience impute unintended meanings."[11]

Certain *issues* generally encourage the use of dramatic devices. Some issues involve concrete matters dividing candidates and voters while others are ambiguous moral and ethical questions on which there is a broad consensus. The latter yield dramatic possibilities. It is relatively easy to dramatize one's stand against the "drug traffic," "organized crime," or "labor racketeers," By playing the hero against symbolically defined forces of evil, a leader confronts wrong, denounces wrongdoers, and professes to stamp out sin wherever he sees it. Thomas E. Dewey, twice nominated as Republican presidential candidate, took advantage of ethical issues; he came to national prominence for his dramatic confrontations with criminals as New York City's district attorney. Ralph Nader has built a national reputation on such issues as safety, quality, and environmental protection; regularly denouncing manufacturers of automobiles, electrical appliances, detergents, and others, he identifies himself as the leader of a crusade to protect the consumer against unsafe, low-quality, polluting products.

Some *political settings* are more conducive to dramatic performances than others. A partisan political convention, for example, is particularly suited because of its avowed symbolism honoring legendary folk heros (such as Abraham Lincoln and Thomas Jefferson), and opportunities for conflict, dramatic encounters, and public denunciations. Congressional hearings also hold dramatic possibilities. In public hearings such as the 1973 Senate inquiry into the Watergate affair, congressional leaders interrogate witnesses, identify with popular figures, denounce villains, and label partisan opponents as fools. Debates, filibusters, and votes in the U.S. Senate are scenes of high drama (witness the drama of the Senate vote failing to convict President Andrew Johnson after impeachment proceedings following the Civil War or the more recent roll calls rejecting President Richard Nixon's appointments of Clement F. Haynsworth in 1969 and G. Harrold Carswell in 1970 to the Supreme Court). And, the judiciary with its adversary system, elaborate ritual, clear definitions of roles, and courtroom props such as flags, elevated bench, and witness stand provides an ideal stage for political drama.

Generally, the most desirable backdrops for dramatic performances are highly visible, permit maximum room for actors to manuever outside the restraints of formal rules and regulations, and provide opportunities for direct appeals to a mass audience. Yet, even bureaucratic agencies — which are less visible to the public eye, steeped in formal procedures, and hierarchically structured — are dramatic settings. Persons act out roles in the hierarchy as superiors and subordinates, roles defined by insignia, titles,

[11]Goffman, *The Presentation of Self in Everyday Life,* p. 66; a detailed description of the rites of passage in American politics can be found in William C. Mitchell, *The American Polity* (New York: Free Press, 1962), pp. 132-39.

and ceremonies as well as by formalized authority and responsibility. Private carpeted offices with special furniture, the privilege of reserved automobile parking (or use of an agency-provided car), and private secretaries are all props superiors use to impress their status upon underlings. Subordinates act a part also and thereby help sustain the drama. They perform to give the dramatic impression that they need to be told what to do and how to do it, are loyal to the organization and its leaders, and are qualified for what they do. Interviews, telephone calls, memos, deferential behavior, and tools of the trade (such props as the engineer's slide rule, the computer specialist's punch card, or the executive's attache case) contribute to believable performances. Subordinates often use "double talk" (reports that say one thing to an immediate superior but quite another to outsiders) to get around superiors without seemingly threatening the play.[12] The so-called "colonels' clique" in the U.S. Department of Defense is an example; these military underlings report that they agree with the Secretary's demands to cut defense expenditures, then confide in Washington journalists or congressmen that stepped-up defense appropriations are essential to military preparedness. Generally, however, the lower-echelon officer's inability to make direct appeals to mass audiences complicates dramatic performances on his own behalf. Think, for example, how the drama of the case of Lieutenant William Calley might have escalated had he been free, when first charged with the murder of Vietnamese civilians at My Lai Village, to proclaim his innocence and make counter-charges on *Meet the Press* rather than wait for a formal court martial.

Few political scenes involve such dramatic exploitation as political campaigns. A case in point was the presidential campaign of 1952 which took place in the setting of the unpopular Korean War. Neither candidate, Republican Dwight Eisenhower nor Democrat Adlai Stevenson, had definite plans for ending that war, but Eisenhower dramatized his willingness to try by promising that, if elected, "I will go to Korea." The announcement employed several dramatic devices:

"His offer had overtones of peripety; i.e., the single plain man would wage war directly against the overwhelming power of bureaucratic mechanics. It also personified the war by indicating that leaders like Eisenhower himself could be held directly responsible and that the war was not doomed by an impersonal fate to drag on hopelessly. These factors produced a level of identification with Eisenhower that any candidate could envy. Finally, the promise set up a ready-made climax composed of those moments when Eisenhower would actually arrive in Korea to survey the situation. How could an electorate on the verge of voting deny itself such an attractive climax by voting for Stevenson?"[13]

[12]Victor A. Thompson, *Modern Organization* (New York: Knopf, 1961), Chapter 7.

[13]Richard M. Merelman, "The Dramaturgy of Politics," *Sociological Quarterly,* Vol. 2 (Spring 1969), 232.

All of the *media of communication* discussed in Chapter Two (see pp. 43-48) have dramatic uses. Roosevelt's fireside chats, the 1960 Kennedy-Nixon debates, televised hearings of congressional committees into the conduct of the Vietnam war — all served as vehicles for politicians who influenced the inferences audiences made about them. The stock-in-trade of many newspaper columnists consists of exploiting dramatic devices, particularly "unmasking" public figures to expose their "real" characters and motives. In late 1971 India and Pakistan waged a brief but costly war in which India victoriously liberated East Pakistan and assisted in establishing the newly independent state of Bangla Desh. In that war the Nixon Administration assumed a public stance generally opposed to India. In early 1972 newspaper columnist Jack Anderson published material from classified government memoranda allegedly revealing the ways U.S. policy makers contrived to blame India for the war. Anderson's efforts to unmask the Nixon administration created an image of duplicity whether such deception actually existed or not. In the 1972 presidential campaign the same Jack Anderson endeavored to unmask the then Democratic vice-presidential nominee, Senator Thomas Eagleton, as an alcoholic who had been arrested for driving while intoxicated. Not being able to prove those charges, Anderson offered a dramatic apology to Eagleton on national television. (The controversy surrounding Eagleton, pertaining to his previous hospitalization for emotional stress, nevertheless led to his resignation from the Democratic ticket.)

Even the published memoirs of public figures can be vehicles for dramatic performance. When former President Lyndon Johnson in 1971 published the first volume in his memoirs, *The Vantage Point,* the event provided an opportunity for a dramatic challenge from Johnsons's opponents that he was twisting history and distorting the facts, thus renewing the dramatic confrontations between pro- and anti-Johnson forces of the 1960s.

Some *events* seem almost destined for dramatic presentation. The disclosure in 1971 of a classified 47-volume, 7000-page study of U.S. involvement in the Vietnam war is an apt example. Known as the "Pentagon Papers" (a symbol with connotations that the report was a product of a civilian-military elite), the study implied that decisions to escalate the war in Vietnam were made well before seeking public support for involvement of American forces. Many people concluded that the American public and Congress had been deceived into believing that no massive commitments would be made. Summaries of the report were published in both *The New York Times* and *The Washington Post* after it had been leaked to the newspapers by "unidentified sources." The U.S. Department of Justice asked the newspapers to return the documents and halt publication as injurious to the "defense interests of the U.S." When the *Times* refused to comply the Justice Department sought a court order against publication. A dramatic confrontation of principles and personages ensued. Members of the news fraternity argued that publication was protected by the people's right to a "free press" and "freedom of information." Government officials responded that the right of "executive privilege" and interests of "national security" were paramount. Within twelve days of the publication of the first installment of the "Pentagon Papers," the case reached the Supreme Court which ruled that the government had failed to justify its case for a permanent injunction against publication. In the meantime Daniel Ellsberg, a former Pentagon aide and at the time a research associate of Massachusetts Institute of Technology, revealed that he had leaked the documents to the press. Subsequently he was indicted, but not convicted, for a violation of the Espionage Act for his unauthorized possession of documents related to national defense.

The controversy over publication of the "Pentagon Papers" had all the ingredients of high political drama. First, the actors in the encounter were clearly identified and symbolized — the "press" (acting on behalf of the "public") versus the "government." Second, the symbols of press and public represented powerful political interests, *The New York Times* and *The Washington Post* versus the past policies of Lyndon B. Johnson and the current policies of President Richard Nixon, Secretary of Defense Melvin Laird, and other administration officials. Third, what began as a conflict between relatively narrow interests, quickly became a symbolic confrontation of principle (the "right of a free press" versus the "national interest"). Fourth, the drama unfolded through several vehicles — in newspapers, magazines, books, and on radio and television — and on several stages — in Congress, in the Supreme Court, and in the Presidency. Fifth, the dramatic mechanism of *peripety* appeared (the situation in which a nobody becomes important or a celebrity falls from grace); to some Daniel Ellsberg became the hero of the antiwar movement while to others he typified the disloyal, radical intellectual. Sixth, the drama played out very quickly. Within a few days after the Supreme Court decision, news of the controversy faded from the headlines; it had been stripped of its dramatic overtones because the suspense and secrecy were gone, dramatic encounters ceased, and a climax had been reached. Finally, the drama of the "Pentagon Papers" illustrates how small is the actual attentive audience for even the most widely publicized political issues; at the height of the controversy, and on the day the Supreme Court announced its decision, a nationwide Gallup Poll revealed only 55 percent of respondents were even aware of the existence of the publication of the papers![14]

[14]News Release, American Institute of Public Opinion, July 2, 1971.

THE ILLUSIONS IN POLITICAL IMAGERY

If political imagery is dramatic, then it shares with drama one other distinguishing quality — make-believe. Expecially in considering the evaluative and expressive uses of political images, we have emphasized that images often have no goal beyond themselves; people have some images of politics which they find satisfying even though those images don't assist them in tangible ways. Political symbols, ceremonies, rituals, encounters, and other dramatistic devices are often means to an end, but frequently they are simply enjoyable in their own right. But where there is dramatic performance for its own sake, there is also the possibility that participants may mistake pretending for reality, and thus enter into a world of fantasy and illusion. All of this is not to say people don't respond to facts. They do. However, they are the facts *as they imagine them.* People perceive and interpret facts in accordance with their images and as those facts are presented through symbols. If the images are so private that they don't match what is "out there" (however that can be determined) or if the symbols communicate political fictions, then political imagery may be illusionary. In the discussion that follows we examine two tendencies in political imagery, conceived as dramatic action, that illustrate illusionary properties. These tendencies at the personal and social levels contrast politics as symbolic play with efforts to achieve social order.

Politics as Symbolic Play

We have seen elsewhere that there are aspects of the development and communication of political images that contribute to a make-believe and playlike quality of politics. Specifically in Chapter Three we distinguished between play and imitation in a person's formation of political images (pp. 54-55). If his mental pictures of the world are confined to mimicking the objects and persons in his environment (if, in other words, he unthinkingly accommodates, or modifies, his images to match new experiences), he is engaged in imitation; but, if he simply assimilates new stimuli into what he has already learned so that new information, data, and experiences have no influence on what he does or thinks, he is in symbolic play. Symbolic play involves protection of the self-image against threatening influences. In symbolic play, information about the environment may entertain and titillate but will not assist a person to adapt to changing conditions. We also know that such play influences image communication (Chapter Two, p. 45); that is, people pay attention to messages they agree with and interact most with people they like or people who are like themselves. If they acquire political information from the media, it is to reinforce their political images, not to alter them. Moreover, much of popular attention to politics stems from a disinterested, voluntary, playlike search for pleasurable ways to express self-images; consequently people turn to political messages for restorative as well as reinforcing reasons.[15]

In addition to these play elements in politics, we have also pointed to other aspects of political images that suggest its make-believe quality. The development of the cognitive content of political images lags behind affective development (see Chapter Three pp. 66-67). Children learn loyalty to their political community before they are able to differentiate their nation from others; they place trust in the President and local policeman before understanding what these officials do; they build an affective tie to the political party of their parents long before knowing what differences there are in party positions on policies. And, as adults, people in the mass hold political opinions that have only minimal information behind them, respond to the personal style of leaders more quickly than to political experience, and have stronger emotional than rational links with political figures, issues, and events (Chapter Four and Five).

For the individuals who comprise the mass, therefore, politics is a playful, expressive drama by which they air needs to be with others, needs to be liked, self-acceptance and self-doubts, aggressions, love, and hate.[16] If the theatrical qualities of political images add up to play the implication is that the development of popular images of politics somehow gets arrested at a precausal and premoral stage. Consequently, instead of facilitating our adaptation to our environments by providing us with accurate perceptions of what the world is like, our political images impress the world with what *we* are like — or at least what we express ourselves as being like. If politics is built upon such illusions associated with symbolic play at the personal level, what consequences does this have for politics as a process of social order?

Politics as Social Order

There are two contrasting conceptions of how political images contribute to the regulation of social conflict. One states that images are manipulated as tools of social control; the other makes the assumption

[15]Jean Piaget, *Play, Dreams, and Imitation in Childhood* (New York: Norton, 1962), pp. 147-212; Brian Sutton-Smith, "Piaget on Play: A Critique," *Psychological Review,* Vol. 73 (1966), 104-10; Mihaly Csikszentmihalyi and Stith Bennet, "An Exploratory Model of Play," *American Anthropologist,* Vol. 73 (February 1971), 45-58; William Stephenson, *The Play Theory of Mass Communication* (Chicago: University of Chicago Press, 1967); Gerhart D. Wiebe, "Two Psychological Factors in Media Audience Behavior," *Public Opinion Quarterly,* Vol. 33 (Winter 1969-1970), 523-36.

[16]Steven R. Brown and John D. Ellithorp, "Emotional Experiences in Political Groups: The Case of the McCarthy Phenomenon," *American Political Science Review,* Vol. 64 (June 1970), 349-66. Robert E. Lane, *Political Thinking and Consciousness* (Chicago: Markham, 1969).

that images are elements of subjective play, and that political arrangements depend less upon the manipulation of symbols by leaders than upon the collective satisfactions people obtain from negotiating and holding similar images. These two conceptions overlap in several respects, but let us examine each separately.

We can label the first conception of the function of politics in achieving social order as that of *social control.*[17] It rests upon the view that societies are collectivities of people organized into hierarchies of different ranks, classes, and status. The *form* of hierarchy reflects human differences and transcends societies generally. There is always a potential for disorder in any particular hierarchy because people disobey, are disloyal, cheat, fight, steal, etc. Man employs his distinctive symbol-using, imagining capacity in the name of hierarchy. Through symbols he sanctifies a given social order (and its expression through hierarchy). The hierarchy is grounded in symbols representing what he believes is the intrinsic nature of man, society, and God. Note, for example, the pertinent references in the American *Declaration of Independence,* a document written to reject one hierarchical order and replace it with another; the dissolution of political bonds is justified on the basis of the "laws of nature and of nature's God," "a decent respect for the opinions of mankind," and a series of truths taken as "self-evident." Meaningful symbols such as these supply the language for the social drama that upholds, destroys, or changes the principles of the existing social order.

Politics plays a crucial role in preserving order, because political authorities portray government to people in ways that dramatize its legitimacy. They accomplish this by manipulating the politically relevant images people have learned to love and cherish, images that have been transmitted from generation unto generation — ways of life, social customs, religious faiths, and political doctrines.

The techniques of social control are by now familiar to us. Leaders endeavor to personify the highest ideals of the community, both while in public office and while trying to attain it: "The local candidate for township engineer assures us that his party will save the city, which in turn will save the nation, which in turn will save the free world, until finally we are saving Christian civilization by voting the local surveyor into office. Such 'mountings' always end in God, and thus, by inference, if we vote for the candidate, we vote for God."[18] Or a leader stages social dramas convincing followers of his majesty and power and identifying himself with the sacred social order: "We observe carefully how rulers stage themselves before different audiences, ranging from the office staff of the boss

[17]Duncan, *Symbols in Society.*

[18]Hugh Dalziel Duncan, *Communication and Social Order* (New York: Oxford University Press, 1962), pp. 139-40.

of a small local institution to the elaborate social dramas in which an emperor, king, or president acts out principles of social order. . . . When the followers have been taught to believe deeply in great transcendent principles which uphold social order, they watch carefully to see that their leaders play their roles in keeping with such principles."[19]

If there are threats to social order political rulers use symbols to convince citizens that dissidents are guilty of "sins" against the prevailing hierarchy of people, customs, and faiths. A favorite dramatic ploy is to find a scapegoat, the symbol of some person or social group to blame for social disturbances. Hence, Hitler placed the blame for social unrest in post-World War I Germany upon the "Jew." The use of the scapegoat device is not restricted to nondemocratic regimes; it is found at all times and places. Taken aback by protests against the 1970 invasion of Cambodia during the Vietnam war the President of the United States referred to student protesters as "bums" in informal remarks but later tempered the reference by stating it applied not to all protesters but only those who "burn buildings," "engage in violence," and "terrorize their fellow students and terrorize the faculty."

The essential feature of social control is that people learn images that support a given social order. Their deep and abiding loyalties to those images and to the social order they represent give leaders an opportunity to manipulate appropriate symbols to enforce obedience to the regime, laws, and authorities. As necessary, political authorities combine propagandistic appeals with threats of force. Some rulers enforce social order by constraint, i.e., by threatening to deprive a population of something deemed valuable such as freedom or wealth. Others achieve social order through inducement — the promise of some indulgence such as greater wealth, physical well-being, respect, or affection. Most combine constraints with inducements, but the degree of deprivation and inducement varies considerably. Deprivation may be as mild as a token tax or as severe as property confiscation, and inducements vary from the promise of the President's autographed photo to a lucrative defense contract. A high degree of constraint and/or inducement results in coercion, whereas a low degree of both constitutes choice.[20]

Contrasted with the social control concept of order is that of *convergent selectivity*. As outlined in Chapter Four, convergent selectivity consists of individuals (each making a choice independently and freely for himself with minimal constraint) reaching a consensus on goals, products, issues, political candidates, or whatever. Whereas the social control conception regards mass opinion as a product of deliberate organization and manipulation by propagandistic appeals, the convergent selectivity view

[19]Duncan, *Symbols in Society*, p. 203.
[20]Lasswell and Kaplan, *Power and Society*, p. 97.

regards people as absorbed in mass communication for pleasurable subjective play. Hence, the choices they make, whether in the market-place
or political arena, are personally pleasing. In social control the object is
to get people to arrive at common decisions (thus enhancing social order)
by mobilizing them through symbol manipulation; in convergent selectivity "the object is to let each person choose something different for
himself" so that social order flows from the convergence of freely made
individual choices.[21]

In both the social control and convergent selectivity conceptions
popular images of politics are basic to social order. In social control politicians mobilize images in support of the political community, its regime, and
its leaders by clever manipulation of the symbols that people respond
to with meaning. Preservation of social order depends upon political elites
who can accurately gauge and guide public sentiment through symbolic
appeals. The hierarchy of the social order is thus marked by clear divisions:
"Throughout human history the upper strata of society leaned more toward
symbolic activities, the lower strata engaged more in physical action, and
the middle classes were in trade. The upper classes achieved their aims
through control of information and physical coercion; the lower classes used
passive resistance (strike) or violence (revolution); and the middle classes
used credit and price manipulation."[22]

Convergent selectivity counters the hierarchical view. The preservation of social order does not rest with symbol-manipulating elites but
results from freely acting individuals making common choices. To be sure,
elites still play a significant role in the social drama. But instead of making
decisions and enforcing them through propaganda and/or coercion, their
role is more akin to the mass merchandiser, i.e., the elites suggest alternatives and compete for support through advertising. Unlike propaganda,
advertising does not address itself to the group, but to single individuals:
advertising "characteristically wants to sell *one* old piano to *one* person."[23]
It transmits possibilities rather than factual information (whether that
information be "disinterested" and objective as in education or "interested"
and biased as in propaganda).[24] The target of advertising is not the
individual in his group setting but the independent, free man before his
television set or reading his newspaper who knows he "only goes around
once in life" so he must get as much "gusto" from it as he can. Advertising

---

[21]Stephenson, *The Play Theory of Mass Communication*, p. 2.

[22]Jurgen Ruesch, "The Social Control of Symbolic Systems," *Journal of Communication*, Vol. 17 (September 1967), 289.

[23]Stephenson, *The Play Theory of Mass Communication*, p. 35.

[24]Terence H. Qualter, *Propaganda and Psychological Warfare* (New York: Random
House, 1962), pp. 26-31.

speaks to individual subjectivity and is "concerned with the ways of impart-
ing a desired meaning to a newly created set of symbols or of adding new
meaning to already existing symbols."[25]

Certainly, we live in an era in America of emphasis on the convergent
selectivity view. Armed with data from public opinion polls and experimental studies of popular images, advertising agencies build sales campaigns for laundry soaps, toothpastes, deodorants, or automobiles to appeal
to each person's unique hope for "a whiter, brighter wash," fear of tooth
decay, or desire to be "cool and dry." Automobile advertising, for instance,
urges each prospective car buyer to purchase a vehicle appropriate to his
particular personality. Research indicates there is a high degree of con-
gruency between a car owner's perception of his automobile and himself, that "automobiles are often expressions of the owner's image of
self."[26] But, advertising is not confined to the sale of commercial products;
few candidates for public office enter electoral contests without the
services of professional image-makers and even such public agencies as
the U.S. Army turn to mass advertising for stepping-up recruiting, telling
young Americans that "We Want to Join You!"

The convergent selectivity conception thus recognizes the capacities
of individuals in mass society for symbolic play. It accepts the premise
that free individuals try to enhance their self-images and respond to symbols
they find pleasurable rather than to those that promise only social
communion. When a sufficient number of individuals in mass society converge in their selection of pleasurable symbols, convergent selectivity may
foster social order. But, contrasted with social control, order rests upon more
than just the manipulation of symbols by elites. Something must be added
to augment convergent selectivity as a device for achieving social order.
There must be the opportunity for people to make free choices from which
to choose, having a diverse, rich, variegated set of alternatives. It is not
enough to say that people may choose any soap they please. There must be
many different soaps available to choose from. When it comes to consumer
goods in mass society, the number and variety of alternatives depend upon
several factors — levels of national economic development, types of economic
controls upon production and sales, the size and diversity of the consumer
audience, etc. With political "goods," however, range of choice is limited
in most regimes. This is precisely what concerns critics of contemporary
politics. Indeed, one argument goes so far as to say that *the very image that
there is choice in contemporary political regimes is the most fundamental
mass illusion of our times.* Let us consider it.

[25]Ruesch, "The Social Control of Symbolic Systems," p. 278.

[26]Al E. Birdwell, "A Study of the Influence of Image Congruence on Consumer
Choice," *Journal of Business,* Vol. 41 (January 1968), 87-88.

The Illusions in Mass Images

Many scholars argue that our political images are illusions, but the principal spokesman for this viewpoint is Jacques Ellul.[27] The argument runs as follows. Throughout history man has used images to explain and justify himself and his "confrontation with reality." These images constitute man's myths about the world. Contemporary mass man is no different. Among current myths are beliefs that Work is redeeming, Progress is inevitable, and Happiness is assured. But the realities are something different. Much of work in mass industrial society is routine, rote, dull, monotonous, and sometimes pointless — at least as demeaning as it is redeeming. The inevitability of human progress is questionable given man's unrelenting pollution of his environment. And, happiness, if defined as a meaningful existence, is never assured but always challenged.

Second, these myths influence all segments of life, including man's political life. And just as the realities of the sustaining myths contradict man's image of the world, the realities of politics contradict these principal illusions. (1) The illusion that man knows what is going on in politics is countered by the fact that most people no longer experience politics directly and concretely but accept instead the appearances of politics in mass communication. If he takes politics seriously, mass man is overwhelmed by information too complex and diverse for him to understand. Hence, he ignores much of politics and deludes himself into believing that his political choices are truly free. (2) Modern man believes he contributes to governmental decisions or at least chooses the politicians who do. Actually he controls politicians only at specified election periods and, even then, he chooses from a limited number of candidates for the higher offices; and, the policy makers that mass man deals with most directly are not elected officials but tax collectors, policemen, and other appointive bureaucrats. (3) Modern man elects politicians and thus selects the decision makers, but politicians are not the key decision makers anyway. The complexities of social problems require the knowledge and skill of qualified technicians — in social welfare, space technology, agriculture, modern weaponry, etc. — who pose social questions in manageable technical terms *for themselves* but in ways far beyond the comprehension of most of the popularly chosen politicians whose task it is to govern the technological society.

In the face of these social and political illusions, there is a growing feeling that the political images that used to facilitate man's adaptation to his environment no longer do so: "The present greatly renewed interest in

[27]Jacques Ellul, "Modern Myths," *Diogenes,* Vol. 23 (Fall 1958), 23-40; Jacques Ellul, *Propaganda: The Formation of Men's Attitudes* (New York: Knopf, 1965), p. 117; Jacques Ellul, *The Political Illusion* (New York: Knopf, 1967); Jacques Ellul, "Technique, Institutions, and Awareness," *American Behavioral Scientist,* Vol. 11 (July-August 1968), 38-42; Jacques Ellul, *The Technological Society* (New York: Knopf, 1965).

symbols is one of the more revealing symptoms of our present discontents. Quite apart from its intrinsic intellectual interest, it is a product of the simple fact that our old symbols are giving us trouble. On the one side, they are losing power because it is suspected that they have no content; on the other side, the reaction is to use those symbols with an increasingly exclusive regard for their feeling-tone alone."[28] There are many images binding us *affectively* to the political environment, but there is a poverty of images that contribute to popular *cognitive* understanding and control over politics.[29]

Of course, there is no empirical evidence that work, progress, and happiness are the galvanizing myths of modern man; nor is there any certainty that people fool themselves regarding how much they know about politics, or fool themselves about the degree of control they have over policy makers, or the technical character of governing. In sum, critics of the illusions in contemporary political images could be wrong. But, even if we discount the major premises of the current critics of modern politics, we still live with the nagging possibility that popular images of politics are fictions, that mass beliefs are false and mass trust misplaced. If people find the dramatic imagery of politics *subjectively* pleasing this does not necessarily mean that political images are objectively real. We need not accept the premise that because a person's political images are *his* political actions that they do or should determine the behavior of others. While political images may perform crucial instrumental, evaluative, and expressive functions for individuals and social groups, those images may not promote adaptive behavior. We must ask the question, under what conditions can political images be both adaptive and gratifying for self-images? Or, putting it another way, how can political images contribute to rational self-competence rather than nonrational self-delusion?

SELF-COMPETENCE AND ADAPTIVE IMAGERY

What is rational behavior? There is no simple answer. Our brief discussion of rationality is neither definitive nor comprehensive. The only intent is to put the topic within the general framework of political images developed throughout this work. In the most straightforward sense, the rational person knows what he wants, calculates alternative ways to get it, and selects the one with the least cost or the most favorable cost. If emotions, such as prejudice, fear, frustration, anger, hate, etc., impair his perceptions of ends and means, he is not acting rationally. Put in the terms

[28]Charles Frankel, "Liberalism and Political Symbols," *Antioch Review,* Vol. 13 (September 1953), 351.

[29]Orrin E. Klapp, *Collective Search for Identity* (New York: Holt, Rinehart & Winston, 1969), Chapter 9.

we have been using, if a person applies his own images too rigidly to external objects, making the outside world fit the needs of his ego (symbolic play), his behavior will be nonrational, closed-minded, and dogmatic;[30] on the other side of the coin, if a person unthinkingly accommodates all of his beliefs, values, and predispositions to symbolic appeals (imitation), his behavior will be nonrational because he is too flexible and he lacks self-autonomy.

Human beings are neither purely rational nor nonrational. In some matters (in the pursuit of wealth, well-being, knowledge, and skill) their political images are cognitive tools for gathering and weighing evidence, reflecting on the political drama, understanding it and acting in it. In other matters such as in the search for status, morality, power, and love, their images are likely to be affective and emotion laden, providing deep meaning but frequently provoking self-gratifying, nonrational responses. Intelligent, political action rests upon a blend of calculated and emotional assessments.

Put in a slightly different way, rational action is minded or self-competent action. If we are *self-competent* we transact with our environment in adaptive ways. There is a reciprocal process of modifying our actions to suit the requirements of a changing environment while we change the environment to suit our dynamic needs. A precise description of the nature of competent behavior depends upon the continuing efforts of biological and behavioral scientists. For our purposes, however, we can piece together the major outlines of such a description from a number of valuable works that explore the dimensions of minded behavior.[31]

We begin by repeating that each person possesses a host of mental representations with distinctive cognitive, affective, and conative qualities. The totality of his images constitute what Kenneth Boulding calls the *Image* — everything he has learned about the world, correct or incorrect.[32] The Image is not a static inner representation, but it changes with a person's new experiences. His behavior depends upon that Image; through it he imagines what he will do. But, he does more than *imagine;* i.e., he behaves in accordance with what he imagines, and in doing this he undertakes a sequence of appropriate actions. This sequence is controlled by his

[30]Milton Rokeach, *The Open and Closed Mind* (New York: Basic Books, 1960); Henry S. Kariel, *Open Systems: Arenas for Political Action* (Itasca, Ill.: Peacock, 1969).

[31]George A. Miller, Eugene Galanter, and Karl H. Pribram, *Plans and the Structure of Behavior* (New York: Holt, Rinehart & Winston, 1960); Irwin D. J. Bross, *Design for Decision* (New York: Macmillan, 1953); Robert C. Carson, *Interaction Concepts of Personality* (Chicago: Aldine, 1969), Chapter 3; Karl W. Deutsch, *The Nerves of Government* (New York: Free Press, 1963); Alfred Kuhn, *The Study of Society* (Homewood, Ill.: Richard D. Irwin, and Dorsey, 1963).

[32]Kenneth E. Boulding, *The Image* (Ann Arbor, Mich.: University of Michigan Press, 1956); Hans G. Furth, *Piaget and Knowledge* (Englewood Cliffs, N.J.: Prentice-Hall, 1969), p. 261.

Plan: "Unless you can use your Image to do something, you are like a man who collects maps but never makes a trip . . . . a Plan is needed in order to exploit the Image."[33] A person's Plans are represented in his Image. They are like computer programs; i.e., the Plans are a series of instructions that control the order for performing a sequence of operations.

An important feature of Plans is that they incorporate feedback loops, that is, *mutual* action-reaction relations. In a feedback relationship A acts on B, while B simultaneously acts on A; the change in A affects B as the change in B affects A and so on. We have seen these mutual action-reaction relations before in image communication, in the development of political images, and elsewhere; indeed, our entire conception of imagery is of such a tranactional process. Feedback loops in computer programs permit the results of an operation to be matched, or tested, with some standard in order to determine what future operations to perform. In *Plans,* feedback provides data about the results of our actions, and this new information then assists us in modifying our subsequent behavior, our future Plans.

Take as a simple example the operation of an automobile. The driver "informs" or "orders" his vehicle to go a certain direction and speed by turning the steering wheel and pressing the accelerator. The orders given by the driver depend upon the driver's intentions, or Plans, and these in turn, flow from his imagining that he will be at a certain place at a certain time (his Image). Assume that he is traveling at high speed (action) and sees he is approaching a sharp curve (feedback); he turns the steering wheel while maintaining his speed (reaction and action) and quickly discerns he cannot negotiate the curve (feedback); he eases up on the accelerator (reaction), finds the going easier (feedback), completes the curve (action), notes the road is straighter (feedback), and proceeds at a higher speed (reaction and action). The driver's actions are at the same time both the cause and the effect of the vehicle's motion and vice versa.[34]

Through his Plans, a person exploits his Image. He visualizes where he was, is, and wants to be in relation to other objects (be they other people, places or events). On the basis of that Image he Plans and acts. From his action he obtains feedback as to its consequence, he matches those results against those he imagined and notes either congruity or incongruity. If the comparison indicates a discrepancy, he acts again to achieve greater correspondence, tests the consequences against intentions, incorporates the information into his Plan, and acts again. The process continues until expectation and realization correspond.

Certainly this outline of the relationship between images, plans, feedback, and action sequences is grossly oversimplified. A detailed

[33]Miller *et al., Plans and the Structure of Behavior,* p. 2.
[34]G. T. Guilbaud, *What is Cybernetics?* (New York: Grove Press, 1960), Chapter 2.

account of the processes underlying human behavior is far beyond the scope of this volume and is more properly the province of the works cited in the accompanying footnotes. However, with just one major qualification the outline provides a framework for considering the qualities of self-competence in political behavior. Perhaps that qualification is obvious — namely, not all Plans are consciously and deliberately formulated and executed. Some become largely routinized and automatic (such as walking, riding a bicycle, and perhaps even voting) and fall in the realm of what the dramatistic analyst calls "motion" rather than "action." Moreover, most people go through their daily lives only dimly aware of many things they do, or they drift from year to year without carefully selected goals or concrete plans for reaching them. There is good reason for this, of course, for if every man's every action followed a conscious goal-plan-act-test-react-replan, act-test-etc. sequence, the psychic costs for living might well be intolerable. Thus, the Image-Plan-Action relationship is not restricted to purposive, deliberate, conscious behavior.

Having recognized this obvious qualification, however, we must not lose sight of the fact that competent behavior does include substantial elements of purposiveness in the formulation and execution of Plans. Competent, minded behavior means *coping* with our environment, creating an active-reactive person-environment exchange.[35] Coping involves both self-awareness and self-modification.

By self-awareness we don't just mean that each of us possesses a self-image (or a series of partisan, ideological, and other self-images) that we express through our response to political symbols. Self-awareness implies that we express a self-image and that we are aware of that expressed self-image. But self-awareness also implies adopting toward our own subjective images and actions the perspective of other people, endeavoring to see ourselves as others do and not simply as we would like to imagine others do. Self-awareness thus relies upon feedback, upon testing, upon being open to others, upon mutually assimilating others' views to our Image and accommodating that Image to their views.

Self-awareness contributes to self-modifying, or learning behavior. The self-aware person is capable of matching his private images against his experiences with others to modify his beliefs, values, and predispositions. There are two types of learning of which the self-competent person is capable. First, he is able to modify his behavior in order to reach a specific immediate goal; he continuously adjusts his Plans in keeping with the feedback he gets in concrete situations. Second, he is also able to make changes in the Image that implied the original goal, again on the basis of feedback; he thus is capable of changing goals as he acquires new infor-

[35]M. Brewster Smith, *Social Psychology and Human Values* (Chicago: Aldine, 1969), p. 237.

mation about his environment. The first type of learning — goal-seeking — involves immediate satisfactions, that is, an internal state in which a person's subjective images are reinforced or restored (as in symbolic play). But goal-changing involves accommodating his internal representations to external forces sufficiently to assure self-preservation.[36]

What has been said about self-competence in general applies to self-competence in political imagery. What does a politically self-competent person look like? It is perhaps easier to begin with what a politically self-competent person does *not* look like. He does not assume that the world as his subjectively experiences it carries the same meaning for others (he does not treat his "map" as the only map of the territory). He does not assume that his private representations of objects are wholly accurate (he does not even treat his map as if it were *the* territory). He does not think in static, fixed categories. "He does not treat as identical all things that have the same name; he does not exhibit two-valued orientations in which absolute good is pitted against absolute evil; he does not confuse reports with inferences, inferences with judgmental statements; he is cautious about applying generalizations to particulars, and so on."[37] In short, the politically self-competent individual copes with political objects by applying a healthy skepticism by which he discounts the "noise" contained both in symbolic messages and in his own subjective appraisals of those messages.

What does the political Image of the politically self-competent person look like? As to cognitive content, it is informed of alternative Images and Plans and open to self-examination and goal-changing. In affective content its categories of right and wrong apply to the consequences of actions rather than to some vaguely perceived moral or immoral qualities in the persons who propose them; moreover it is empathetic, capable of evaluating itself as others do. In its conative content it is expressive, but forthrightly so to the extent that private motives are revealed for public scrutiny and feedback, not to rationalize behavior; the expression of the competent self-image says that its holder has confidence in his own efficacy, has self-respect and personal initiative, and takes individual responsibility for his actions.[38]

To recommend self-competence is easier than to achieve it. Self-awareness, self-evaluation, and self-modification are hard tasks for all of us. It is no easy thing to know what we want, to compute realistically the probable ways and costs of achieving it, and to act to achieve it. This is so in any area of collective life — and particularly so in politics. One of the

[36]Deutsch, *The Nerves of Government*, pp. 91-93; David Elkind, ed., *Six Psychological Studies by Jean Piaget* (New York: Random House, 1967), Chapter 4.

[37]S. I. Hayakawa, *Symbol, Status, and Personality* (New York: Harcourt, Brace & World, 1953), pp. 52-53.

[38]Robert E. Lane, *Political Thinking and Consciousness* (Chicago: Markham, 1969), pp. 218-23.

reasons competent behavior is so hard, for political communities as well as for their citizens, is that we don't yet have Plans for how to achieve all the political ends enumerated in our Constitution's Preamble — a more perfect union, justice, domestic tranquility, common defense, general welfare, and the blessings of liberty. But, if we have no Plans we also have no Image. How do we imagine an unpolluted environment, an equitable welfare system, adequate health care, a progressive tax structure, efficient law enforcement, a fair judiciary, a representative government, or even liberty, justice, and equality? Would we recognize the Good Life if we encountered it?

The fact that it is hard to achieve adaptive imagery raises the question of what social conditions facilitate it. Social scientists and philosophers concerned with that question have suggested numerous conditions which we can summarize as opportunity, respect, resources, and risk.[39] A society provides *opportunity* when it gives us hope that, with appropriate efforts, we can expect desired outcomes; hope for improvement supplies the background in which we are free to imagine and to plan. *Respect* refers to a theme repeated many times in this volume, that is, our perceptions that others, including political authorities, take us seriously; we will perceive that politicians are unconcerned unless leaders provide substantive evidence that citizens count in policy making. By *resources* we mean sufficiently broad allocations of values in a population to guarantee us access to opportunities and enduring self-respect, as well as the respect of our fellows. Finally, if there are hope, respect, and resources, then there is the possibility for us to take *risks* without fearing that everything will be lost if we fail. We must be willing to risk changing even our most sacred political images in the face of contradictory messages from a changing environment:

> "It is the first step in sociological wisdom to recognize that the major advances in civilization are processes which all but wreck the societies in which they occur: — like unto an arrow in the hand of a child. The art of a free society consists first in the maintenance of the symbolic code; and secondly in fearlessness of revision, to secure that the code serves those purposes which satisfy an enlightened reason. Those societies which cannot combine reverence to their symbols with freedom of revision, must ultimately decay either from anarchy, or from the slow atrophy of a life stifled by useless shadows."[40]

Politics is dramatic action, and the images through which we play our roles, like the drama itself, are sometimes authentic and sometimes illusory. Political self-competence begins with our willingness to recognize the

---

[39]Smith, *Social Psychology and Human Values,* Chapter 15.

[40]Alfred North Whitehead, *Symbolism: Its Meaning and Effect* (New York: Macmillan, 1927), p. 88.

difference between the authentic and the illusory and explore the subtle ways that political action arises from a combination of the actor's rational understanding of the nature of politics and his emotional responses to the political situation.

a bibliographic note

More than half a century ago Edward Sapir, a pioneer in the systematic study of linguistics and social communication, urged us to investigate man's use of symbols in order to understand his behavior. Sapir went on to call for a *science of symbols*. In 1956 in his very provocative little book, *The Image* (Ann Arbor: University of Michigan Press, 1956), Kenneth E. Boulding also suggested such a science which he labeled "Eiconics," — a cross-disciplinary investigation of the "message-image" relationship. Message-image relationship refers to how images are modified by symbolically presented information and how they in turn influence symbolically presented information. Neither Sapir's science of symbols nor Boulding's eiconics exist as separate disciplines today, but the study of symbols and images is the focal point of interests unifying scholars in such widely diverse disciplines as biology, communications engineering, the various social and behavioral sciences, and the humanities. The purpose of this bibliographic note is to introduce the reader to the principal works of these disciplines that are most pertinent to the concerns touched upon in this book.

This note is neither comprehensive nor exhaustive. The reader should supplement it by following up on the citations contained in the footnotes to the various chapters. It consists of bibliographic observations in six major areas. The first section touches upon works that indicate the similarity of interests in efforts of persons who study images, symbols, and attitudes. Section two lists major works pertaining to the communication of images, particularly political images. The third suggests references from learning, attitude-change, and developmental theories that provide insights into the formation and adoption of political images. The fourth section is devoted to surveying a few of the major empirical studies of mass attitudes that fairly may be treated within the framework of political images. The fifth section deals with alternative frameworks for the study of imagery, expecially from dramaturgical and cybernetic theories. The final section lists works discussing the principal techniques employed for studying political images. Roughly, the first section consists of references related to Chapter One; section two contains references employed in Chapter Two; section three parallels Chapter Three; section four lists studies that round out the surveys of popular images contained in Chapters Four and Five; and the fifth section of this note reviews material relevant to the dramatistic theory reviewed in Chapter Six.

The reader will notice in examining the suggested works that many of them do not make explicit reference to images of politics but talk about symbols, beliefs, values, opinions, attitudes, orientations, and so on. This should not be surprising for, as pointed out in the Introduction of this work, it has been our task to use the notion of images as a rubric under which we might organize, integrate, and synthesize a great deal of research pertaining to the symbolic and subjective aspects of politics. In performing that task, we have therefore ranged across several disciplines to discover those studies which might best illustrate the character of political imagery even though the studies were originally undertaken with different purposes in mind. The reader is free to determine for himself how relevant such studies are to enhancing his understanding of the images of politics.

IMAGES, SYMBOLS, AND ATTITUDES: CONCEPTS AND PERSPECTIVES

Although there is a great deal of interest expressed by political journalists in image-candidates, image-making, image-merchandising, etc., social scientists have made relatively little use of either the concept of images or imagery in studying human behavior. There are exceptions as, for instance, Robert Jervis, *The Logic of Images in International Relations* (Princeton: Princeton University Press, 1970), but generally political scientists have preferred to employ such concepts as symbolism, attitudes, and symbolic behavior. It is an underlying assumption of this text that the notion of imagery is a useful synthesizing concept in studying political activity and that discussion of political images should not be monopolized by political columnists. With this in mind we shall list in this section some of the major works that provide systematic introductions to imagery and/or symbolism in human behavior.

The beginning point for acquiring an understanding of the rich possibilities in studying images is the afore-mentioned work by Kenneth E. Boulding, *The Image*. In it he employs the distinction between the overlapping and interdependent aspects of an image — the symbolic and subjective — that has been used throughout our discussion of political images. Boulding explores images in biological organisms, social collectivities, politics, economics, history, and philosophy. A less systematic but still insightful use of the image notion is in Daniel J. Boorstin, *The Image, Or What Happened to the American Dream* (New York: Atheneum, 1962). A few of the problems connected with the unsystematic use of the concept of images are discussed by Leo P. Crespi in "Some Observations on the Concept of Images," *Public Opinion Quarterly*, Vol. 25 (Spring 1961), 115-20. Public relations specialists have long used notions of images in their work; for how they approach the subject see Albert J. Sullivan, "Toward a Philosophy of Public Relations: Images," in Otto Lerbinger and Albert J. Sullivan, eds., *Information, Influence, and Communication* (New York: Basic Books, 1965), pp. 240-52. Consult Rudolf Arnheim, *Visual Thinking* (London: Faber and Faber, 1969) and Mardi Jon Horowitz, *Image Formation and Cognition* (New York: Appleton-Century-Crofts, 1971), for ways in which the concept is used in the study of visual perception. And, in noting works that contribute to the development of image as a concept, we should not ignore Walter Lippmann's discussion of stereotypes in *Public Opinion* (New York: Macmillan, 1922).

In studying any organism one of the principal foci of interest is the exchanges that occur between that organism and its environment. The organism's image provides a convenient way for organizing these transactions. A useful discussion of the nature of such transactions is Heinz von Foerster, "From Stimulus to Symbol: The Economy of Biological Computation," in Walter Buckley, ed., *Modern Systems Research for the Behavioral Scientist* (Chicago: Aldine, 1968). In our discussion imagery has been viewed from a transactional perspective; i.e., images consist of a person's subjective appraisals of symbolic stimuli with the symbolic-subjective taken together rather than as independent isolated units. The nature of such a transactional perspective in studying human behavior can best be understood by consulting two difficult but rewarding works: Arthur F. Bentley, *Behavior, Knowledge, Fact* (Bloomington, Ind.: Principia Press, 1935) and John Dewey and Arthur F. Bentley, *Knowing and the Known* (Boston: Beacon Press, 1949). Applications of this perspective, either explicit or implicit, can be found in Hadley Cantril et al., "Psychology and Scientific Research, III, The Transactional View in Psychological Research," *Science*, Vol. 110 (1949), 517-22; Hans Toch and Malcolm S.

MacLean, Jr., "Perception, Communication and Educational Research: A Transactional View," *Audio-Visual Communication Review,* Vol. 10 (July 1970), 55-76; W. R. Bion, *Experiences in Groups* (New York: Basic Books, 1961); Kenneth J. Gergen, *The Psychology of Behavior Exchange* (Reading, Mass.: Addison-Wesley, 1969); Arthur F. Bentley, *The Process of Government* (Chicago: University of Chicago Press, 1908); and William Stephenson, *The Study of Behavior* (Chicago: University of Chicago Press, 1953).

The body of writing on symbolism is much greater than that explicitly on imagery. The classic introduction is Edward Sapir's article entitled "Symbolism" in the *Encyclopedia of the Social Sciences* (New York: Macmillan, 1930), pp. 492-95. Most writers on the subject distinguish between *sign* and *symbol.* For some a sign is simply any action that elicits a response and a symbol denotes the sign plus its meaning. The variety of distinctions can be sampled by examining Alfred North Whitehead, *Symbolism: Its Meaning and Effect* (New York: Macmillan, 1927); the excellent discussion and illustration by W. Lloyd Warner, *The Living and the Dead* (New Haven: Yale University Press, 1959); Heinz Werner and B. Kaplan, *Symbol Formation* (New York: John Wiley, 1963); Suzanne Langer's description of the overlap in symbols and images in *Philosophy in a New Key: A Study in the Symbolism of Reason, Rite, and Art* (Cambridge, Mass.: Harvard University Press, 1942); Anselm Strauss, *Mirrors and Masks: The Search for Identity* (Glenco, Ill.: Free Press, 1959); Chapter 10, "Symbol Spheres," of Hans Gerth and C. Wright Mills, *Character and Social Structure* (New York: Harcourt, Brace, & World, 1953); Thomas Luckmann, *The Invisible Religion: The Transformation of Symbols in Industrial Society* (New York: Macmillan, 1967); Edward T. Hall. *The Silent Language* (New York: Fawcett, 1959); Martin Foss, *Symbols and Metaphor in Human Experience* (Princeton: Princeton University Press, 1949); Lyman Bryson, ed., *Symbols and Values: An Initial Study* (New York: Harper, 1954); and Theodore Thass-Thienemann, *Symbolic Behavior* (New York: Washington Square Press, 1968). Some of these works, such as Werner or Gerth and Mills, reflect a sociological perspective; others are philosophical (Whitehead) or psychological (Thass-Theinemann). The works of Ernst Cassirer offer even a more general definition of symbolism as characterizing all human activity. See his *Philosophy of Symbolic Forms* (New Haven: Yale University Press, 1944). Finally, just to get an idea of how pervasive symbolism has been in the life of man, the reader should browse through J. E. Cirlot's *A Dictionary of Symbols* (New York: Philosophical Library, 1962); if the student prefers to learn something about symbolism in America, he should consult Ernst Lehner, *American Symbols* (New York: William Penn Publishing, 1957).

The school of symbolic interaction in sociology is one of the major sources for many of the views expressed in our discussion of political imagery. The classic work to consult is George Herbert Mead's *Mind,*

Self, and Society (Chicago: University of Chicago Press, 1934). For those who prefer shorter descriptions of the symbolic interactionist's perspective three excellent summaries are Arnold M. Rose, "A Systematic Summary of Symbolic Interaction Theory," in his edited volume, *Human Behavior and Social Processes: An Interactionist Approach* (Boston: Houghton, Mifflin, 1962), pp. 3-19; Bernard N. Meltzer, "Mead's Social Psychology," in Jerome G. Manis and Bernard N. Meltzer, eds., *Symbolic Interaction* (Boston: Allyn & Bacon, 1967), pp. 5-24; and Herbert Blumer, "Society as Symbolic Interaction," in Manis and Meltzer, eds., *Symbolic Interaction,* pp. 139-48. In the same volume Blumer spells out the research implications of the symbolic interactionist position in "Sociological Analysis and 'The Variable,' " pp. 84-94. Other useful works include Walker Percy, "Symbol Consciousness and Intersubjectivity," *Journal of Philosophy,* Vol. 34 (December 1970), 922-34; Tamotsu Shibutanti, *Society and Personality* (Englewood Cliffs, N. J.: Prentice-Hall, 1961); and Peter McHugh, *Defining the Situation: The Organization of Meaning in Social Interaction* (New York: Bobbs-Merrill, 1968). For a lively and informative discussion of the wedding of symbolic interactionist and ethnomethodology approaches in sociology read Sanford M. Lyman and Marvin B. Scott, *A Sociology of the Absurd* (New York: Appleton-Century-Crofts, 1970).

A number of social scientists have explored the role of symbolism in politics. Among the most insightful analyses are Walter Bagehot, *The English Constitution* (New York: Oxford University Press, 1933) which discusses the significance of rite and ritual in political order. Graham Wallas's *Human Nature in Politics* (Lincoln: University of Nebraska Press, Bison Edition, 1962) is an excellent account of the function of emotion in politics. Any reader interested in symbols in politics should consult the works of Harold D. Lasswell; these include Lasswell et al., *Language of Politics* (New York: George W. Stewart, 1949), Lasswell et al., *The Comparative Study of Symbols* (Stanford: Stanford University Press, 1952), and Lasswell, *World Politics and Personal Insecurity* (New York: McGraw-Hill, 1935). Brief treatments of symbolism in politics can be found in Carl Joachim Friedrich, *Man and His Government* (New York: McGraw-Hill, 1963), pp. 94-136; Samuel Beer et al., on "Emotional Attitudes and Symbolism," in Beer et al., *Patterns of Government* (New York: Random House, 1962), pp. 42-45 (an excellent succinct discussion within an over-all descriptive framework); Charles Merriam, "The Credenda and Miranda of Power," in *Political Power* (New York: McGraw-Hill, 1934) is still worthwhile.

The political scientist who has concerned himself most directly with the analysis of the symbolic aspects of politics is Murray Edelman. In his *The Symbolic Uses of Politics* (Urbana: University of Illinois Press, 1964) he discusses how governing interests utilize symbols, language, ritual, drama, etc. to pacify masses with symbolic gratifications while pursuing tangible rewards for themselves; as a critique of this point of view one might wish to consult Michael N. Zald, "Politics and Symbols: A Review Article," *Sociological Quarterly,* Vol. 7 (Winter 1966), 85-91. Edelman extends his analysis to how symbols are used to arouse masses in *Politics as Symbolic Action: Mass Arousal and Quiescence* (Chicago: Markham, 1971).

Although ruling interests may placate their constituencies by substituting symbolic for material satisfactions, this does not make the symbolic rewards any less meaningful. Joyce M. Mitchell and William C. Mitchell argue that it is the task of governments to distribute *both* symbolic and material goods; see their chapter entitled "Symbolic Public Goods: Identification, Status and Morality," in *Political Analysis and Public Policy* (Chicago: Rand McNally, 1969), pp. 135-64. In his work *Symbolic Crusade* (Urbana: University of Illinois Press, 1966), Joseph R. Gusfield demonstrates that in some cases symbolic recognition of status may be far more meaningful in politics than simple material gain. An earlier treatise, Thurmond Arnold's *The Symbols of Government* (New Haven: Yale University Press, 1935) also describes the many uses of symbols in politics. Among other works available see Michael Walzer, "On the Role of Symbolism in Political Thought," *Political Science Quarterly,* Vol. 82 (June 1967), 191-204; Victor A. Thompson's discussion of dramaturgy in administrative organizations in *Modern Organization* (New York: Knopf, 1961), Chapter 7; Daniel Lerner, *The Passing of Traditional Society* (New York: Free Press, 1958); and Roger Cobb and Charles Elder, "Individual Orientations in the Study of Political Symbolism," *Social Science Quarterly,* Vol. 53 (June 1972), 79-90. A useful discussion of how symbols are used to expand political conflicts from narrow, private interests to wider, public groups is found in Roger W. Cobb and Charles D. Elder, *Participation in American Politics: The Dynamics of Agenda-Building* (Boston: Allyn & Bacon, 1972), Chapters 8 and 9. Recently a sociologist has offered a succinct summary of the relevance of treating politics as symbolic interaction; see Peter M. Hall, "A Symbolic Interactionist Analysis of Politics," *Sociological Inquiry,* Vol. 42 (1972).

One of the major themes developed in Chapter One of this book stressed the varieties of political imagery and their personal and social functions. The ideas on which that discussion is based are drawn from a large body of literature concerning the study of attitudes. Personal images and attitudes are essentially similar constructs referring to clusters of perceptions, beliefs, values, and predispositions. To explore the various definitions of the nature of attitudes, readers should consult the following: Marvin E. Shaw and Jack M. Wright, *Scales for the Measurement of Attitudes* (New York: McGraw-Hill, 1967), Chapter 1, and Bernard Berelson and Gary A. Steiner, *Human Behavior: An Inventory of Scientific Findings*

(New York: Harcourt, Brace & World, 1964), Chapter 14. The working distinction between attitudes and images is drawn by William Stephenson in *The Play Theory of Mass Communication* (Chicago: University of Chicago Press, 1967), Chapter 3.

The function that attitudes, and thereby images, perform for individuals is discussed in M. Brewster Smith, "The Personal Setting of Public Opinions: A Study of Attitudes Toward Russia," *Public Opinion Quarterly,* Vol. 11 (Winter 1947), 295-305; M. Brewster Smith, Jerome S. Bruner, and Robert W. White, *Opinions and Personality* (New York: John Wiley, 1956); and Daniel Katz, "Attitude Formation and Public Opinion," *The Annals of the American Academy of Political and Social Science,* Vol. 367 (September 1966), 150-62. The relationship between attitudes and behavior is always difficult to define, but the most helpful discussions are Ulf Himmelstrand, "Verbal Attitudes and Behavior: A Paradigm for the Study of Message Transmission and Transformation," *Public Opinion Quarterly,* Vol. 24 (Summer 1960), 224-50 and Howard J. Ehrlich, "Attitudes, Behavior, and the Intervening Variables," *The American Sociologist,* Vol. 4 (February 1969), 29-34.

The arbitrary division of the dimensions of images — the cognitive, affective, and conative — is based upon a long tradition in the study of attitudes. For a review of this tradition see Thomas M. Ostrom, "The Emergence of Attitude Theory: 1930-1950," in Anthony G. Greenwald, Timothy C. Brock, and Thomas M. Ostrom, eds., *Psychological Foundations of Attitudes* (New York: Academic, 1968), pp. 1-32. In the same volume one should also read Anthony G. Greenwald's "On Defining Attitude and Attitude Theory" for a summary of how the three dimensions relate to various theories of attitude-change. The content of the various dimensions of political attitudes are explored specifically in John H. Kessel, "Cognitive Dimensions and Political Activity," *Public Opinion Quarterly* (February 1965), pp. 377-89 and Lester Milbrath, "The Nature of Political Beliefs and the Relationship of the Individual to the Government," *American Behavioral Scientist,* Vol. 12 (November/December 1968), 28-36.

In typifying the varieties of imagery as instrumental, evaluative, and expressive, our discussion draws primarily upon the distinctions made by Talcott Parsons and Edward A. Shils in their chapter entitled "Systems of Value-Orientation," in Parsons and Shils, eds., *Toward a General Theory of Action* (New York: Harper & Row, Torchback Edition, 1962), pp. 159-89; also consult Parson's complex work, *The Social System* (Glencoe, Ill.: Free Press, 1951). The discussion of the social functions of imagery in Chapter Two, particularly the focus upon the images manifested through social hierarchies, is based on Harold D. Lasswell and Abraham Kaplan, *Power and Society* (New Haven: Yale University Press, 1950) and Hugh Dalziel Duncan, *Symbols in Society* (New York: Oxford University Press, 1968).

THE COMMUNICATION OF POLITICAL IMAGES

There are several excellent introductory works concerning the nature of effects of human communication. Among the most readable and easily grasped are David K. Berlo, *The Process of Communication* (New York: Holt, Rinehart & Winston, 1960) and J. L. Aranguren, *Human Communication* (New York: McGraw-Hill, 1967); Melvin L. DeFleur, *Theories of Mass Communication* (New York: McKay, 1966), and Charles R. Wright, *Mass Communication* (New York: Random House, 1964). Also excellent although more complex is Lee Thayer, *Communication and Communication Systems* (Homewood, Ill.: Richard D. Irwin, 1968); Lee Richardson, *Dimensions of Communication* (New York: Appleton-Century-Crofts, 1969); and Alex S. Edelstein, *Perspectives in Mass Communication* (Copenhagen: Einar Harcks Forlag, 1970). There are two excellent anthologies of theoretical approaches to the study of communications: Lee Thayer, ed., *Communication: Concepts and Perspectives* (Washington, D.C.: Spartan Books, 1967) and Frank E. X. Dance, *Human Communication Theory: Original Essays* (New York: Holt, Rinehart & Winston, 1967). A succinct readable review of the major theories of communication is available in Donald Cushman and George C. Whiting, "An Approach to Communication Theory: Toward Consensus on Rules," *The Journal of Communication,* Vol. 22 (September 1972), 217-38. Readers will also find the selections helpful in Dean C. Barnlund's edited volume, *Interpersonal Communication* (Boston: Houghton Mifflin, 1968).

Reviews of the known effects of mass communications on behavior include Joseph T. Klapper, *The Effects of Mass Communication* (Glencoe: Free Press, 1961); Otto N. Larsen, "Social Effects of Mass Communication," in Robert E. L. Faris, ed., *Handbook of Modern Sociology* (Chicago: Rand McNally, 1964), pp. 349-81; Percy Tannenbaum and Bradley Greenberg, "Mass Communication," in Paul R. Farnsworth, *The Annual Review of Psychology,* Vol. 19 (1968), 351-86; Bruce H. Westley, "Communication and Social Change," *American Behavioral Scientist,* Vol. 14 (May/June 1971), 719-46; and Walter Weiss, "Effects of Mass Media of Communication," in Gardner Lindzey and Elliot Aronson, *The Handbook of Social Psychology,* 2nd ed. (Reading, Mass.: Addison-Wesley, 2nd ed., 1969), pp. 77-195.

The semiotic of communication-semantics, syntactics, and pragmatics is distinguished in Charles W. Morris's volume, *Signs, Language and Behavior* (New York: Prentice-Hall, 1946). The divisions owe much to the work of Charles S. Peirce, as demonstrated by James K. Feibleman, *An Introduction to the Philosophy of Charles S. Peirce* (Cambridge, Mass.: M.I.T. Press, 1946) and Charles Morris, *The Pragmatic Movement in American Philosophy* (New York: Braziller, 1970). Among the works exploring the semantics of communication are S. I. Hayakawa, *Symbol, Status, and Personality* (New York: Harcourt, Brace, & World, 1963); C. K. Ogden and I. A. Richards, *The Meaning of Meaning* (New York: Harcourt, Brace & World, 1923); and Noam Chomsky, *Syntactic Structures* (New York: Gregory Lounz, 1957). Considered within the context of image communication, syntactics has been used to refer to transmission of messages. Information theories of message transmission are explained in J. R. Pierce, *Symbols, Signals, and Noise* (New York: Harper & Row, 1961); Colin Cherry, *On Human Communication* (New York: M.I.T. Press, 1957); Claude E. Shannon and Warren Weaver, *The Mathematical Theory of Communication* (Urbana: The University of Illinois Press, 1963); and Wilbur Schramm, "Information Theory and Mass Communication," *Journalism Quarterly* (Spring 1955), 131-46. The place of languages in message transmission is discussed in George N. Gordon, *The Lanauages of Communication* (New York: Hastings House, Publishers, 1970) and Ray L. Birdwhistell, *Kinesics and Context* (Philadelphia: University of Pennsylvania Press, 1970). A readable popularization of some of Birdwhistell's ideas can be found in Julius Fast, *Body Language* (New York: M. Evans and Company, 1970). The homophily-heterophily principle in communication is surveyed by Everett M. Rogers and Dilip K. Bhowmik, "Homophily-Heterophily: Rational Concepts for Communication Research," *Public Opinion Quarterly* Vol. 34 (Winter 1970-71), 523-38. An excellent pictorial summary of the way symbols have been employed by political interests to mobilize mass populations is Gary Yanker's *Prop Art* (New York: Darien House, 1972).

Many of the ideas expressed about the communication of political images have been drawn from the work undertaken into the pragmatics of communication. The best single introduction to that subject is Paul Watzlawick, Janet Beavin, and Don Jackson, *Pragmatics of Human Communication* (New York: Norton, 1967). There the reader will encounter the principle that "one cannot not communicate" that is the basis of much of image communication. The Watzlawick work also distinguishes between analogic and digital communication, a distinction worth considering in another context in Bronislaw Malinowski, *Magic, Science, and Religion* (Glencoe, Ill.: Free Press, 1948). A related work that should be consulted is the special issue of the *American Behavioral Scientist,* Vol. 10 (April 1967) edited by John H. Weakland and Janet Beavin and entitled "Communication in Behavior and Behavioral Science." In coming to grips with the pragmatics of image communication the reader should also consult John W. Fox, "The Concepts of Image and Adoption in Relation to Interpersonal Behavior," *Journal of Communication,* Vol. 17 (1967), 147-51; Harley C. Shands synthesizing article entitled "Outline of a General Theory of Communication: Implications of Normal and Pathological Schizogenesis," in Thayer, *Communication: Concepts and Perspectives,* pp.

97-134; and Robert C. Carson, *Interaction Concepts of Personality* (Chicago: Aldine, 1969). Two very readable works on the subject are George A. Miller, *The Psychology of Communication* (New York: Basic Books, 1967) and Don Fabun's handy little primer, *Communications: The Transfer of Meaning* (Beverly Hills, Cal.: Glencoe Press, 1968).

Few persons have had more impact on the terminology of discussing image communication than Marshall McLuhan. Among his important works are *The Gutenberg Galaxy* (Toronto: University of Toronto Press, 1962) and *Understanding Media: The Extensions of Man* (New York: New American Library, 1964). Some of McLuhan's notions are drawn from Harold A. Innis, *The Bias of Communication* (Toronto: University of Toronto Press, 1951). For an excellent introduction to the thoughts of both McLuhan and Innis see James W. Carey, "Harold Adam Innis and Marshall McLuhan," *Antioch Review* (Spring 1967), pp. 5-39. A healthy critique of McLuhan's notions is Kenneth Burke's "Medium as 'Message' " in Burke, *Language as Symbolic Action* (Berkeley, Cal.: University of California Press, 1968), pp. 410-18.

The parasocial and playlike character of mass communication is best spelled out by William Stephenson, *The Play Theory of Mass Communication*. Donald Horton and R. Richard Wohl provide a seminal piece on the subject in "Mass Communication and Para-Social Interaction," *Psychiatry,* Vol. 19 (1956), 215-29. Using Piaget's notions about the stages of development, Gerhart D. Wiebe discusses the ego-centered aspects of mass communications and distinguishes between directive, reinforcing, and restorative communications in "Two Psychological Factors in Media Audience Behavior," *Public Opinion Quarterly,* Vol. 33 (Winter 1969-70), 523-36. Hugh Dalziel Duncan spells out the symbolic nature of communication in *Communication and Social Order* (New York: Oxford University Press, 1962). Herbert E. Krugman has developed a thesis regarding how people passively learn their images from television because of its playlike character; see his "The Impact of Television: Learning without Involvement," *Public Opinion Quarterly,* Vol 29 (Fall 1965), 349-57 and "Passive Learning Through Television," written with Eugene L. Hartley, *Public Opinion Quarterly,* Vol. 34 (Summer 1970), 184-90. Krugman's thesis has been critiqued by Ivan L. Preston, "A Reinterpretation of the Meaning of Involvement in Krugman's Models of Advertising Communication," *Journalism Quarterly,* Vol. 47 (Summer 1970), 287-95.

The area of political communication generally has been explored in a number of works. One of the most useful is Kurt Lang and Gladys Engel Lang, *Politics and Television* (Chicago: Quadrangle Books, 1968). A provocative empirical analysis of the effects of television on voting is Jay G. Blumler and Denis McQuail, *Television in Politics* (Chicago: University of Chicago Press, 1969). A perspective for studying the effects of mass communication upon politics has been suggested by Herbert

Blumer, "Suggestions for the Study of Mass Media Effects," in Eugene Burdick and Arthur J. Brodbeck, *American Voting Behavior* (Glencoe, Ill.: Free Press, 1959), pp. 197-219. More general treatments of political communication are Ulf Himmelstrand, *Social Pressures, Attitudes and Democratic Processes* (Stockholm: Almquist and Wicksell, 1960) and Richard R. Fagen's survey, *Politics and Communication* (Boston: Little, Brown, 1968). For comparative purposes the reader should consult Leonard W. Doob, *Communication in Africa* (New Haven: Yale University Press, 1961); W. Phillips Davison, *International Political Communication* (New York: Frederick A. Praeger, 1965) and Lucian W. Pye, ed., *Communications and Political Development* (Princeton, N. J.: Princeton University Press, 1963).

THE FORMATION OF POLITICAL IMAGES

The learning of political images is a process that overlaps personality growth, social learning, attitude-change, and child development. Among the works dealing with personality growth the following have been especially helpful in providing a background for the discussion of image formation: Gordon W. Allport, *The Person in Psychology* (Boston: Beacon Press, 1968); A. Bandura and R. H. Walters, *Social Learning and Personality Development* (New York: Holt, Rinehart & Winston, 1963); H. J. Eysenck, *The Biological Basis of Personality* (Springfield, Ill,: Charles C Thomas, 1967); and Eugene A. Southwell and Michael Merbaum, eds., *Personality: Theory and Research* (Belmont, Cal.: Wadsworth Publishing, 1964). Intelligence as a factor influencing personality is considered in J. P. Guilford, *The Nature of Human Intelligence* (New York: McGraw-Hill, 1967); the implications of variations in intelligence for the formation of political attitudes is discussed in S. K. Harvey and T. G. Harvey, "Adolescent Political Outlooks: The Effects of Intelligence as an Independent Variable," *Midwest Journal of Political Science,* Vol. 14 (November 1970), 565-95. A. H. Maslow discusses the motivational background of personality growth in *Motivation and Personality* (New York: Harper & Row, 1954); see also David C. McClelland et al., *The Achievement Motive* (New York: Appleton, 1953). Among the works of political scientists tracing the influence of personality upon political attitudes are Robert E. Lane, *Political Ideology* (New York: Free Press, 1962); Lane's *Political Thinking and Consciousness* (Chicago: Markham, 1969); and Fred I. Greenstein's introductory survey, *Personality and Politics* (Chicago: Markham, 1969).

Social psychologist M. Brewster Smith presents a paradigm of the relationship between personality and politics in his "Personality in Politics: A Conceptual Map with Application to the Problem of Political

Rationality," in Oliver Garceau, ed., *Political Research and Political Theory* (Cambridge: Harvard University Press, 1969). Two useful applications of political psychology in empirical research are Giuseppe Di Palma and Herbert McClosky, "Personality and Conformity: The Learning of Political Attitudes," *American Political Science Review*, Vol. 64 (December 1970), 1054-73, and Steven R. Brown and John D. Ellithorp, "Emotional Experiences in Political Groups: The Case of the McCarthy Phenomenon," *American Political Science Review*, Vol. 64 (June 1970).

In addition to Bandura and Walters, *Social Learning and Personality Development,* and Berelson and Steiner, *Human Behavior,* another excellent survey of learning theory is Ernest R. Hilgard and Gordon H. Bower, *Theories of Learning* (New York: Appleton-Century-Crofts, 1966). In general, political scientists have conducted studies of the socialization of children into political attitudes with relatively little concern for social learning theories. There are, however, notable exceptions. For example, an application of the Bandura-Walters's approach in political socialization is in Herbert Hirsch, *Poverty and Politicization* (New York: Free Press, 1971). A useful outline of the basic elements of learning theory as they relate to politics is to be found in Richard Merelman, "Learning and Legitimacy," *American Political Science Review,* Vol. 60 (September 1966), 548-61.

The literature pertaining to attitude-change is voluminous and growing larger. Among the best introductory surveys to the subject are the following: Charles A. Kiesler, Barry E. Collins, and Norman Miller, *Attitude Change* (New York: John Wiley, 1969); Chester A. Insko, *Theories of Attitude Change* (New York: Appleton-Century-Crofts, 1967); Arthur R. Cohen, *Attitude Change and Social Influence* (New York: Basic Books, 1964) and Philip Zimbardo and Ebbe E. Ebbesen, *Influencing Attitudes and Changing Behavior* (Reading, Mass.: Addison-Wesley, 1969). There are two general bodies of literature in attitude-change. The first deals with cognitive-affective-conative consistency in changing attitudes. Among the works discussing the better-known variants of consistency theory are Leon Festinger, *A Theory of Cognitive Dissonance* (Evanston, Ill.: Row Peterson, 1957); Fritz Heider, *The Psychology of Interpersonal Relations* (New York: John Wiley, 1958); Muzafer Sherif and C. I. Hovland, *Social Judgment* (New Haven: Yale University Press, 1961); and Carolyn W. Sherif, Muzafer Sherif, and Roger E. Nebergall, *Attitude and Attitude Change* (Philadelphia: Saunders, 1965). The second body of literature deals with relating attitude-change to learning processes. The best single work here is the volume edited by Anthony G. Greenwald et al., *Psychological Foundations of Attitudes,* especially the article by William J. McGuire, "Personality and Attitude Change: An Information Processing Theory," pp. 171-96.

The discussion of image adoption in this volume borrows a great deal from the concepts and theories of Jean Piaget's developmental psychology.

Such notion as stages of development, adaptive behavior, assimilation-accommodation, play, and imitation are Piaget's. For the essence of developmental theories of image formation the reader should, therefore, turn first to the work of Piaget. The place to begin is with commentaries on Piaget's work. The best of these are: Hans G. Furth, *Piaget and Knowledge: Theoretical Foundations* (Englewood Cliffs, N. J.: Prentice-Hall, 1969); J. H. Flavell, *The Developmental Psychology of Jean Piaget* (New York: Van Nostrand, 1963); Alfred L. Baldwin, *Theories of Child Development* (New York: John Wiley, 1968), pp. 171-300 containing the section entitled "The Theory of Jean Piaget"; Eleanor Maccoby, "The Development of Moral Values and Behavior in Childhood," in John A. Clausen, *Socialization and Society* (Boston: Little, Brown, 1968), pp. 227-69; and Albert Mehrabian, *An Analysis of Personality Theories* (Englewood Cliffs, N. J.: Prentice-Hall, 1968), Chapter 5, entitled "Cognitive-Developmental Approaches to Personality Theory." The reader should then read the important works of Piaget: he discusses his general approach in "A Theory of Development," *International Encyclopedia of the Social Sciences* (New York: Macmillan, 1970), pp. 140-47; an overview of these theories can be found in the volume edited by David Elkind, *Six Psychological Studies of Jean Piaget* (New York: Random House, 1967); Piaget explains cognitive development in his *The Origins of Intelligence in Children* (New York: Norton, 1952); he treats moral development in *The Moral Judgment of the Child* (New York: Free Press, 1965); and the essentials of his notions of adaptive behavior versus play and imitation are in *Play, Dreams, and Imitation in Childhood* (New York: Norton, 1962). But developmental theory is not the monopoly of Piaget and at least two other researchers should be consulted in rounding out the discussion in this volume of image formation. Two works of Lawrence Kohlberg are noteworthy: "Development of Moral Character and Moral Ideology," in Martin L. Hoffman and L. W. Hoffman, eds., *Child Development Research*, Vol. 1 (New York: Russell Sage, 1964), 383-41, and "The Development of Children's Orientations Toward a Moral Order: I. Sequence in the Development of Moral Thought," *Vita Humana* (1963), 11-33. The works of Uriel G. Foa are also important including "Perception of Behavior in Reciprocal Roles: The Ringex Model," *Psychological Monographs*, Vol. 80 (1966), 1-21 and "New Developments in Facet Design and Analysis," *Psychological Review*, Vol. 72 (1965), 262-74.

Among political scientists who have applied developmental perspectives to their work the leading one is Richard Merelman. See his "The Development of Political Ideology: A Framework for the Analysis of Political Socialization," *American Political Science Review*, Vol. 63 (September 1969), 750-67, and "The Development of Policy Thinking in Adolescence," *American Political Science Review*, Vol. 65 (December 1971), 1033-47. Charles F. Andrian has applied developmental theory to the learning of political attitudes; see his *Children and Civic Awareness* (Columbus, Ohio: Charles E. Merrill, 1971). Robert E. Lane makes use of Kohlberg's model in *Political Thinking and Consciousness,* pp. 192-212. Piaget turns his attention to a problem of political learning in "The Development in Children of the Idea of the Homeland and of Relations with Other Countries," *International Social Science Bulletin,* Vol. 3 (1951), 561-78; for a critique of his theory and methods see Gustav Jahoda, "Children's Concepts of Nationality: A Critical Study of Piaget's Stages," *Child Development,* Vol. 35 (1964), 1081-92.

The empirical studies on which we have relied for data regarding the formation of political images are those conducted by political scientists under the rubric of political socialization. There is a large body of research in this area. Among the introductory surveys, which vary considerably in quality, are the following: Herbert Hyman, *Political Socialization* (Glencoe, Ill.: Free Press, 1959); Kenneth P. Langton, *Political Socialization* (New York: Oxford University Press, 1969), which reports a comparative study of American and Jamaican children as well as reviewing the basic literature; and Richard E. Dawson and Kenneth Prewitt, *Political Socialization* (Boston: Little, Brown, 1969). In addition, there are numerous anthologies and readers such as Norman Adler and Charles Harrington, eds., *The Learning of Political Behavior* (New York: Scott, Foresman, 1970); and Roberta Sigel, *Learning About Politics* (New York: Random House, 1970). Two special volumes of professional journals worth consulting are "Youth and Society," *Social Science Quarterly,* Vol. 49 (September 1968) and "Political Socialization: Its Role in the Political Process," *The Annals of the American Academy of Political and Social Science,* Vol. 361 (September 1965).

The leading book-length studies reporting empirical research in political socialization, in addition to the Andrian and Hirsch volumes mentioned previously in this section, are Fred I. Greenstein, *Children and Politics* (New Haven: Yale University Press, 1965); Robert Hess and Judith Torney, *The Development of Political Attitudes in Children* (Chicago: Aldine, 1967); and David Easton and Jack Dennis, *Children in the Political System: Origins of Political Legitimacy* (New York: McGraw-Hill, 1969). There are far too many article-length studies to permit the compilation of a representative list here. For those most relevant to the discussion of image formation, the reader is advised to check the footnotes in Chapter 3. The impact of mass communications upon political socialization has not been explored extensively, but useful insights can be found in the following: Steven H. Chaffee, L. Scott Ward, and Leonard P. Tipton, "Mass Communication and Political Socialization," *Journalism Quarterly,* Vol. 47 (Winter 1970), 647-59; the special issue of the *American Behavioral Scientist* entitled "Mass Communication and Youth: Some Current Perspectives," Vol. 14 (January/February, 1971); and Seymour Feshbach and

Robert D. Singer, *Television and Aggression* (San Francisco: Jossey-Bass, 1971).

IMAGES OF PUBLIC SUPPORTS AND CONCERNS

Chapters Four and Five rest upon the view that it is useful to distinguish between certain elements in a mass society — the mass, the attentives, and the elites. William Kornhauser's *The Politics of Mass Society* (Glencoe, Ill.: Free Press, 1959) is useful in contrasting mass societies with other social collectivities. Also very valuable is Herbert Blumer's essay, "The Mass, the Public, and Public Opinion," in Alfred McClung Lee, *New Outline of the Principles of Sociology* (New York: Barnes & Noble, 1946), pp. 185-93. The concept of attentive publics is developed in the following: Gabriel A. Almond, *The American People and Foreign Policy* (New York: Praeger, 1960); James N. Rosenau, *Public Opinion and Foreign Policy* (New York: Random House, 1961); and Donald J. Devine, *The Attentive Public* (Stokie, Ill.: Rand McNally, 1970). Devine's recent work, *The Political Culture of the United States* (Boston: Little, Brown, 1972) is the best single work available surveying the distribution of values that contribute to the preservation of the American political regime. An excellent introduction to the role of elites in mass society is Suzanne Keller, *Beyond the Ruling Class: Strategic Elites in Modern Society* (New York: Random House, 1963). Several works provide a comparative account, using empirical data, of the political supports and concerns manifested by mass populations. Among the principal ones on which the discussion in this text has relied are Hadley Cantril, *The Pattern of Human Concerns* (New Brunswick, N. J.: Rutgers University Press, 1965); Gabriel A. Almond and Sidney Verba, *The Civic Culture* (Princeton, N.J.: Princeton University Press, 1963); Guiseppe Di Palma, *Apathy and Participation: Mass Politics in Western Societies* (New York: Free Press, 1970); George Katona, Burkhard Strumpel, and Ernest Zahn, *Aspirations and Affluence* (New York: McGraw-Hill, 1971); and Lucian Pye and Sidney Verba, eds., *Political Culture and Political Development* (Princeton, N.J.: Princeton University Press, 1965).

Discussions of political support usually rely upon the conceptualization of the systems model developed by David Easton. His thinking is spelled out in *A Systems Analysis of Political Life* (New York: John Wiley, 1965). William A. Gamson has done a great deal to focus attention upon political trust; see his *Power and Discontent* (Homewood, Ill.: Dorsey, 1968) and his essay, "Political Trust and Its Ramifications," in Gilbert Abcarian and John W. Soule, eds., *Social Psychology and Political Behavior* (Columbus, Ohio: Charles E. Merrill, 1971), pp. 41-55. See also James C. Davies, *Human Nature in Politics* (New York: John Wiley, 1963). Joel D. Aberbach and Jack L. Walker have provided two reports of empirical research into the bases of political trust; see their "Political Trust and Racial Ideology," *American Political Science Review*, Vol. 64 (December 1970), pp. 1199-1219 and "The Meanings of Black Power: A Comparison of White and Black Interpretations of a Political Slogan," *American Political Science Review*, Vol. 64 (June 1970), 367-88. Milton Rokeach and Seymour Parker provide data related to the sources of political trust in "Values as Social Indicators of Poverty and Race Relations in America," *The Annals of the American Academy of Political and Social Science*, Vol. 388 (March 1970), 97-111.

There are several studies of how symbolism is used to promote national unity. Certainly one of the best is Edward Shils and Michael Young, "The Meaning of the Coronation," *Sociological Review*, Vol. 1 (December 1953), 63-81. Herbert Feith describes how political elites exploit symbols to obtain the support of masses in his "Indonesia's Political Symbols and their Wielders," *World Politics*, Vol. 16 (October 1963), 79-97. Other studies of particular interest are Bernard Barber, "Place, Symbol, and Utilitarian Function in War Memorials," *Social Forces*, Vol. 28 (October, 1949), pp. 64-68; A. Parel, "Symbolism in Gandhian Politics," *Canadian Journal of Political Science*, Vol. 2 (December 1969), pp. 13-27; and M. Servin, "Religious Aspects of Symbolic Acts of Sovereignty," Vol. 13 (January 1957), 255-67. The leading work in the content analysis of symbols as indicators of national integration is Richard L. Merritt, *Symbols of American Community*, 1735-1775 (New Haven: Yale University Press, 1966).

Diffuse support for American political institutions has become a topic of increasing interest for political scientists in recent years. Edward N. Muller outlines the theoretical problem and provides empirical evidence in his "Correlates and Consequences of Beliefs in the Legitimacy of Regime Structures," *Midwest Journal of Political Science*, Vol. 14 (August 1970), pp. 392-412 and "The Representation of Citizens by Political Authorities: Consequences for Regime Support," *American Political Science Review*, Vol. 64 (December 1970), 1149-66. The matter is more generally discussed by John C. Wahlke, "Policy Demands and System Support: The Role of the Represented," *British Journal of Political Science*, Vol. 1 (July 1971), 271-91. Diffuse support for legislative systems is explored in G. R. Boynton et al., "The Structure of Public Support for Legislative Institutions," *Midwest Journal of Political Science*, Vol. 12 (February 1968), 163-80 and Samuel C. Patterson et al., "Perceptions and Expectations of the Legislature and Support for It," *American Journal of Sociology*, Vol. 745 (July 1969), 62-76. The judiciary comes in for its share of attention in Walter Murphy and Joseph Tanenhaus, "Public Opinion and the United States Supreme Court," *Law and Society Review*, Vol. 1 (1968), 357-84 and Harry P. Stumpf, "Political Efficacy of Judicial Symbolism," *Western Political Quarterly*, Vol. 19 (June 1966), 293-303. Merlin Gustafson in his "The Religious Role of the President," *Midwest Journal of Political Science*, Vol. 14 (November 1970) traces one source of diffuse support for the presidency. The only broad empirical study of views of the federal bureaucracy is Franklin P. Kilpatrick et al., *The Image of the Federal Service* (Washington, D.C.: Brookings Institution, 1964). Jack Dennis has explored diffuse support for two major political institutions in America in "Support for the Party System by the Mass Public," *American Political Science Review*, Vol. 40 (September 1966), 600-615 and "Support for the Institution of Elections by the Mass Public," *American Political Science Review*, Vol. 64 (September 1970), pp. 600-615.

Orrin E. Klapp is a sociologist who has focused a great deal of interest upon the phenomenon of symbolic leadership. His works are useful and easy to read: *Heroes, Villains and Fools* (Englewood Cliffs, N. J.: Prentice-Hall, 1962) and *Symbolic Leaders* (Chicago: Aldine, 1964). William C. Mitchell demonstrates how American politicians engage in symbolic leadership in *The American Polity* (New York: Free Press, 1962), pp. 123-44. John E. Mueller provides useful data in "Presidential Popularity from Truman to Johnson," *American Political Science Review*, Vol. 64 (March 1970), 18-34. D. R. Stewart and T. C. Smith indicate one form of symbolic leadership in "Celebrity Structure of the Far Right," *Western Political Quarterly*, Vol. 17 (June 1964), 349-55. And, for a fascinating account of the techniques of public denunciation open to political leaders read Harold Garfinkel, "Conditions of Successful Degradation Ceremonies," *American Journal of Sociology*, Vol. 61 (March 1956), 420-24.

The imagery and/or symbolism of social movements and ideologies has given rise to several studies. Joseph Gusfield's *Symbolic Crusade* is certainly one of the most interesting. Leon Festinger et al., *When Prophesy Fails*, has many insights into the images of people who believe that the world is coming to an end. The agrarian movement's use of imagery is discussed in Louis Galambos, "Agrarian Image of the Large Corporation, 1879-1920: A Study of Social Accommodation," *Journal of Economic History*, Vol. 28 (September 1968), 341-62. Jerry L. Simmons provides a discussion of popular images of movements that do not conform to social norms in *Deviants* (San Francisco: Glendessary Press, 1969). Considering works most useful for acquiring an acquaintance with the nature of images in mass ideologies and belief systems one should begin with Philip E. Converse's oft-quoted article, "The Nature of Belief Systems in Mass Publics," in David E. Apter, ed., *Ideology and Discontent* (New York: Free Press, 1964), pp. 205-56. Compare this to the argument made by Giovanni Sartori in "Politics, Ideology, and Belief Systems," *American Political Science Review*, Vol. 63 (June 1969), 398-411; Steven R. Brown in "Consistency and the Persistence of Ideology: Some Experimental Results," *Public Opinion Quarterly*, Vol. 34 (Spring 1970), 60-68; and John Osgood Field and Ronald E. Anderson, "Ideology in the Public's Conception of the 1964 Election," *Public Opinion Quarterly*, Vol. 33 (February

1969), 380-98. Sophisticated discussions of the nature of ideologies are found in Charles Geertz, "Ideology as a Cultural System," in Apter, *Ideology and Discontent,* pp. 47-76 and Ben Halpern, " 'Myth' and 'Ideology' in Modern Usage," *History and Theory,* Vol. I (1961), 129-49. Discussions of the role of ideological self-images in American politics include R. S. Brooks, "Self and Political Role: A Symbolic Interactionist Approach to Political Ideology," *Sociological Quarterly,* Vol. 10 (Winter 1969), 22-31; Lloyd A. Free and Hadley Cantril, *The Political Beliefs of Americans* (New Brunswick, N. J.: Rutgers University Press, 1967); and Robert E. Lane, *Political Ideology* (New York: Free Press, 1962).

Political scientists in America and other political systems have devoted a great deal of time, money, and energy in recent decades to the study of voting behavior. In the process they have generated a large body of data, interpretations, and theories about the relative impact of partisan self-images, party images, candidate images, and issue images upon voting. The most relevant of the voting studies for understanding images of politics have been cited in the footnotes of Chapter 5 and little could be gained by reviewing them here. In preference to that we will list here only the major studies that have dealt in reasonably specific ways with images and voting behavior. These include the three major volumes rising out of the studies of the Survey Research Center, University of Michigan: Angus Campbell, Gerald Gurin, and Warren E. Miller, *The Voter Decides* (New York: Harper, Row, 1954); Angus Campbell, Philip E. Converse, Warren E. Miller, and Donald E. Stokes, *The American Voter* (New York: John Wiley, 1960); and Angus Campbell, Philip E. Converse, Warren E. Miller, and Donald E. Stokes, *Elections and the Political Order* (New York: John Wiley, 1966). In addition, Bernard R. Berelson, Paul F. Lazarsfeld, and William N. McPhee, *Voting* (Chicago: University of Chicago Press, 1954) deals with popular perceptions of issues, candidates, and parties. The effects of the campaign upon perceptions of the candidates in the 1964 presidential campaign is discussed in John H. Kessel, *The Goldwater Coalition* (Indianapolis: Bobbs-Merrill, 1968), Chapter 9. A useful report of data gathered during the 1968 presidential campaign regarding political images is The American Institute for Political Communication publication, *Anatomy of a Crucial Election* (Washington, D.C., 1970). Two major studies have dealt with political images in British elections: Blumler and McQuail, *Television in Politics,* and David Butler and Donald Stokes, *Political Change in Britain* (New York: St. Martin's, 1969). Since some readers may be interested in more popularly written accounts (which are sometimes misleading, however) of the role of image-making in elections, they might want to consult Gene Wyckoff, *The Image Candidates* (New York: Macmillan, 1968) and the controversial work by Joe McGinniss, *The Selling of the President 1968* (New York: Trident Press, 1969).

FRAMEWORKS FOR THE STUDY OF POLITICAL IMAGERY

There are two principal frameworks within which the relationship between symbolic and subjective images, both in politics and other areas, has been considered. One is the dramatistic approach, which also incorporates ideas of role theory, play, etc. The other is the cybernetic approach, which looks at the role of images (defined as patterns of data) in facilitating self-controlling behavior and competence.

Any person seriously interested in exploring the application of the dramatistic perspective to the study of symbolic-subjective imagery must become at least passingly familiar with the views of Kenneth Burke. This is no easy task for his writing is complex and filled with references to and illustrations from literary works which are frequently difficult to follow. Nonetheless, the body of Burke's writings is the major source of the dramatistic approach. A good place to begin in understanding Burke's views is with his article entitled "Dramatism" published in Thayer, *Communication: Concepts and Perspectives*, pp. 327-60. This should be followed by the essays in his *Language as Symbolic Action*, for the style there is reasonably clear. After this the reader may want to tackle his *A Grammar of Motives* (Berkeley: University of California Press, 1969) and *A Rhetoric of Motives* (Berkeley: University of California Press, 1969); both are recent editions of earlier published works. It is in this body of writing that Burke distinguishes between motion and activity; the grammar, rhetoric, and symbolics of motives; and the elements of act, agent, agency, scene, and purpose in dramatic performance. Erving Goffman has also contributed a great deal to the dramatistic perspective, especially with his concept that everyday living is a series of dramatic performances. His major theories are available in *The Presentation of Self in Everyday Life* (Garden City, N. Y.: Doubleday, 1959); *Behavior in Public Places* (New York: Free Press, 1963); *Encounters* (Indianapolis: Bobbs-Merrill, 1961); *Strategic Interaction* (Philadelphia: University of Pennsylvania Press, 1970) and *Relations in Public* (New York: Basic Books, 1971). Finally, the dramatistic perspective is summarized by Sheldon L. Messinger and Robert D. Towne, "Life as Theater: Some Notes on the Dramaturgic Approach to Social Reality," *Sociometry*, Vol. 25 (1962), 98-110; note in the piece, however, the tendency to speak of the approach as a metaphor, a view certainly not that of Burke.

Several social scientists have endeavored to apply the dramatistic approach to their work. Hugh Dalziel Duncan makes the most explicit use of Burke's notions in *Communication and Social Order; Symbols in Society;* and also in his *Symbols and Social Theory* (New York: Oxford University Press, 1969). Orrin E. Klapp's *Symbolic Leaders,* and his *Collective Search for Identity* (New York: Holt, Rinehart & Winston, 1969) are also applications of the dramatistic perspective by a sociologist. The work by Bill Kinser and Neil Kleinman, *The Dream That Was No More A Dream: A Search for Aesthetic Reality in Germany, 1890-1945* (New York: Harper & Row, 1969) is an excellent study of the drama surrounding the rise of the Nazi regime. Among the political scientists who have employed dramatistic analysis is Richard Merelman, "The Dramaturgy of Politics," *Sociological Quarterly*, Vol. 10 (Spring 1969), 216-41; Victor A. Thompson, *Modern Organization;* Edelman in *The Symbolic Uses of Politics*, also incorporates dramatistic notions. Gusfield's *Symbolic Crusade*, develops a dramatistic model in the final chapter. In his *The Dramas of Politics* (Boston: Little, Brown, 1973) James N. Rosenau argues that the stable patterns of politics are dramatic and should be so approached by students.

Dramatism implies role-playing and, for an introduction to the use of role concepts, see Patricke Johns Heine, *Personality in Social Theory* (Chicago: Aldine, 1971); J. Milton Yinger, *Toward a Field Theory of Behavior* (New York: McGraw-Hill, 1965); Bruce Biddle and Edwin Thomas, *Role Theory* (New York: John Wiley, 1966); and Neal Gross, Ward S. Mason, and Alexander W. McEachern, *Explorations in Role Analysis* (New York: John Wiley, 1958), Part I. The play characteristics related to dramatic activity are systematically traced in Johan Huizinga, *Homo Ludens: A Study of the Play Element in Culture* (Boston: Beacon Press, 1950); Jacques Ehrmann, ed., *Game, Play, Literature* (Boston: Beacon Press, 1968); Piaget, *Play, Dreams, and Imitation in Childhood;* Brian Sutton-Smith, "Piaget on Play: A Critique," *Psychological Review*, Vol. 73 (1966), 104-10; Mihaly Csikszentmihalyi and Stith Bennett, "An Exploratory Model of Play," *American Anthropologist*, Vol. 73 (February 1971), pp. 45-58; and Stephenson, *The Play Theory of Mass Communication.*

Concern with the possibility that popular images of politics are more illusory than "real" has been expressed by many writers. The most articulate of such writers is Jacques Ellul. See his "Modern Myths" in *Diogenes*, Vol. 23 (Fall 1958), 23-40; "Techniques, Institutions, and Awareness," *American Behavioral Scientist*, Vol. 11 (July/August 1968), 38-42; *The Political Illusion* (New York: Knopf, 1967); and *Propaganda* (New York: Knopf, 1965). Herbert Marcuse has also been an outspoken critic of popular illusions; see his *One-Dimensional Man* (Boston: Beacon Press, 1969). A critique of reigning images of the nature of democracy can be found in Peter Bachrach, *The Theory of Democratic Elitism* (Boston: Little, Brown, 1967).

The cybernetic approach to the study of images is best exemplified by the work of George A. Miller, Eugene Galanter, and Karl H. Pribram, *Plans and the Structure of Behavior* (New York: Holt, Rinehart & Winston, 1960). In this work the authors distinguish between Images and Plans, discuss the basic test-operate-test (TOTE) unit involved in problem-solving, and apply their framework in several areas. Alfred Kuhn employs a cybernetic model to discuss all social transactions in his *The Study of Society* (Homewood, Ill.: Dorsey, 1963). Karl Deutsch offers a cybernetic model of politics in *The Nerves of Government* (New York: Free Press, 1963). For the basic concepts involved in cybernetic approaches consult Norbert Wiener, *Cybernetics, or Control and Communication in the Animal and the Machine* (Cambridge, Mass.: M.I.T. Press, 1948) and G. T. Guilbaud, *What is Cybernetics?* (New York: Grove Press, 1969).

The problems of self-competence and rationality as outlined in this text are explored more fully in M. Brewster Smith, *Social Psychology and Human Values* (Chicago: Aldine, 1969); Henry S. Kariel, *Open Systems: Arenas for Political Action* (Itasca, Ill.: F. E. Peacock, 1969); Robert E. Lane, *Political Thinking and Consciousness;* Milton Rokeach, *The Open and Closed Mind* (New York: Basic Books, 1960); and Jean Piaget, *Science of Education and the Psychology of the Child* (New York: Viking, 1970).

STUDYING POLITICAL IMAGES

Over the course of several decades social scientists have developed a variety of techniques for gathering data about attitudes, beliefs, and values. These techniques, sometimes experimental and sometimes employing sample surveys, usually involve personal interviews, questionnaires, tests, scales, and other instruments. Any good methodological primer will introduce readers to such techniques. Among these are Fred N. Kerlinger, *Foundations of Behavioral Research* (New York: Holt, Rinehart & Winston, 1964); Claire Selltiz et al., *Research Methods in Social Relations* (New York: Henry Holt, one vol. ed., 1960); and Leon Festinger and Daniel Katz, *Research Methods in the Behavioral Sciences* (New York: Holt, Rinehart & Winston, 1953). Introductions to survey research include Frederick J. Stephan and Philip J. McCarthy, *Sampling Opinions* (New York: John Wiley, 1963); Charles H. Backstrom and Gerald D. Hursh, *Survey Research* (Evanston, Ill.: Northwestern University Press, 1963); and sections of E. Terrence Jones, *Conducting Political Research* (New York: Harper & Row, 1971). Experimental techniques are introduced in Donald T. Campbell and Julian C. Stanley, *Experimental and Quasi-Experimental Designs for Research* (Chicago: Rand McNally, 1963). For a description of various techniques of learning about attitudes see Gene F. Summers, ed., *Attitude Measurement* (Skokie, Ill.: Rand McNally, 1970).

Generally the techniques for investigating images have been derived from those employed to study attitudes. One of the major techniques, however, is the use of the semantic differential, originally developed to determine what concepts mean to people. For a discussion of the semantic differential, and an application in the study of images of political figures, see Charles E. Osgood et al., *The Measurement of Meaning* (Urbana:

University of Illinois Press, 1957). A technique rarely used in the study of political images thus far, but having definite possibilities, is that underlying George A. Kelley's personal construct theory. Consult his *The Psychology of Personal Constructs* (Philadelphia: Norton, 1955). Also useful, but seldom used, is the interpersonal check list; for a succinct introduction, see Thomas W. Madron, *Small Group Methods and the Study of Politics* (Evanston, Ill.: Northwestern University Press, 1969).

One of the most promising techniques for studying political images that is gradually becoming more widely used by social scientists is the technique associated with *Q*-methodology. *Q*-methodology is the creation of William Stephenson; he explains its theory and applications in two major works that should be read by anyone interested in studying attitudes, opinions, and images: *The Study of Behavior* (Chicago: University of Chicago Press, 1953) and *The Play Theory of Mass Communication* (Chicago: University of Chicago Press, 1967). Readers will find in both works a point of view about images that squares well with the underlying assumptions about symbolic-subjective transactions that appear in Boulding, Bentley, and others cited in the first section of this bibliographic note. Stephenson specifically attacks the problem of imagery in an unpublished 1960 paper, "Methodology of 'Imagery' Measurement: MR Redefined," but readers will be able to get some flavor of his thinking on the matter by looking at his two books and by reading two major articles on related questions: "Application of Q-Method to the Measurement of Public Opinion," *The Psychological Record,* Vol. 14 (1964), 265-73 and "Application of the Thompson Schema to the Current Controversy Over Cuba," *The Psychological Record,* Vol. 14 (1964), 275-90.

index